D0282398

75086

Faulkner, new perspectives / edited by
Richard H. Brodhead. -- Englewood
Cliffs, N.J. : Prentice-Hall, [1983]
viii, 216 p. ; 21 cm. -- (Twentieth
century views)
"A Spectrum book."
Bibliography: p. [213]-216.
ISBN 0-13-308288-1

1. Faulkner, William, 1897-1962--
Criticism and interpretation--
Addresses, essays, lectures.
I. Brodhead, Richard H., 1947-

25 OCT 83.   9324055   OMMMxc   83-3330

TWENTIETH CENTURY VIEWS

The aim of this series is to present the best in contemporary critical opinion on major authors, providing a twentieth century perspective on their changing status in an era of profound revaluation.

Maynard Mack, *Series Editor*
Yale University

⟩

FAULKNER

NEW PERSPECTIVES

Edited by
Richard H. Brodhead

Prentice-Hall, Inc. A SPECTRUM BOOK *Englewood Cliffs, N.J.*

Library of Congress Cataloging in Publication Data

Main entry under title:
Faulkner, new perspectives.

(Twentieth century views)
"A Spectrum Book."
Bibliography: p.
1. Faulkner, William, 1897–1962—Criticism and
interpretation—Addresses, essays, lectures.   I. Brodhead,
Richard H., date.   II. Series.
PS3511.A86Z78321116   1983   813′.52   83–3330
ISBN 0-13-308288-1
ISBN 0-13-308270-9 (pbk.)

10 9 8 7 6 5 4 3 2 1

ISBN 0-13-308288-1

ISBN 0-13-308270-9 {PBK.}

Editorial/production supervision: Marlys Lehmann
Cover wood engraving by Vivian Berger © 1983
Manufacturing buyer: Cathie Lenard

This book is available at a special discount when ordered in
bulk quantities. Contact Prentice-Hall, Inc., General
Publishing Division, Special Sales, Englewood Cliffs, N.J. 07632.

Prentice-Hall International, Inc., *London*
Prentice-Hall of Australia Pty. Limited, *Sydney*
Prentice-Hall Canada Inc., *Toronto*
Prentice-Hall of India Private Limited, *New Delhi*
Prentice-Hall of Japan, Inc., *Tokyo*
Prentice-Hall of Southeast Asia Pte. Ltd., *Singapore*
Whitehall Books Limited, *Wellington, New Zealand*
Editora Prentice-Hall do Brasil Ltda., *Rio de Janeiro*

In memory of Larry Holland

Contents

I wish to thank the many students of Faulkner who have assisted me in the making of this collection. Three have been especially helpful and deserve special mention: James B. Meriwether, Eric Sundquist, and Robert Dale Parker.

Grateful acknowledgment is made to Random House, Inc., to Curtis Brown Ltd., to the author's literary estate, and to Chatto & Windus Ltd. for permission to quote the copyrighted works of William Faulkner.

Lines from "The Municipal Gallery Revisited" are reprinted by permission of Macmillan Publishing Company and A. P. Watt Ltd. from *Collected Poems* of W. B. Yeats. Copyright 1940 by Georgie Yeats, renewed 1968 by Bertha Georgie Yeats, Michael Butler Yeats, and Anne Yeats.

Introduction:
Faulkner and the Logic of Remaking

by Richard H. Brodhead

I

Robert Penn Warren called his introduction to the first volume of this anthology, published sixteen years ago, "Faulkner: Past and Present." His title gives a measure of how quickly time passes in literary history. At this writing, we have moved what might have seemed only a short way beyond Warren's present, but already the past that extends out behind Faulkner has completely changed in shape. When Warren wrote, the battle for recognition of Faulkner—a battle in which Warren was one of the great heroes —was still recent history. In his essay he still savors Faulkner's modern stature as a triumph newly won, and still freshly remembers what Faulkner and his champions had had to struggle against—a reading public that let Faulkner's entire output go out of print by 1945; a literary establishment that labeled his writing degenerate, sadistic, obscurantist, and dull; the pronouncements even by critics who would later become Faulkner's best readers that his work was monstrous—"curiously dull, furiously commonplace, and often meaningless, suggesting some ambiguous irresponsibility and exasperated sullenness of mind"; in any case, too bizarre to be taken quite seriously—"most of his books are Gothic ruins, impressive only by moonlight." [1]

American literature has a perverse habit of saving its most honored places for authors (Melville, Whitman, Thoreau, and Dickinson are examples) to whom it denied recognition at the time of their writing; and Warren does not exaggerate the extent

---

[1] The quotations are from Alfred Kazin and Malcolm Cowley, as cited in Robert Penn Warren, "Faulkner: Past and Present," *Faulkner: A Collection of Critical Essays* (Englewood Cliffs, N.J.: Prentice-Hall, 1966), pp. 13 and 7.

to which Faulkner, the principal twentieth-century heir to this pattern, was reviled and ignored when his work was new. And yet the dark days that Warren still freshly recalls in 1966 have by now become so remote as to take on the character of a historical curiosity. To look back from this moment the same distance Warren looked back in 1966 is to see almost the reverse of what he saw: the spectacle not of an author struggling to be recognized but of an author massively encased in recognition, an author whose greatness has been put beyond dispute (even beyond discussion), an author whose stature has been not just established but powerfully institutionalized. By the 1950s Faulkner had already been confirmed in the roles of American literary great and giant of literary modernism—positions that have been consolidated, since then, by the fading of his competition (first Wolfe and Dos Passos; more recently, Hemingway and Fitzgerald). In consequence the author who was once largely unread has, for the last twenty or thirty years, been read widely, even compulsorily. *(The Sound and the Fury* and *As I Lay Dying,* in particular, have attained something like the status *The House of the Seven Gables* and *Silas Marner* once had, as inevitable entries in high school and college curricula.) The author who was once out of print is now annually reprinted, and, for that matter, continues to come into print. (Although long dead, Faulkner has become, in the last few years alone, the author of [among other things] a volume of letters, a new play, *The Marionettes,* and new versions of two familiar novels, *Sartoris* and *Sanctuary;* with the appearance of his *Uncollected Stories,* he has even succeeded in getting published all the short stories he was unable to place in his lifetime.) Above all the author once denied serious critical attention has become the subject of uncountable lectures, essays, dissertations, book-length studies, annual conferences, special issues, and reviews of research—an outpouring of critical attention such as no other writer, it may be, in the whole history of letters has received so near the time of his work, and such as only a few writers have received at any time.

With the consolidation of Faulkner's fame, the grosser errors of his original reception have been set to rights. But his new situation brings with it problems of its own. Nowadays Faulkner shows signs of suffering the harm that comes not from being misunderstood or unesteemed but from being understood and esteemed too readily. The trouble with Faulkner's early readers, it is easy for us now to say, is that they did not know how to read him. The trouble with current readers is more likely to be that they *do* know how to read him—that, armed with the weapons that Faulkner criticism and academic instruction have made standard issue, they can move right along towards a satisfactory "reading" of Faulkner, without having to confront the difficulties (beauties too), often quite alien to what criticism describes, of Faulkner's texts themselves. Similarly we can say, smugly but with much justice, that Faulkner's early readers failed to recognize his greatness. Our own problem is more likely to be that we take his greatness as a given—that we find him important because he is important, losing the sense, even as we scour his work with our attention, of what gave his work a claim on our attention in the first place.

When Faulkner's worth was still in doubt, it was essential to locate and bring together (as the early anthologies of Faulkner criticism did) the critical writing through which his claims to value could be most persuasively established. In our own situation, when those claims have been established so powerfully, it may be no less essential to have Faulkner put back into question, and his right to our interest established over again. On this assumption, the present collection brings together a group of essays having little in common except the vigor they bring to the task of rethinking Faulkner. It publishes them not to the end of making a new set of critical views prevail over an old one, but rather in the hope of encouraging the spirit that gives all great visions of Faulkner, past, present, or future, their power: a spirit bold enough to see afresh what Faulkner's writings do, and to say anew why his writings matter.

II

What makes the fiction we know as Faulkner's? How does Faulkner make his claim on us? Faulkner himself—who might be said to have spent the first half of his career doing his work, and the second half trying to say how he did it—gave many answers to these questions, and we could do worse than to begin with one of his explanations. In a 1945 letter he writes:

All my writing life I have been a poet without education, who
possessed only instinct and a fierce conviction and belief in the
worth and truth of what he was doing, and an illimitable courage
for rhetoric (personal pleasure in it too: I admit it) and who
knew and cared for little else.[2]

What makes this statement striking is that where we might expect
Faulkner to ground his work in the subjects it explores (I write
to tell the story of the South, or to weigh the burden of the past,
or to chronicle "the old verities and truths"—love and honor and
pity and pride and so on), he makes no mention of them. Instead
he identifies his work's primary impulse simply with a strong
literary will, a fierce urge to assert what language, irrespective
of its content, can make.

The aptness of this self-description comes clear each time we
start back into Faulkner. For although from instruction and previous reading we know to think of Faulkner as the master of
certain great themes, when we start reading him what meets us is
always a raw act of style. I think of *The Sound and the Fury,*
which greets us not with a history of family decline but with a
string of too-simple words, grouped into strange compound sentences that fail to join their elements except into unintelligible
sequences of unmotivated gestures: "They took the flag out, and
they were hitting. Then they put the flag back and they went
to the table, and he hit and the other hit. Then they went on,
and I went along the fence. Luster came away from the flower
tree and we went along the fence and they stopped and we
stopped. . . ." Or I think of *Sanctuary,* a book we might make
into a critique of modernity and its unnaturalness, but that presents itself as a set of studiously unnatural conceits: "against the
sunny silence, in his slanted straw hat and his slightly akimbo
arms, he had that vicious depthless quality of stamped tin"; "his
tight suit and stiff hat all angles, like a modernistic lampstand";
"he smells like that black stuff that ran out of Bovary's mouth
and down upon her bridal veil when they raised her head." Or
I think of "The Bear," a story that does tell of initiation in the
woods, but only after it initiates us into a wilderness of prose—
the prolix and proliferating high-Faulknerian sentence, where

[2] Joseph Blotner, ed., *Selected Letters of William Faulkner* (New York:
Random House, 1977), pp. 188.

every element gets compounded and recompounded, and every noun throws off extended families of dependent clauses.

Faulkner's writing, whatever its style, always insists on its style.[3] Its language never lets us forget that it is contrived—contrived in the sense of being something the work has devised (sentences like these, Faulkner's works all tell us, you can find nowhere but here); contrived too in the sense of being visibly, even flagrantly, artificial. Each of the passages just mentioned advertises its refusal to put things together in their natural or normal ways, insists on relating them only in ways *it* invents—as the Benjy style in *The Sound and the Fury* puts mere succession where we used to know causation: as *Sanctuary*'s willful similes *make* like what were never like before. This writing does not fail, eventually, to project a world through its words, but it is a world that has been radically recomposed. And recomposed, the writing tells us, *by* the writing: the world not as it is, but as an act of style has made it.

Faulkner's fierce exploitation of the writer's powers of making, and his insistence that what he gives us be recognized as the yield of his compositional act, put their marks on all his work. We can read them as clearly in the forms of his novels as in the forms of his sentences—the fracturing and interleafing of two fully separate stories in *The Wild Palms* is a spectacular example of his will to break the orders natural to his materials, then make a new one that is visibly the product of his own making power. But if this aggressive display of making is characteristic of Faulkner, it is just as characteristic that where such making leads is to an equally aggressive remaking—the undoing of his work's con-trivance, so that he can contrive it anew. Everyone agrees that *The Sound and the Fury* is the book in which Faulkner first fully discovers how to write like Faulkner. Part of the reason is that it is the novel in which he latches onto his distinctive rhythm of recreation—calculating, with great deliberateness and ingenuity, a style in which his work can be rendered (what we call the characters or points of view of *The Sound and the Fury*—

---

[3] My phrasing echoes Conrad Aiken's, in his important early essay "William Faulkner: The Novel as Form," reprinted in Warren, ed., *Faulkner: A Collection of Critical Essays,* pp. 46–52. On the aggressively constructed quality of Faulkner's style, see also the conclusion of Calvin Bedient's essay "Pride and Nakedness: *As I Lay Dying,*" reprinted in this volume.

Benjy, Quentin, Jason—are really so many distinctive ways of composing a world through words), then giving a virtuoso performance in that style, then abruptly abolishing it and going on to construct another (and another, and another [4]) in its place. During the astonishingly productive years that begin with *The Sound and the Fury,* this restless refashioning, not just of his materials but of the principles on which they are composed, becomes the most salient feature of Faulkner's creativity. His great novels—*The Sound and the Fury* (1929), *As I Lay Dying* (1930), the revised *Sanctuary* (1931), *Light in August* (1932), *Absalom, Absalom!* (1936), *The Hamlet* (1940), and *Go Down, Moses* (1942)—succeed each other not as continuations of previous efforts, not even as modifications or extensions of previous plans, but as so many reinventions of the novel form itself, each repudiating its predecessors' designs to draw a new one of its own.

This prodigious power of formal inventiveness and this ruthlessness toward his own prior inventions are traits Faulkner shares with his great predecessors in American fiction. The course of his novels shows the same repeated revolutionizing of plan that leads Melville, for instance, from *Typee* and *Omoo* through the renewed experiments of *Mardi, Moby-Dick, Pierre, The Piazza Tales,* and *The Confidence-Man,* or that leads James from his early international novels to the realist experiments of the 1880s, to the dramatic experiments of the 1890s, to the masterpieces (more experimental still) of his late style. Faulkner resembles James and Melville in nothing so much as his persistent

---

[4] All of Faulkner's many accounts of the writing of *The Sound and the Fury* emphasize his repeated discovery, after completing each section, that he would need to tell his story another way. See James B. Meriwether and Michael Millgate, eds., *Lion in the Garden: Interviews with William Faulkner* (New York: Random House, 1968), pp. 146–148. Elsewhere Faulkner describes trying it over as the working plan of his entire writing:

> I'm trying primarily to tell a story, in the most effective way I can think of, the most moving, the most exhaustive. But I think even that is incidental to what I am trying to do, taking my output (the course of it) as a whole. I am telling the same story over and over, which is myself and the world. . . . I am trying to say it all in one sentence, between one Cap and one period. I'm still trying, to put it all, if possible, on one pinhead. I don't know how to do it. All I know to do is to keep on trying in a new way.

Blotner, ed., *Letters,* p. 185.

radicalism, his inability to engage a formula for his work without bringing it up for revision. This might be said to be his deepest bond, not just to the line of American fiction, but to the American literary tradition in general. Faulkner does sometimes treat persistent American themes (like the wilderness, in *Go Down, Moses*) and work familiar American forms (like the Gothic romance, in *Absalom, Absalom!*). But the essential thing he shares with the greatest American writers—both ones he read and used, like Melville and James, and ones he mostly ignored, like Whitman and Emerson—is an attitude toward literary work itself: the sense that his medium is not something he may move in but something he must make; and above all the sense that he must keep remaking even his own boldest creations.

／ Faulkner criticism, while it boasts of his formal experimentalism, tends to treat it as a somewhat secondary trait, a byproduct of his wrestling with the great nonliterary subjects that haunt him. But this line of thinking is misleading. For one thing, it understates the role that a sheer passion for formal rearrangement, quite independent of any end it can be said to serve, plays in the making of Faulkner's fiction. More important, it also gives an inverted picture of how Faulkner's work unfolds. In a sense it would be more accurate to say that Faulkner's searching treatments of his obsessive themes are a byproduct of his literary experimentation. For in Faulkner the work of formal construction involves far more than finding how to express what the author already knows: it is itself the means by which he finds and grasps his subjects.

Regina Fadiman's recent study of Faulkner's revision of *Light in August* gives an instructive example of this. The *Light in August* manuscript, as Fadiman says, shows signs of several stages of drafting, and repeated reorderings of its contents. Her attempt to reconstruct the sequence of its composition leads her to a rather startling discovery. This is that Joe Christmas as we now know him was a late addition to *Light in August,* an idea that apparently came to Faulkner as he wrote. In an earlier draft still detectable in the manuscript, Fadiman establishes, Lena Grove, Reverend Hightower, and Byron Bunch were Faulkner's main characters, and Joe Christmas, then confirmed to be black of blood, was a marginal figure, never seen from within. The narrative of Christmas's life history in the current chapters 6 through 12 was

written independently at a later stage, she shows, and inserted into
the older material, which was then revised to accommodate it.
(Revised, among other ways, by having Christmas's race made un-
determinable.[5])

Fadiman's description of the *Light in August* manuscript gives
stunning evidence of Faulkner's habit of working and reworking
his materials. If her reconstruction is right, it also gives stunning
evidence of what that reworking yields. It suggests that the drama
now at the center of the novel—the forging and enactment of the
doom that flows from Joe Christmas's problematic origins—is
not part of Faulkner's original conception of *Light in August,* but
is rather something he attains to—something, exactly, he is enabled *to* conceive— through the compositional process itself.[6] Of
course what we see Faulkner grasping by this process is much
more than a character, however memorable. In embellishing a
history for Joe Christmas, then also for Joanna Burden, in his
later draft, Faulkner is composing into being the past itself as
Light knows it, and recomposing the novel's present in such a
way as to make it the past's leaving: something that issues from
and is densely determined by a long history. In reimagining
Christmas, Faulkner also for the first time moves race to the
center of a novel, and discovers how action could draw its deeper
energies from the opposition of black and white. Race itself gets
crucially reconceived in this process. In the early draft of *Light*
(as in Faulkner's earlier fiction) race is a given, something you are,
by birth. (Joe *is* a negro.) In the revision, Faulkner transforms
it from a genetic attribute to a structure of consciousness, a
violently charged field of psychic conflict that is yours (or better,
that is *you*) regardless of genetic facts. Then in another brilliant
new imagining, Faulkner further redefines race as a taking within
of the whole fabric of a culture. In telling the new Christmas
story Faulkner plots how racial terms, as they enter Joe's mind,

[5] See Regina K. Fadiman, *Faulkner's Light in August: A Description and
Interpretation of the Revisions* (Charlottesville: The University Press of
Virginia, 1975).

[6] Compare Faulkner's comment that "that story began with Lena Grove,
the idea of the young girl with nothing, pregnant, determined to find her
sweetheart," but that "as I told the story I had to get more and more into
it." Frederick L. Gwynn and Joseph L. Blotner, eds., *Faulkner in the University* (Charlottesville: The University Press of Virginia, 1959), p. 74.

become fatally aligned with the other fierce polarities of Southern Protestant culture: black/white, female/male, nature/transcendence, mercy/justice, and so on.

These are significantly new understandings for Faulkner. They are not evident in his books before *Light*. And once he wrests them to expression there, they become the bases for his later works. The encumbering of the present with a long-drawn-out past, a past lost to memory but still so potent that it dooms the present to repeat it; the establishment, then transgression of racial boundaries in the past, such that personal history is tangled in invisible coils of racial strife: these become the essential realities in Faulkner after *Light in August*. His next great works reach a crisis of final knowledge when they break through into a forgotten past and uncover the racial crossings hidden there—as Quentin and Shreve, in the climactic eighth chapter of *Absalom, Absalom!*, penetrate to a lower layer of Sutpen family history, where they can see that the sin Charles Bon threatens to revisit on the family is that of miscegenation; as Ike McCaslin, in the climactic fourth section of "The Bear" in *Go Down, Moses,* reads the ledgers that make his a history of ancestral miscegenation and incest regularly renewed. The final product of the crisis of composition Faulkner undergoes in inventing Joe Christmas, this is to suggest, is the shape of understanding that governs his last major works. And he reaches this understanding, it is worth repeating, through the vigorous making and remaking of a story.

After *Light in August* Faulkner seems increasingly to recognize that the way of making that has always been his practice also serves him as a means to deepened knowledge. This new recognition can be seen in the preface to *The Sound and the Fury* (reprinted in this volume) that he wrote soon after completing *Light,* a preface that boldy declares that writing is a knowledge-breeding labor: "I wrote this book and learned to read." [7] The recognition is also clearly visible in his later fiction. Faulkner's innovation in *Absalom, Absalom!* is to take his own compositional process and stage it as an action within the text. He contrives this novel as a series of multiple tellings, each of which makes up what it seeks to know, then gets propelled, by its inventions, into a process of continuing reinvention in which the story gets

---

[7] See Faulkner's introduction on p. 20.

embellished, extended, then radically revised. This method is new
to Faulkner's fiction in *Absalom!*; but the real novelty of the book
is that it presents the act of persistently repeated reinvention
as a form of divination: as the means, and the only means, by
which consciousness can retrieve the lost material without which
human experience makes no sense. As Donald Kartiganer argues
in his essay in this volume, whether or not Quentin knew what
Sutpen told Henry from a source outside his telling, *Absalom!*
emphatically presents that knowledge as the yield of his and
Shreve's increasingly passionate narrative imagining—as it presents Shreve's last discovery, of the reason why Bon put his octoroon mistress's face in the locket Judith would find on his corpse,
as having the superior authority ("Aint that right? Aint it? By
God, ain't it?") not of corroborated assertion but of sufficiently
passionate surmise. At the peak of his powers Faulkner's is a world
where (as James said of "The Turn of the Screw") "nothing is
right save as we rightly imagine it" [8]—and where nothing is rightly
imagined save as it is imagined again and again.

The will to renovation becomes somewhat less urgent in
Faulkner's fiction after *Absalom, Absalom!* Especially after the
six-year gap in his writing following *Go Down, Moses,* Faulkner
becomes less and less interested in wrenching free from his own
designs, more and more eager to revive his earlier work and con-
solidate it into a whole. But his care for the act of reimagining,
and for the value of what it produces, gets if anything more
pronounced. Faulkner's late works are haunted by the specter of
their end. As Gary Stonum shows,[9] Mink Snopes's revenge quest
in *The Mansion* expresses Faulkner's sense of his own late work:
a struggle, in a changed world, and absurdly late in the day, to
complete a project willed long before. *Requiem for a Nun* shows
even more powerfully Faulkner's fear that the world he wrote of
will soon have vanished, and that the things that pertained to it
(his work included) will be understood no more. In "The Jail"
he gloomily reviews the daily realities that have been erased by
the "outland invasion" of Yoknapatawpha's traditional, indigenous culture. At first Cecilia Farmer, the figure he keeps return-
ing to, seems to epitomize his region's doom: the incarnation, in

---

[8] Henry James, *The Art of the Novel,* ed. Richard P. Blackmur (New York:
Charles Scribner's Sons, 1934), p. 171.
[9] In "Faulkner's Last Phase," reprinted in this volume.

her time, of the patient, persistent spirit in which right old Southerners worked their land, she survives now only as a name carved on a windowpane, displayed for uncomprehending Yankee tourists to stare at. But once Faulkner introduces Cecilia Farmer she keeps engaging him, with the result that he tells her story over, then tells it over—and with the result that this emblem of the irretrievable, unknowable past gets known again and again. Faulkner's ability to reinvent Cecilia Farmer seems to change his own mood. For when he moves, in "The Jail," toward his final vision of what will happen when the leavings of his South fall into the hands of strangers, he reads this situation in a reversed way. Before he had lamented that the outlanders who will fill his land will inevitably fail to understand its traces: "they could even repeat some of its legend and history . . . but they had had no contact with it; it was not a part of their lives; they had automatic stoves and furnaces and milk deliveries and lawns the size of installment-plan rugs." But in the final version his point is exactly that they *will* understand—and understand not because they share the past's life already, but because the past's traces will provoke them to imagine its life: as Cecilia's signature, in the concluding paragraphs of "The Jail," provokes the Yankee tourist to imagine her back into being. Because it will incite those who follow to feats of this sort, the name on the window becomes a sign not that the past is unintelligible, but rather that it can always be made intelligible again, by a renewed imaginative act.[10]

In the ponderous atmosphere of late Faulkner, the will to make and remake that has always informed Faulkner's art itself gets newly understood, as a special case of the most general of human wills. In Faulkner's later works men make—a name, a book— in order to leave their mark: to express through a relic they have wrought the fact that they once did exist. Remaking becomes, finally, simply the necessary complement to this act, the means by which men bring other mens' makings back to life—as the Yankee stranger, having reconstructed Cecilia Farmer in his mind, can then read what her carved name really says: "*'Listen, stranger; this was myself: this was I.'*"

[10] By far the best reading of this section of *Requiem for a Nun,* and one to which I am indebted here, is in Noel Polk's *Faulkner's Requiem for a Nun: A Critical Study* (Bloomington: Indiana University Press, 1981), pp. 160–187.

Faulkner criticism continues the rhythm of creation and recreation that his work began, and Faulkner helps explain why this is so. His writings have the same status for us as readers that the shreds of the Sutpen record have for Quentin and his father, or that the name on the pane has for the Yankee in *Requiem for a Nun:* they affect us with power, the source of which we cannot know unless we go to work constructing an account of it. The Faulkner we possess, Faulkner helps us understand, is always and necessarily one his readers have helped to make. And their makings inevitably lead onward to revision. One reason is that, in Faulkner criticism as in the interpretive drama of *Absalom, Absalom!*, each new formulation of one phase of the subject makes it possible to reformulate other phases as well. Another is that, again as in *Absalom!*, the inquiry is always being joined by fresh hands. Each new worker in the field of Faulkner sets the subject in his own frame of expectations and needs, seen within which features that were formerly prominent suddenly fade, and other sets of features come to the fore. "Let me play," each new critic, Shreve-like, says to his predecessors—a gesture that prepares for him later to say: "because your old man was wrong here, too."

The works in this anthology show many times over how this renovation takes place. I include Cleanth Brooks's "William Faulkner: Vision of Good and Evil" because it summarizes so many of the central insights of Brooks's *William Faulkner: The Yoknapatawpha Country* (1963)—with Michael Millgate's *The Achievement of William Faulkner,* the most distinguished and widely accepted work of Faulkner criticism from the 1960s. Like the strongest criticism of that time, Brooks's essay organizes its Faulkner in accordance with certain critical assumptions. With considerable oversimplification, these might be described as the assumptions that an author's works, both singly and as a whole, are at their most significant level unified, not fragmented; that what unifies them is the existence within them of organizing themes; that themes have a hierarchy of importance, with ethical ones being most important; and therefore that the critic can best get at Faulkner by abstracting his works' ethical statements, which individual texts can then be used to exemplify.

Organizing Faulkner within these framing assumptions permits Brooks to display a set of features that are (or are, at least, after

Brooks has taught us to see them) absolutely central to Faulkner
—particularly the sharp opposition he posits between a natural,
feminine, generative principle on the one hand and a rigid,
masculine order asserted against the natural on the other. (Brooks's
essay beautifully captures the jointly sexual and cultural [South-
ern Calvinist] aspects of this opposition, as well as Faulkner's
ambivalence toward both its sides.) Indeed what Brooks uncovers
is so central as to help conceal the fact that his Faulkner is being
made: so resonant are his findings that they make the organization
he uses to compose Faulkner seem like Faulkner's own.

The nearly equal number of readers who felt liberated and
infuriated by John Irwin's *Doubling and Incest/Repetition and
Revenge* (1975) would no doubt agree that it was the only book
published on Faulkner in the 1970s that had an influence comparable to Brooks's. There are two related reasons for its impact.
The first is that it was the first book to bring the new artillery
of post-structuralist criticism to bear on a major American author.
The second is that it was the first book to show that an equally
compelling picture of Faulkner could be drawn without reference
to values or themes. Irwin, of course, gets his Faulkner not by
"finding" him but by constructing him within a different frame
of assumptions—the assumption (to oversimplify once more) that
literary works are not autonomous wholes but need to be read for
their relations to (even identify with) other literary works and
works in other disciplines (psychology, philosophy); that the
work's essential relation is not to moral realities like good and
evil but to the reality of time; that the essential feature of its
relation to time (here the influence of Freud and Nietzsche as
mediated by Harold Bloom and Paul de Man comes clear) is
that it wishes to master time, indeed to make time, yet also knows
that it comes after a time that lies outside its control; that it expresses its wish for originality and its knowledge of secondariness
in every available literary structure simultaneously; and therefore that the critic can best get at the work by tracing the whole
complex of interchangeable terms in which it brings its attitude
toward temporality to expression.

Whether this set of assumptions is more or less valid than, say,
Cleanth Brooks's is not my subject here. In any case the real
interest of Irwin's assumptions lies less in their possible validity
than in what he can do with them. This is, silently and quite
unpolemically, to obliterate the familiar Faulkner of the '60s and

early '70s. When Faulkner gets rethought in Irwin's terms, the ethical and thematic structures that had come to seem so familiar and so essential in his fiction simply disappear. Another set of structures—Oedipal triangles, spatial and temporal doublings, patterns of displaced revenge; structures equally recurring, and just as arguably "in" his works—emerge in their place, to become what Faulkner *is*.

Doubling and Incest is still a recent book. But enough time has passed since its publication to make clear that the effect of its brave new making will be not to freeze a new Faulkner in place but to set the process of making in motion again. David Wyatt, whose essay "Faulkner and the Burdens of History" (1979) is reprinted in this volume, is one of many recent critics who take up where Irwin left off. Clearly, when Wyatt looks at Faulkner he sees what Irwin showed him—an author whose primary problem is unconsummated revenge, which is associated with a pattern of genealogical repetition, both of which in turn raise the question of the power or impotence of the writer's act. Just as clearly, what Wyatt is doing is extending an Irwinian kind of analysis to regions Irwin did not touch. But as Faulkner might have led us to expect, the apparently passive act of extension produces automatically and immediately a revision. Pushing his inquiry both earlier (back to *Sartoris)* and later (forward to *The Unvanquished)* in Faulkner than Irwin goes, Wyatt finds that Faulkner's attitude toward time's and the writer's power is in fact not constant—that these are questions Faulkner works through, achieves a changed stance to, through his work itself. Even more critically, by pushing his inquiry across the bounds of Faulkner's writing into his biography, Wyatt finds that Faulkner's work on these subjects does not flow from his wrestling with a universal, eternal predicament of Man in Time. His way of formulating them and their urgency to his imagination derive instead, Wyatt argues, from Faulkner's lived experience of a completely particularized biographical situation: his place in his family's own curiously repetitious drama of attempted and failed revenge. To correct Irwin in this way is at least implicitly to change not details of a portrait but rather the very terms in which Faulkner is to be known. In Wyatt's work Faulkner comes to life again, this time neither as a profound literary ethicist nor as a struggler with temporality, but as a writer whose meditations on those and every other subject come out of the heat of a lived, personal life.

In one mood we might be tempted to see a sequence of views such as I have been tracing as a path of progress, in which criticism brings us ever closer to the truth about Faulkner. In another we might see it as a depressing succession of mere fictions, each momentarily persuasive, but all equally remote from Faulkner's reality. Keeping a book like *Absalom!* in mind helps us toward a more interesting reading. It helps us see that each critical version of Faulkner is indeed a fabrication, someone's making, not bare truth; but that they are not for that reason incapable of yielding truth—since the "truth" of Faulkner can never be known anyway except as it is fashioned by his interpreters.[11] Further, it helps us understand that the reversals in which one reading of Faulkner casts an older one out have their real value not as breakthroughs to truth or as renewals of illusion but as revivals of power: moments in which inquiry recovers its passionate energy, the perpetual renewal of which, Faulkner suggests, is the condition for genuine knowledge to take place at all.

I have kept this notion in mind in selecting the works to be included in this volume. My first aim, of course, has been simply to choose the best writing done on Faulkner since Robert Penn Warren composed the first volume of this anthology. (I do include two pieces written prior to that date: Brooks's, because it summarizes a body of work the usefulness of which shows no sign of being exhausted; and Irving Howe's discussion of Faulkner and race, still the most penetrating treatment of that crucial subject.[12]) While I have tried to arrange for most of Faulkner's

---

[11] Faulkner's famous response to a question at the University of Virginia is pertinent here:

> Q. Mr. Faulkner, in *Absalom, Absalom!* does any one of the people who talks about Sutpen have the right view, or is it more or less a case of thirteen ways of looking at a blackbird with none of them right?
> A. That's it exactly. I think no one individual can look at truth. It blinds you. You look at it and you see one phase of it. Someone else looks at it and sees a slightly awry phase of it. But taken all together, the truth is in what they saw though nobody saw the truth intact.

Faulkner in the University, pp. 273–274.

[12] For more recent and quite different accounts of Faulkner's racial imaginings, see Myra Jehlen, *Class and Character in Faulkner's South* (New York: Columbia University Press, 1976), especially pp. 75–132, and Lee Jenkins, *Faulkner and Black-White Relations: A Psychoanalytic Approach* (New York: Columbia University Press, 1981).

major themes and works to be touched on (there are inevitably
lapses: I regret the absence of an essay on *The Hamlet*), I have
also insisted that, whatever their immediate subject, the essays
included here also push toward some more general statement
about Faulkner—as Calvin Bedient's beautiful reading of *As I
Lay Dying*, to cite just one instance, also pushes toward a statement about human isolation in Faulkner, and the meaning of
human work. But above all I have tried to recapture some of the
transformative violence by which Faulkner has been remade in
our time. Taken together the essays collected here repeat the
centrally Faulknerian action by which some critical subject, already fully explained, gets brought up for rethinking, then is
explained in a new way—as Faulknerian revenge, brilliantly explicated by John Irwin, then gets explicated quite differently by
David Wyatt; as the Faulknerian family, imaginatively described
by David Minter, then gets described quite otherwise by Calvin
Bedient; as Faulknerian value, its scheme laid out by Cleanth
Brooks, gets redefined as not a scheme but a process, by Gary
Stonum; or as the Faulknerian labor of reconstructing the past,
understood as a generally human work of knowing by Donald
Kartiganer, gets reseen as the product of a specifically twentieth-
century social transformation by Susan Willis.

I might add that while I have never let it override the wish to
reprint the best of Faulkner criticism, in making this selection I
have also given some thought to remedying that criticism's greatest
current lack: its lack of a strong sense of the wider connectedness
of Faulkner's work. Recent literary-critical protocols and the
modern academic organization of knowledge into fields have
cooperated to close Faulkner's writing in upon itself, and to
efface its connections to anything external to it. The result has
been to produce prodigies of internal analysis of his work, but
also an almost total suppression of interest in where that work
came from and what it effected. With the appearance of Joseph
Blotner's gargantuan biography, for instance, nearly every docu-
mentable fact about Faulkner's life has been firmly established.
But we still have only the most rudimentary knowledge of the inward system of dispositions and compulsions that was Faulkner's
character, or of the nature of the economy by which he trans-
ferred certain energies of his life into that other life we call his
work. Rampant misogyny has been amply demonstrated in Faulk-

ner's fiction, for example;[13] but we know as little as ever about how the misogyny of the fiction mirrors or perhaps relieves a misogyny in his life. To cite another case, it has long been known that two of the great transformative crises in Faulkner's fiction coincided in time with two of his greatest personal crises: the writing of *Light in August,* that novel of parents in search of children and children deprived of parents, with the birth and death of Faulkner's first child, his daughter Alabama; and the completion of *Absalom, Absalom!,* that novel of brotherly love and brotherly murder, with the death of his brother Dean, in the airplane Faulkner had given him and urged him to learn to fly. But criticism has been either too uninterested or simply too embarrassed by personal matters to ask how these sets of events fit together, or more generally how Faulkner recreated intensities in his life as intensities in his work. David Minter's and David Wyatt's essays in this collection are examples of a new kind of biographical criticism (made possible by Blotner's biography) that we need much more of: a criticism that will treat Faulkner's life as a living inward process, to be known not by amassing facts but through feats of intuitive invention; and that will treat his work not as a passive reflection of his factual "life" but as an act of life itself, passionately expressing personal conflicts and perhaps even helping to resolve them.

Faulkner criticism has been even more deficient in relating Faulkner to his social and cultural context. He is celebrated—it is the greatest truism about him—for his especially intimate relation to the life of his region. But what passes for the South in most recent Faulkner criticism is a vague specter projected from within his novels themselves, or, at best, worked up from a few good sourcebooks. And even when criticism presents early-twentieth-century Deep Southern culture with any density of detail, it still tends to assume that Faulkner's writing rather passively mirrors its factual environment. Susan Willis's "Aesthetics of the Rural Slum" is a rare attempt to reimagine, independent of Faulkner's fiction, the deep strains in the social world that surrounded that fiction (she helps remind us, for one thing,

---

[13] The charge, over forty years old, is thoroughly (and unaccusingly) documented in Albert J. Guerard, *The Triumph of the Novel* (New York: Oxford University Press, 1976), pp. 109–135.

how nearly his great writing coincided with the Great Depression); then to suggest how Faulkner's fiction expresses its culture's tensions in its every aspect, even when the links are not immediately apparent.[14] We will need many more such efforts to reconstruct the real historical ground of Faulkner's fiction if we are fully to appreciate how he both draws on and invents the life of his place.

Finally, we need to know more about Faulkner's relation to the context of literature. The myth of Faulkner as literary natural or poet without education has by now been thoroughly dispelled, and we have long lists of the authors Faulkner read and drew on for his work.[15] But we still lack a fully discriminated account of how his sense of literary tradition changed over the course of his career, or how his deepening knowledge of such tradition extended the resources of his work. Hugh Kenner's "Faulkner and the Avant-Garde" gives a fascinating glimpse of how Faulkner domesticated, even provincialized, the literary methods made available by international modernism;[16] many other phases of this subject remain to be looked into. Full consideration of the literary context that enabled and formed Faulkner's writing would also need to look at his relation to his markets. Unlike Melville, Faulkner succeeded in writing very popular magazine fiction the whole time he was producing his very unpopular novels; unlike James in the theater, he even had some success writing for the great mass entertainment medium of his time, the screen. (Who remembers that *Absalom, Absalom!* was completed in Hollywood?) How the resulting differentiation among the forms of his writing (novel, story, script) shaped his conception of his work within each form has not, so far as I know, been

---

[14] Another work that attempts these projects, with results very different from Willis's, is Jehlen's *Class and Character in Faulkner's South.*

[15] The most authoritative treatment of Faulkner's literary influences is Richard P. Adams's "The Apprenticeship of William Faulkner," reprinted in Linda W. Wagner, ed., *William Faulkner: Four Decades of Criticism* (East Lansing: Michigan State University Press, 1973), pp. 7–44. See also Arthur F. Kinney, *Faulkner's Narrative Poetics* (Amherst: University of Massachusetts Press, 1978), pp. 37–67. Faulkner's preface to *The Sound and the Fury,* reprinted in this volume, is by far the most revealing of his many statements on his sense of literary tradition.

[16] Kenner discusses Faulkner's somewhat similar transformation of his first style, that of *fin-de-siecle* aestheticism, in *A Homemade World* (New York: Knopf, 1975), pp. 194–210.

seriously considered.[17] Neither has the effect on Faulkner's writing of his great final market, the literary-critical one. It is clear that when the American literary establishment and the academy latched onto him in his last years, Faulkner got good at discussing his work in the way his new admirers were discussing it; and we might wonder whether the pronounced ethical thematics of his late writings are not products of a kind of reincorporation back into his fiction of the literary notions of its last institutional home. But again such questions, far from being answered, have scarcely begun to be asked.

All of which is to say that, even two anthologies later, there is still as great a need as ever for Faulkner to be known anew. This fact should not be dismaying. For if Faulkner has anything to teach, it is that he will always need to be reimagined: that it is only as he gets known anew that he can ever be really known at all.

---

[17] Attention has begun to be paid to at least one part of Faulkner's non-canonical writing, his work in film. See Bruce F. Kawin, *Faulkner and Film* (New York: Frederick Ungar, 1977), and Tom Dardis, *Some Time in the Sun* (New York: Charles Scribner's Sons, 1976).

An Introduction to
The Sound and the Fury

by *William Faulkner*

[For a new edition of *The Sound and the Fury* that was proposed by Random House but later abandoned, Faulkner wrote, during the summer of 1933, an introduction that survives in several partial and complete versions and drafts. This extraordinarily revealing document, never published during Faulkner's lifetime, was first brought into print in the early 1970s, when James B. Meriwether succeeded in reassembling the typescript of what was apparently Faulkner's final version. This text, reprinted below, first appeared in *The Southern Review*, 8 (Autumn 1972), pp. 708–710. Meriwether then edited a second, also complete but very different, version of the introduction, which was printed in *The Mississippi Quarterly*, 26 (Summer 1973), pp. 410–15. It is also reprinted here, under the heading "Another Version." For a full account of the circumstances under which these pieces were written and of their subsequent history, see James B. Meriwether, "An Introduction for *The Sound and the Fury*," *The Southern Review*, 8 (Autumn 1972), pp. 705–708.]

I wrote this book and learned to read. I had learned a little about writing from Soldiers' Pay—how to approach language, words: not with seriousness so much, as an essayist does, but with a kind of alert respect, as you approach dynamite; even with joy, as you approach women: perhaps with the same secretly unscrupulous intentions. But when I finished The Sound and The Fury I discovered that there is actually something to which the shabby term Art not only can, but must, be applied. I discovered then that I had gone through all that I had ever read, from Henry

James through Henty to newspaper murders, without making any distinction or digesting any of it, as a moth or a goat might. After The Sound and The Fury and without heeding to open another book and in a series of delayed repercussions like summer thunder, I discovered the Flauberts and Dostoievskys and Conrads whose books I had read ten years ago. With The Sound and The Fury I learned to read and quit reading, since I have read nothing since.

Nor do I seem to have learned anything since. While writing Sanctuary, the next novel to The Sound and The Fury, that part of me which learned as I wrote, which perhaps is the very force which drives a writer to the travail of invention and the drudgery of putting seventy-five or a hundred thousand words on paper, was absent because I was still reading by repercussion the books which I had swallowed whole ten years and more ago. I learned only from the writing of Sanctuary that there was something missing; something which The Sound and The Fury gave me and Sanctuary did not. When I began As I Lay Dying I had discovered what it was and knew that it would be also missing in this case because this would be a deliberate book. I set out deliberately to write a tour-de-force. Before I ever put pen to paper and set down the first word, I knew what the last word would be and almost where the last period would fall. Before I began I said, I am going to write a book by which, at a pinch, I can stand or fall if I never touch ink again. So when I finished it the cold satisfaction was there, as I had expected, but as I had also expected that other quality which The Sound and The Fury had given me was absent: that emotion definite and physical and yet nebulous to describe: that ecstasy, that eager and joyous faith and anticipation of surprise which the yet unmarred sheet beneath my hand held inviolate and unfailing, waiting for release. It was not there in As I Lay Dying. I said, It is because I knew too much about this book before I began to write it. I said, More than likely I shall never again have to know this much about a book before I begin to write it, and next time it will return. I waited almost two years, then I began Light in August, knowing no more about it than a young woman, pregnant, walking along a strange country road. I thought, I will recapture it now, since I know no more about this book than I did about The Sound and The Fury when I sat down before the first blank page.

It did not return. The written pages grew in number. The story was going pretty well: I would sit down to it each morning without reluctance yet still without that anticipation and that joy which alone ever made writing pleasure to me. The book was almost finished before I acquiesced to the fact that it would not recur, since I was now aware before each word was written down just what the people would do, since now I was deliberately choosing among possibilities and probabilities of behavior and weighing and measuring each choice by the scale of the Jameses and Conrads and Balzacs. I knew that I had read too much, that I had reached that stage which all young writers must pass through, in which he believes that he has learned too much about his trade. I received a copy of the printed book and I found that I didn't even want to see what kind of jacket Smith had put on it. I seemed to have a vision of it and the other ones subsequent to The Sound and The Fury ranked in order upon a shelf while I looked at the titled backs of them with a flagging attention which was almost distaste, and upon which each succeeding title registered less and less, until at last Attention itself seemed to say, Thank God I shall never need to open any one of them again. I believed that I knew then why I had not recaptured that first ecstasy, and that I should never again recapture it; that whatever novels I should write in the future would be written without reluctance, but also without anticipation or joy: that in The Sound and The Fury I had already put perhaps the only thing in literature which would ever move me very much: Caddy climbing the pear tree to look in the window at her grandmother's funeral while Quentin and Jason and Benjy and the negroes looked up at the muddy seat of her drawers.

This is the only one of the seven novels which I wrote without any accompanying feeling of drive or effort, or any following feeling of exhaustion or relief or distaste. When I began it I had no plan at all. I wasn't even writing a book. I was thinking of books, publication, only in the reverse, in saying to myself, I wont have to worry about publishers liking or not liking this at all. Four years before I had written Soldiers' Pay. It didn't take long to write and it got published quickly and made me about five hundred dollars. I said, Writing novels is easy. You dont make much doing it, but it is easy. I wrote Mosquitoes. It wasn't quite so easy to write and it didn't get published quite as quickly and it made me about four hundred dollars. I said,

Apparently there is more to writing novels, being a novelist, than I thought. I wrote Sartoris. It took much longer, and the publisher refused it at once. But I continued to shop it about for three years with a stubborn and fading hope, perhaps to justify the time which I had spent writing it. This hope died slowly, though it didn't hurt at all. One day I seemed to shut a door between me and all publishers' addresses and book lists. I said to myself, Now I can write. Now I can make myself a vase like that which the old Roman kept at his bedside and wore the rim slowly away with kissing it. So I, who had never had a sister and was fated to lose my daughter in infancy, set out to make myself a beautiful and tragic little girl.

[*Another version:*]

Art is no part of southern life. In the North it seems to be different. It is the hardest minor stone in Manhattan's foundation. It is a part of the glitter or shabbiness of the streets. The arrowing buildings rise out of it and because of it, to be torn down and arrow again. There will be people leading small bourgeois lives (those countless and almost invisible bones of its articulation, lacking any one of which the whole skeleton might collapse) whose bread will derive from it—polyglot boys and girls progressing from tenement schools to editorial rooms and art galleries; men with grey hair and paunches who run linotype machines and take up tickets at concerts and then go sedately home to Brooklyn and suburban stations where children and grandchildren await them—long after the descendents of Irish politicians and Neapolitan racketeers are as forgotten as the wild Indians and the pigeon.

And of Chicago too: of that rythm not always with harmony or tune; lusty, loudvoiced, always changing and always young; drawing from a river basin which is almost a continent young men and women into its living unrest and then spewing them forth again to write Chicago in New England and Virginia and Europe. But in the South art, to become visible at all, must become a ceremony, a spectacle; something between a gypsy encampment and a church bazaar given by a handful of alien mummers who must waste themselves in protest and active self-defense until there is nothing left with which to speak—a single week, say, of furious endeavor for a show to be held on Friday night and then struck and vanished, leaving only a paint-stiffened smock or a worn out typewriter ribbon in the corner and perhaps a small bill for cheesecloth or bunting in the hands of an astonished and bewildered tradesman.

Perhaps this is because the South (I speak in the sense of the indigenous dream of any given collection of men having something in common, be it only geography and climate, which shape their economic and spiritual aspirations into cities, into a pattern of houses or behavior) is old since dead. New York, whatever it may believe of itself, is young since alive; it is still a logical and unbroken progression from the Dutch. And Chicago even boasts of being young. But the South, as Chicago is the Middlewest and New York the East, is dead, killed by the Civil War. There is a thing known whimsically as the New South to be sure, but it is not the south. It is a land of Immigrants who are rebuilding the towns and cities into replicas of towns and cities in Kansas and Iowa and Illinois, with skyscrapers and striped canvas awnings instead of wooden balconies, and teaching the young men who sell the gasoline and the waitresses in the restaurants to say O yeah? and to speak with hard r's, and hanging over the intersections of quiet and shaded trees where no one save Northern tourists in Cadillacs and Lincolns ever pass at a gait faster than a horse trots, changing red-and-green lights and savage and peremptory bells.

Yet this art, which has no place in southern life, is almost the sum total of the Southern artist. It is his breath, blood, flesh, all. Not so much that it is forced back upon him or that he is forced bodily into it by the circumstance; forced to choose, lady and tiger fashion, between being an artist and being a man. He does it deliberately; he wishes it so. This has always been true of him and of him alone. Only Southerners have taken horsewhips and pistols to editors about the treatment or maltreatment of their manuscript. This—the actual pistols—was in the old days, of course, we no longer succumb to the impulse. But it is still there, still within us.

Because it is himself that the Southerner is writing about, not about his environment: who has, figuratively speaking, taken the artist in him in one hand and his milieu in the other and thrust the one into the other like a clawing and spitting cat into a croker sack. And he writes. We have never got and probably will never get, anywhere with music or the plastic forms.

We need to talk, to tell, since oratory is our heritage. We seem to try in the simple furious breathing (or writing) span of the individual to draw a savage indictment of the contemporary scene or to escape from it into a makebelieve region of swords and magnolias and mockingbirds which perhaps never existed anywhere. Both of the courses are rooted in sentiment; perhaps the ones who write savagely and bitterly of the incest in clay-floored cabins are the most sentimental. Anyway, each course is a matter of violent partizanship, in which the writer unconsciously writes into every line and phrase his violent despairs and rages and frustrations or his violent prophesies of still more violent hopes. That cold intellect which can write with calm and complete detachment and gusto of its contemporary scene is not among us; I do not believe there lives the Southern writer who can say without lying that writing is any fun to him. Perhaps we do not want it to be.

I seem to have tried both of the courses. I have tried to escape and I have tried to indict. After five years I look back at *The Sound and The Fury* and see that that was the turning point: in this book I did both at one time. When I began the book, I had no plan at all. I wasn't even writing a book. Previous to it I had written three novels, with progressively decreasing ease and pleasure, and reward or emolument. The third one was shopped about for three years during which I sent it from publisher to publisher with a kind of stubborn and fading hope of at least justifying the paper I had used and the time I had spent writing it. This hope must have died at last, because one day it suddenly seemed as if a door had clapped silently and forever to between me and all publishers' addresses and booklists and I said to myself, Now I can write. Now I can just write. Whereupon I, who had three brothers and no sisters and was destined to lose my first daughter in infancy, began to write about a little girl.

I did not realise then that I was trying to manufacture the sister which I did not have and the daughter which I was to lose, though the former might have been apparent from the fact that Caddy had three brothers almost before I wrote her name on paper. I just began to write about a brother and a sister splashing one another in the brook and the sister fell and wet her clothing and the smallest brother cried, thinking that the sister was conquered or perhaps hurt. Or perhaps he knew that he was the baby and that she would quit whatever water battles to comfort him. When she did so, when she quit the water fight and stooped in her wet garments above him, the entire story, which is all told by that same little brother in the first section, seemed to explode on the paper before me.

I saw that peaceful glinting of that branch was to become the dark, harsh flowing of time sweeping her to where she could not return to comfort him, but that just separation, division, would not be enough, not far enough. It must sweep her into dishonor and shame too. And that Benjy must never grow beyond this moment; that for him all knowing must begin and end with that fierce, panting, paused and stooping wet figure which smelled like trees. That he must never grow up to where the grief of bereavement could be leavened with understanding and hence the alleviation of rage as in the case of Jason, and of oblivion as in the case of Quentin.

I saw that they had been sent to the pasture to spend the afternoon to get them away from the house during the grandmother's funeral in order that the three brothers and the nigger children could look up at the muddy seat of Caddy's drawers as she climbed the tree to look in the window at the funeral, without then realising the symbology of the soiled drawers, for here again hers was the courage which was to face later with honor the shame which she was to engender, which Quentin and Jason could not face: the one taking refuge in suicide, the other in vindictive rage which drove him to rob his bastard niece of the meagre sums which Caddy could send her. For I had already gone on to night and the bedroom and Dilsey with the mud-stained drawers scrubbing the naked backside of that doomed little girl—trying to cleanse with the sorry byblow of its soiling that body, flesh, whose shame they symbolised and prophesied, as though she already saw the dark future and the part she was to play in it trying to hold that crumbling household together.

Then the story was complete, finished. There was Dilsey to be the future, to stand above the fallen ruins of the family like a ruined chimney, gaunt, patient and indomitable; and Benjy to be the past. He had to be an idiot so that, like Dilsey, he could be impervious to the future, though unlike her by refusing to accept it at all. Without thought or comprehension; shapeless, neuter, like something eyeless and voiceless which might have lived, existed merely because of its ability to suffer, in the beginning of life; half fluid, groping: a pallid and helpless mass of all mindless agony under sun, in time yet not of it save that he could nightly carry with him that fierce, courageous being who was to him but a touch and a sound that may be heard on any golf links and a smell like trees, into the slow bright shapes of sleep.

The story is all there, in the first section as Benjy told it. I did not try deliberately to make it obscure; when I realised that the story might be printed, I took three more sections, all longer than Benjy's, to try to clarify it. But when I wrote Benjy's section, I was not writing it to be printed. If I were to do it over now I would do it differently, because the writing of it as it now stands taught me both how to write and how to read, and even more: It taught me what I had already read, because on completing it I discovered, in a series of repercussions like summer thunder, the Flauberts and Conrads and Turgenievs which as much as ten years before I had consumed whole and without assimilating at all, as a moth or a goat might. I have read nothing since; I have not had to. And I have learned but one thing since about writing. That is, that the emotion definite and physical and yet nebulous to describe which the writing of Benjy's section of *The Sound and The Fury* gave me—that ecstasy, that eager and joyous faith and anticipation of surprise which the yet unmarred sheets beneath my hand held inviolate and unfailing—will not return. The unreluctance to begin, the cold satisfaction in work well and arduously done, is there and will continue to be there as long as I can do it well. But that other will not return. I shall never know it again.

So I wrote Quentin's and Jason's sections, trying to clarify Benjy's. But I saw that I was merely temporising; That I should have to get completely out of the book. I realised that there would be compensations, that in a sense I could then give a final turn to the screw and extract some ultimate distillation. Yet it took me better than a month to take pen and write *The day dawned bleak and chill* before I did so. There is a story somewhere about an old Roman who kept at his bedside a Tyrrhenian vase which he loved and the rim of which he wore slowly away with kissing it. I had made myself a vase, but I suppose I knew all the time that I could not live forever inside of it, that perhaps to have it so that I too could lie in bed and look at it would be better; surely so when that day should come when not only the ecstasy of writing would be gone, but the unreluctance and the something worth saying too. It's fine to think that you will leave something behind you when you die, but it's better to have made something you can die with. Much better the muddy bottom of a little doomed girl climbing a blooming pear tree in April to look in the window at the funeral.

OXFORD.
19 AUGUST, 1933.

William Faulkner: Vision of Good and Evil

by Cleanth Brooks

Professor Randall Stewart, in his very stimulating little book *American Literature and Christian Doctrine,* asserts that "Faulkner embodies and dramatizes the basic Christian concepts so effectively that he can with justice be regarded as one of the most profoundly Christian writers in our time. There is everywhere in his writings the basic premise of Original Sin: everywhere the conflict between the flesh and the spirit. One finds also the necessity of discipline, of trial by fire in the furnace of affliction, of sacrifice and the sacrificial death, of redemption through sacrifice. Man in Faulkner is a heroic, tragic figure." This is a view with which I am in basic sympathy. I agree heartily with Professor Stewart on the matter of Faulkner's concern with what he calls "original sin," and with Faulkner's emphasis upon discipline, sacrifice, and redemption. But to call Faulkner "one of the most profoundly Christian writers in our time" seems somewhat incautious. Perhaps it would be safer to say that Faulkner is a profoundly religious writer; that his characters come out of a Christian environment, and represent, whatever their shortcomings and whatever their theological heresies, Christian concerns; and that they are finally to be understood only by reference to Christian premises.

Probably the best place to start is with the term "original sin." The point of reference might very well be T. E. Hulme, one of the profoundly seminal influences on our time, though a critic and philosopher whom Faulkner probably never read. In "Humanism and the Religious Attitude" Hulme argued for a return to orthodox doctrine. His concern with religion, however, had nothing to do with recapturing what he called "the sentiment of Fra Angelico." Rather, "What is important," he asserted, "is

Reprinted with permission from Cleanth Brooks, *The Hidden God* (New Haven: Yale University Press, 1963), pp. 22–43.

what nobody seems to realize—the dogmas like that of Original Sin, which are the closest expression of the categories of the religious attitude. That man is in no sense perfect, but a wretched creature, who can apprehend perfection. It is not, then, that I put up with the dogma for the sake of the sentiment, but that I may possibly swallow the sentiment for the sake of the dogma."

Hulme's position as stated here would seem to smack of scholastic Calvinism rather than of the tradition of Catholic Christianity. His emphasis at least suggests that nature is radically evil and not merely gone wrong somehow—corrupted by a fall. But if Hulme's passage is so tinged, that very fact may make it the more relevant to Faulkner, who shows, in some aspects, the influence of Southern Puritanism.

Be that as it may, Hulme's is not a didactic theory of literature, which stresses some direct preachment to be made. On the contrary, his "classicism" derives from a clear distinction between religious doctrine and poetic structure. It is romantic poetry which blurs that distinction, competing with religion by trying to drag in the infinite. With romanticism we enter the area of "split religion," and romantic "damp and fugginess." For Hulme, the classic attitude involves a recognition of man's limitations—his finitude. Since the classical view of man recognizes his limitations and does not presume upon them, the classical attitude, Hulme argues, is a religious attitude. For Hulme is quite convinced that man, though capable of recognizing goodness, is not naturally good. It is only by discipline that he can achieve something of value.

The whole point is an important one, for Faulkner's positive beliefs are often identified with some kind of romantic primitivism. Thus his concern with idiots and children and uneducated rural people, both white and Negro, is sometimes interpreted to mean that man is made evil only by his environment with its corrupting restrictions and inhibitions, and that if man could only realize his deeper impulses, he would be good.[1]

Allied to this misconception is another, namely that Faulkner's characters have no power of choice, being merely the creatures of their drives and needs, and that they are determined by their

---

[1] Faulkner, a few years ago, in defining his notion of Christianity, called it a "code of behavior by means of which (man) makes himself a better human being than his nature wants to be, if he follows his nature only" (*Paris Review*, Spring 1956, p. 42).

environment and are helplessly adrift upon the tides of circumstance. It is true that many of his characters are obsessed creatures or badly warped by traumatic experiences, or that they are presented by Faulkner as acting under some kind of compulsion. But his characters are not mere products of an environment. They have the power of choice, they make decisions, and they win their goodness through effort and discipline.

If Faulkner does not believe that man is naturally good and needs only to realize his natural impulses, and if he does believe that man has free will and must act responsibly and discipline himself, then these beliefs are indeed worth stressing, for they are calculated to separate him sharply from writers of a more naturalistic and secularistic temper. But I grant that to attribute to Faulkner a belief in original sin or in man's need for discipline would not necessarily prove him a Christian. The concept of grace, for example, is either lacking or at least not clearly evident in Faulkner's work.

Let us begin, then, by examining Faulkner's criticism of secularism and rationalism. A very important theme in his earlier work is the discovery of evil, which is part of man's initiation into the nature of reality. That brilliant and horrifying early novel *Sanctuary* is, it seems to me, to be understood primarily in terms of such an initiation. Horace Benbow is the sentimental idealist, the man of academic temper, who finds out that the world is not a place of moral tidiness or even of justice. He discovers with increasing horror that evil is rooted in the very nature of things. As an intellectual, he likes to ponder meanings and events, he has a great capacity for belief in ideas, and a great confidence in the efficacy of reason. What he comes to discover is the horrifying presence of evil, its insidiousness, and its penetration of every kind of rational or civilized order. There is in this story, to be sure, the unnatural rape of the seventeen-year-old girl by the gangster Popeye, and the story of Popeye's wanton murder of Tommy, but Horace Benbow might conceivably accept both of these things as the kinds of cruel accidents to which human life is subject. What crumples him up is the moral corruption of the girl, which follows on her rape; she actually accepts her life in the brothel and testifies at the trial in favor of the man who had abducted her. What Horace also discovers is that the forces of law and order are also corruptible. His opponent in the trial, the district attorney, plays fast and loose with the evidence and actually ensures that the innocent man will not only be convicted but burned to death by a mob. And what perhaps Horace himself does not discover (but it is made plainly evident to the reader) is that Horace's betrayal at the trial is finally a bosom betrayal: Horace's own sister gives the district attorney the tip-off that will allow him to defeat her brother and make a mockery of justice. Indeed, Horace's sister, the calm and serene Narcissa, is, next to Popeye, the most terrifying person in the novel. She simply does not want her brother associated with people like the accused man, Lee Goodwin, the bootlegger, and his common-law wife. She exclaims to her brother, "I don't see that it makes any difference who [committed the murder]. The question is, are you going to stay mixed up with it?" And she sees to it with quiet and efficient ruthlessness that the trial ends at the first possible date, even though this costs an innocent man's life.

Sanctuary is clearly Faulkner's bitterest novel. It is a novel in which the initiation which every male must undergo is experienced in its most shattering and disillusioning form. Horace not only discovers the existence of evil: he experiences it not as an abstract idea but as an integral portion of reality. After he has had his interview with Temple Drake in the brothel, he thinks: "Perhaps it is upon the instant that we realize, admit, that there is a logical pattern to evil, that we die," and he thinks of the expression he had once seen in the eyes of a dead child and in the eyes of the other dead: "the cooling indignation, the shocked despair fading, leaving two empty globes in which the motionless world lurked profoundly in miniature."

One of the most important connections has already been touched upon in what I have said earlier. Horace Benbow's initiation into the nature of reality and the nature of evil is intimately associated with his discovery of the true nature of woman. His discovery is quite typical of Faulkner's male characters. In the Faulknerian notion of things, men have to lose their innocence, confront the hard choice, and through a process of initiation discover reality. The women are already in possession of this knowledge, naturally and instinctively. That is why in moments of bitterness Faulkner's male characters—Mr. Compson in *The Sound and the Fury,* for example—assert that women are not innocent. Mr. Compson tells his son Quentin: "Women are like that[;] they don't acquire knowledge of people[. Men] are for that[. Women] are just born with a practical fertility of suspicion. . . . they have an affinity for evil[—]for supplying whatever the evil lacks in itself[—]drawing it about them instinctively as you do bed clothing in slumber. . . ." Again, "Women only use other people's codes of honour."

I suppose that we need not take these Schopenhauerian profundities of the bourbon-soaked Mr. Compson too seriously. It might on the whole be more accurate to say that Faulkner's women lack the callow idealism of the men, have fewer illusions about human nature, and are less trammeled by legalistic distinctions and niceties of any code of conduct.

Faulkner's view of women, then, is radically old-fashioned—even medieval. Woman is the source and sustainer of virtue and also a prime source of evil. She can be either, because she is, as man is not, always a little beyond good and evil. With her powerful natural drives and her instinct for the concrete and personal, she does not need to agonize over her decisions. There is no code for her to master—no initiation for her to undergo. For this reason she has access to a wisdom which is veiled from man; and man's codes, good or bad, are always, in their formal abstraction, a little absurd in her eyes. Women are close to nature; the feminine principle is closely related to the instinctive and natural: woman typically manifests pathos rather than ethos.

A little later I shall have something more to say about Faulkner's characters in confrontation with nature. At this point, however, I want to go back and refer to another aspect of *Sanctuary*. The worst villains in Faulkner are cut off from nature. They have in some profound way denied their nature, like Flem Snopes in *The Hamlet,* who has no natural vices, only the unnatural vice of a pure lust for power and money. In *Sanctuary* Popeye is depicted as a sort of *ludus naturae*. Everybody has noticed the way in which he is described, as if he were a kind of automation, with eyes like "two knobs of soft black rubber." As Horace watches him across the spring, Popeye's "face had a queer, bloodless color, as though seen by electric light; against the sunny silence, in his slanted straw hat and his slightly akimbo arms, he had that vicious depthless quality of stamped tin." Faulkner's two figures of speech are brilliantly used here. They serve to rob Popeye of substance and to turn him into a sinister black silhouette against the spring landscape. The phrase "as though seen by electric light" justifies the description of his queer, bloodless color, but it does more than this. Juxtaposed as it is to the phrase "against the sunny silence," it stresses the sense of the contrived, the artificial, as though Popeye constituted a kind of monstrous affront to the natural scene. These suggestions of a shadowy lack of substance are confirmed at the end of the sentence with the closing phrase: "depthless quality of stamped tin." Faulkner relentlessly forces this notion of the unnatural: Popeye deliberately spits into the spring, he cringes in terror from the low swooping owl, he is afraid of the dark.

Popeye has no natural vices either. He cannot drink. Since he is impotent, he is forced to use unnatural means in his rape of Temple. As a consequence, some readers take Popeye to be a kind of allegorical figure, a representation of the inhumanly mechanistic forces of our society. We may say that Popeye is quite literally a monster, remembering that the Latin *monstrum* signifies something that lies outside the ordinary course of nature.

Though Popeye represents an extreme case, in this matter he is typical of all of Faulkner's villains. For example, Thomas Sutpen, in *Absalom, Absalom!*, is a man of great courage and heroic stature, who challenges the role of a tragic protagonist. Yet he has about him this same rigid and mechanical quality. Sutpen, as an acquaintance observes, believes "that the ingredients of morality were like the ingredients of pie or cake and once you had measured them and balanced them and mixed them and put them into the oven it was all finished and nothing but pie or cake could come out."

Sutpen has a great plan in mind, his "design," he calls it—which involves his building a great plantation house and setting up a dynasty. As he tells General Compson, "I had a design. To accomplish it I should require money, a house, and a plantation, slaves, a family—incidentally, of course, a wife." But when he finds later that his wife has a trace of Negro blood, he puts her aside, and he does it with an air of honest grievance. He says "[Her parents] deliberately withheld from me the one fact which I have reason to know they were aware would have caused me to decline the entire matter, otherwise they would not have withheld it from me—a fact which I did not learn until after my son was born. And even then I did not act hastily. I could have reminded them of these wasted years, these years which would now leave me behind with my schedule. . . ." (The last term is significant: Sutpen, modern man that he is, works in accordance with a timetable.) He tells General Compson that when he put aside his wife and child, "his conscience had bothered him somewhat at first but that he had argued calmly and logically with his conscience until it was settled." General Compson is aghast at this revelation of moral myopia. He calls it "innocence," and by the term he means a blindness to the nature of reality. And since the writer is Faulkner, the blindness involves a blindness to the nature of woman. For Sutpen has actually believed that by providing a more than just property settlement he could reconcile his wife to his abandoning her. General Compson had thrown up his hands and exclaimed: "Good God, man . . . what kind of conscience [did you have] to trade with which would have warranted you in the belief that you could have bought immunity from her for no other coin but justice?—"

Evil for Faulkner, then, involves a violation of nature and runs counter to the natural appetites and affections. And yet, as we have seen, the converse is not true; Faulkner does not consider the natural and instinctive and impulsive as automatically and necessarily good. Here I think rests the best warrant for maintaining that Faulkner holds an orthodox view of man and reality. For his men, at least, cannot be content merely with being natural. They cannot live merely by their instincts and natural appetites. They must confront the fact of evil. They are constrained to moral choices. They have to undergo a test of their courage, in making and abiding by the choice. They achieve goodness by discipline and effort. This proposition is perhaps most fully and brilliantly illustrated in Faulkner's story "The Bear." Isaac McCaslin, when he comes of age, decides to repudiate his inheritance. He refuses to accept his father's plantation and chooses to earn his living as a carpenter and to live in a rented room. There are two powerful motives that shape this decision: the sacramental view of nature which he has been taught by the old hunter, Sam Fathers, and the discovery of his grandfather's guilt in his treatment of one of his slaves: the grandfather had incestuously begotten a child upon his own half-Negro daughter.

"The Bear" is thus a story of penance and expiation, as also of a difficult moral decision made and maintained, but since it is so well known and has received so much commentary, I want to illustrate Faulkner's characteristic drama of moral choice from a less familiar story, "An Odor of Verbena," which is the conclud-

ing section of Faulkner's too little appreciated but brilliant novel
The Unvanquished. As this episode opens, word has come to
Bayard Sartoris, a young man of twenty-four off at law school,
that his father has been assassinated by a political enemy. Ringo,
the young Negro man of his own age and his boyhood compan-
ion, has ridden to the little town where Bayard is at law school
to bring the news. Bayard knows what is expected of him—the
date is 1874, the tradition of the code of honor still lingers,
the devastating Civil War and the Reconstruction have contorted
the land with violence, and Bayard knows that the community
expects him to call his father's assassin to account. Even the quiet
and gentle Judge Wilkins with whom he is studying law expects
him to do so, and though he speaks to the boy with pity ("Bayard, my son, my dear son"), he offers him not only his horse
but his pistol as well. Certainly also Bayard's father's Civil War
troop expect him to avenge his father. Bayard's young step-
mother, eight years older than he, expects it. Speaking in a
"silvery ecstatic voice" like the priestess of a rite wrought up to
a point of hysteria, she offers Bayard the pistols when he returns
to the family home. Even Ringo expects it.

Some years before, when Bayard and Ringo were sixteen, at
the very end of the Civil War, when the region had become a
no-man's land terrorized by bushwhackers, Bayard's grandmother
had been killed by a ruffian named Grumby, and Bayard and
Ringo had followed him for weeks until finally they had run
him down and killed him. Bayard had loved his grandmother,
and was resolved that her murderer should be punished. But there
was no law and order in this troubled time to which he could
appeal; the two sixteen-year-old boys had to undertake the
punishment themselves.

Now as the two young men ride back to Jefferson, Ringo says
to Bayard, "We could bushwhack him. . . . Like we done Grumby
that day. But I reckon that wouldn't suit that white skin you
walks around in." Bayard in fact has resolved that he will not
kill again.

The motive for this decision is complex. For one thing, he
realizes that his father had become a proud and abstracted and
ruthless man. Bayard had loved his father but is well aware that
his father had pressed his opponent, Redmond, far too hard.
George Wyatt, the countryman who had served under his father,
earlier had in fact come to Bayard to ask him to restrain his father:

" 'Right or wrong,' he said, 'us boys and most of the other folks in this country know John's right. But he ought to let Redmond alone. I know what's wrong: he's had to kill too many folks, and that's bad for a man. We all know Colonel's brave as a lion, but Redmond ain't no coward either and they ain't any use in making a brave man that made one mistake eat crow all the time. Can't you talk to him?' "

Another powerful motive is evidently the psychic wound that Bayard has suffered in the killing of Grumby. He has executed vengeance once, and in that instance there were extenuating circumstances to justify his taking the law into his own hands. But this case is different, and as he says to himself before he begins his journey home, "If there [is] anything at all in the Book, anything of hope and peace for [God's] blind and bewildered spawn," the command " '*Thou Shalt not kill*' must be it." Finally, and not least, there is the example of his own father. Even his father had decided that there had been too much killing. Two months before, he had told Bayard: "Now I shall do a little moral house cleaning. I am tired of killing men, no matter what the necessity or the end." Thus Bayard, in resolving not to avenge his father, may be said to be following his father's own resolve.

But Bayard, as a member of a tightly knit community, does not want to be branded as a coward; he respects his community's opinion, and he feels compelled to live up to what the community expects of him. And so he resolves, though the reader does not learn of it until late in the story, to face Redmond, but to face him unarmed.

There is one person who understands his dilemma and can support him in his decision. It is his Aunt Jenny, who tells him when he arrives home that night: " 'Yes. All right. Don't let it be Drusilla, poor hysterical young woman. And don't let it be [your father], Bayard, because he's dead now. And don't let it be George Wyatt and those others who will be waiting for you tomorrow morning. I know you are not afraid.' 'But what good will that do?' I said. 'What good will that do?' . . . 'I must live with myself, you see.' 'Then it's not just Drusilla? Not just him? Not just George Wyatt and Jefferson?' 'No,' I said."

It is indeed not just Drusilla and George Wyatt and the other outsiders that are forcing Bayard to take his proposed course of action. As he tells his aunt, it is not enough that *she* knows that he is not afraid. He must prove it to himself. "I must live with myself," he says. This is the situation of many a Faulkner character. He must live with himself. He must prove to himself that he possesses the requisite courage.

Bayard is fortunate. The man that he goes to meet is also brave, also decent. He has decided that, having killed the father, he will not kill the young son. Thus, when Bayard walks up the stairs past the small faded sign *"B. J. Redmond, Atty at Law"* and opens the door, he sees Redmond sitting "behind the desk, not much taller than Father, but thicker as a man gets that spends most of his time sitting and listening to people, freshly shaven and with fresh linen; a lawyer yet it was not a lawyer's face—a face much thinner than the body would indicate, strained (and yes, tragic; I know that now) and exhausted beneath the neat recent steady strokes of the razor, holding a pistol flat on the desk before him, loose beneath his hand and aimed at nothing." Redmond fires twice but Bayard can see that the gun was not aimed at him and that the misses are deliberate. Then Redmond gets up from his desk, blunders down the stairs and walks on out past George Wyatt and the six other members of Colonel Sartoris' old troop. He "walked through the middle of them with his hat on and his head up (they told me how someone shouted at him: 'Have you killed that boy too?') saying no word, staring straight ahead and with his back to them, on the station where the south-bound train was just in and got on it with no baggage, nothing, and went away from Jefferson and from Mississippi and never came back."

George Wyatt rushes up to Bayard, mistakenly thinking that he had taken Redmond's pistol away from him and then missed him, missed him twice. "Then he answered himself . . . 'No; wait. You walked in here without even a pocket knife and let him miss you twice. My God in heaven.' " But he adds, " 'You ain't done anything to be ashamed of. I wouldn't have done it that way, myself. I'd a shot at him once, anyway. But that's your way or you wouldn't have done it." And even Drusilla, the wrought-up priestess of violence, before she leaves the house forever to go back to her kinsfolk in Alabama, leaves on Bayard's pillow a sprig of verbena because it is the odor of courage, "that odor which she said you could smell alone above the smell of horses," as a token that she too has accepted his act as brave and honorable.

One further observation: as I have already remarked, it is the men who have to be initiated into the meaning of reality, who have to observe a code of conduct, who have to prove themselves worthy. Aunt Jenny, as a woman, is outside the code. Indeed she sees the code as absurd and quixotic, though she knows that Bayard as a man will have to observe it. And what shall we say of Drusilla, who is a woman, and yet is the very high priestess of the code? Drusilla is the masculinized woman, who as a type occurs more than once in Faulkner. Drusilla's story is that she has lost her fiancé early in the war and finally in her boredom and despair has actually ridden with the Confederate cavalry. She is brave and Faulkner gives her her due, but he is not celebrating her as a kind of Confederate Joan of Arc. Her action exacts its penalty and she ends a warped and twisted woman, truly a victim of the war.

I realize that I am risking oversimplification in pressing some of these issues so hard—for example, the contrast between man and woman, in their relation to nature and to their characteristic roles as active and passive. One may be disposed to doubt that even a traditional writer writing about a traditional society would stylize these relationships as much as I have suggested Faulkner has. Yet I am very anxious to sketch in, even at the risk of over-bold strokes, the general nature of Faulkner's conception of good and evil, and so I mean to stand by this summary: Faulkner sees the role of man as active; man makes choices and lives up to the choices. Faulkner sees the role of woman as characteristically fostering and sustaining. She undergirds society, upholding the family and community mores, sending her men out into battle, including the ethical battle. This generalization I believe, is, if oversimplified, basically true. And I should like to relate it to Faulkner's "Calvinistic" Protestantism. In so far as his Calvinism represents a violent repression and constriction of natural impulse, a denial of nature itself, Faulkner tends to regard it as a terrible and evil thing. And the natural foil to characters who have so hardened their hearts in accordance with the notion of a harsh and vindictive God is the feminine principle as exemplified by a person like Lena Grove, the heroine of *Light in August*. Lena has a childlike confidence in herself and in mankind. She is a creature of warm natural sympathies and a deep instinctive commitment to her natural function.

But Faulkner has still another relation to Calvinistic Protestantism. Insofar as the tradition insists that man must be brought

ιe urgency of decision, must be set tests of courage and
ce, must have his sinews strung tight for some moral
ι捕ρ oι his back braced so as to stand firm against the push of
circumstance, Faulkner evidently derives from this tradition.
From it may be derived the very necessity that compels his male
characters to undergo an initiation. The required initiation may
be analogous to the crisis of conversion and the character's
successful entrance into knowledge of himself, analogous to the
sinner's experiencing salvation.

On the conscious level, Faulkner is obviously a Protestant
anticleric, fascinated, but also infuriated, by some of the more
violently repressive features of the religion that dominates his
country. This matter is easily illustrated. One of his masterpieces, *Light in August,* provides a stinging criticism of the harsher
aspects of Protestantism. Indeed a basic theme in *Light in August*
is man's strained attempt to hold himself up in a rigid aloofness
above the relaxed female world. The struggle to do so is, as
Faulkner portrays it in this novel, at once monstrous, comic, and
heroic, as the various characters take up their special postures.

In a character like old Doc Hines, there is a definite distortion
and perversion. His fury at "bitchery and abomination" is the
fury of a crazed man. In her conversation with Bunch and
Hightower, Mrs. Hines states quite precisely what has happened
to her husband: he began "then to take God's name in vain and
in pride to justify and excuse the devil that was in him." His
attribution of his furies to God is quite literally a taking of God's
name in vain, blasphemy. The tendency to call one's own hates
the vengeance of a just God is a sin to which Protestantism has
always been prone. But not merely Southern Protestantism and,
of course, not merely Protestantism as such.

Calvin Burden represents another instance of the militant
Protestant, but this man's heartiness and boisterous energy have
something of the quality of comedy. He is the son of a Unitarian
minister; but when he runs away to the West, he becomes a
Roman Catholic and lives for a year in a monastery. Then, on
his marriage, he repudiates the Catholic Church, choosing for
the scene of his formal repudiation "a saloon, insisting that every
one present listen to him and state their objections." Then,
though he cannot read the English Bible—he had learned from
the priests in California to read Spanish—he begins to instruct
his child in the true religion, interspersing his readings to the

child in Spanish with "extemporised dissertations composed half of the bleak and bloodless logic which he remembered from his father on interminable New England Sundays and half of immediate hellfire and tangible brimstone." Perhaps he differs from the bulk of doctrinaire hellfire and brimstone Protestants in not being a "proselyter" or a "missionary." But everything else marks him as truly of the breed: his intensity, his stern authoritarianism, and his violence. He has killed a man in an argument over slavery and he threatens to "frail the tar" out of his children if they do not learn to hate what he hates—hell and slaveholders.

The case of the Rev. Gail Hightower is one of the most interesting of all. He is the only one of these Protestants who has had formal theological training. Because of that fact one might expect him to be the most doctrinaire. He is not. He seems at the beginning of the book the most tolerant and pitying of all the characters, the one who recoils in horror at man's capacity for evil and man's propensity to crucify his fellows: he is a man whose only defense against violence is nonresistance. One may be inclined to say that Hightower had rebelled against his Calvinist training and repudiated the jealous and repressive God. Certainly, there is truth in this notion. Hightower is a disillusioned man and a man who has learned something from his sufferings. But there is a sense in which he has never broken out of the mold: he still stresses a God of justice rather than of mercy, for his sincerest belief is that he has somehow "bought immunity." He exclaims: "I have paid. I have paid"—in confidence that God is an honest merchant who has receipted his bill and will honor his title to the precious merchandise he has purchased at such cost.

Lastly there is the case of Joe Christmas, the violent rebel against hellfire Protestantism. His detachment from any kind of human community is shocking. Here is a man who has no family ties, no continuity with the past, no place in any community whatsoever. He is a man who has literally tried to kick the earth out from under his feet. Yet his very alienation and his insistence upon his own individual integrity are touched with the tragically heroic. As a child he is conscious that he is being hounded by old Doc Hines; he resists stubbornly the discipline imposed by his foster father McEachern, whom he finally brains with a chair; and when his paramour, Joanna Burden, threatens him with hell and insists that he kneel with her and pray for forgiveness, he decapitates her. Yet there is a most important sense in which Joe

Christmas is the sternest and most doctrinaire Calvinist in the book.

He imbibes more from the training of his foster father than he realizes. For all that he strains in fierce resistance against him, he "could depend" on "the hard, just, ruthless man." It is the "soft kindness" of the woman, his foster mother that he abominates. If one mark of the Calvinists in this novel is their fear and distrust of women and their hatred of the female principle, then Joe Christmas is eminently qualified to take a place among them. He even has affinities with his old childhood ogre, Doc Hines, and Hines' fury at the bitchery of women and the abomination of Negro blood. Joe, hearing the "fecundmellow" voices of Negro women, feels that he and "all other manshaped life about him" had been returned to the "lightless hot wet primogenitive Female" and runs from the scene in a kind of panic.

Christmas too wants not mercy but justice, is afraid of the claims of love and its obligations, and yearns only for a vindication of his identity and integrity—a vindication made the more difficult by his not really knowing precisely what he would vindicate. When he puts aside the temptation to marry Joanna and win ease and security, he does it by saying: "If I give in now, I will deny all the thirty years that I have lived to make me what I chose to be." Finally, Joe is something of a fatalist, and his fatalism is a kind of perversion of Calvinist determinism. On his way to murder Joanna, "he believed with calm paradox that he was the volitionless servant of the fatality in which he believed that he did not believe." But so "fated" is his act of murder that he keeps saying to himself "I had to do it"—using the past tense, as if the act had already been performed.

Lena (along with Eula of *The Hamlet*) has sometimes been called an earth goddess. The description does have a certain aptness when applied to Eula, especially in some of the more rhapsodic passages of *The Hamlet*. But it is a little highfalutin for Lena. It is more accurate to say that Lena is one of Faulkner's several embodiments of the female principle—indeed one of the purest and least complicated of his embodiments. Her rapport with nature is close. She is never baffled as to what course of action to take. She is never torn by doubts and indecisions. There is no painful introspection. This serene composure has frequently been put down to sheer mindlessness, and Lena, to be sure, is a very simple young woman. But Faulkner himself undoubtedly attributes most of Lena's quiet force to her female nature. In this novel the principal male characters suffer alienation. They are separated from the community, are in rebellion against it—and against nature. But Lena moves serenely into the community, and it gathers itself about her with protective gestures. Its response to her, of course, is rooted in a deep and sound instinct: Lena embodies the principle upon which any human community is founded. She is the carrier of life and she has to be protected and nurtured if there is to be any human community at all.

I have said that *Light in August* depicts man's strained attempt to hold himself up in rigid aloofness above the relaxed female world. In terms of the plot, Lena is the direct means by which Byron Bunch and the indirect means by which Hightower are redeemed from their pallid half lives and brought back into the community. This coming back into the community is an essential part of the redemption. Unless the controlling purposes of the individuals are related to those that other men share, and in which the individual can participate, he is indeed isolated, and is forced to fall back upon his personal values, with all the risk of fanaticism and distortion to which such isolation is liable.

The community is at once the field for man's action and the norm by which his action is judged and regulated. It sometimes seems that the sense of an organic community has all but disappeared from modern fiction, and the disappearance accounts for the terrifying self-consciousness and subjectivity of a great deal of modern writing. That Faulkner has some sense of an organic community still behind him is among his most important resources as a writer.

In *Light in August* Faulkner uses Lena to confirm an ideal of integrity and wholeness in the light of which the alienated characters are judged; and this is essentially the function of Dilsey, the Negro servant in *The Sound and the Fury,* regarded by many people as Faulkner's masterpiece. Dilsey's role, to be sure, is more positive than Lena's. She has affinities not with the pagan goddess but with the Christian saint. She is not the young woman and young mother that Lena is. She is an older woman and an older mother, and she is the sustaining force—the only possible sustaining force of a broken and corrupted family.

Yet Dilsey's primary role is generally similar to Lena's: she affirms the ideal of wholeness in a family which shows in every other member splintering and disintegration. *The Sound and the*

Fury can be regarded as a study in the fragmentation of modern man. There is Benjy, the idiot brother who represents the life of the instincts and the unreflective emotions; there is Quentin, the intellectual and artistic brother, who is conscious of his own weakness and failure and yet so hagridden by impossible ideals that he finally turns away from life altogether and commits suicide; and there is Jason, the brother who represents an aggressive and destructive rationalism that dissolves all family and community loyalties and attachments. There has been a somewhat strained attempt to portray the brothers in Freudian terms: Benjy as the *id,* Quentin as the tortured *ego,* and Jason as the tyrannical and cruel *super-ego.* Faulkner's own way of regarding the three brothers (as implied in the appendix he supplied for the Modern Library edition) is interesting. Benjy is an idiot, of course; Quentin, in his obsession, is obviously half-mad; and Jason is perfectly sane, the first "sane" Compson for generations. Faulkner's mocking choice of the term "sane" to characterize Jason's coldly monstrous self-serving (all of Faulkner's villains, let me repeat, are characterized by this devouring and destructive rationalism) is highly significant. It is as if Faulkner argued that mere sanity were not enough—indeed that pure sanity was inhuman. The good man has to transcend his mere intellect with some overflow of generosity and love.

But we ought not to confine ourselves to the three brothers, for Dilsey is being contrasted not merely with them but with the whole of the family. There is Mr. Compson, who has been defeated by life and has sunk into whisky and fatalism. There is Mrs. Compson, the mother, whom Faulkner calls a "cold, weak" person. She is the whining, self-centered hypochondriac who has poisoned the whole family relationship. She is evidently a primary cause of her husband's cynicism; she has spoiled and corrupted her favorite son, Jason; and she has withheld her love from the other children. Quentin, on the day of his suicide, can say to himself bitterly, "If I only had a mother." Mrs. Compson is all that Dilsey is not. It is the mother role that she has abandoned that Dilsey is compelled to assume. There is lastly the daughter of the family, Candace, who in her own way also represents the dissolution of the family. Candace has become a wanton. Sex is her particular escape from an unsatisfactory home, and she is subject to her own kind of specialization, the semiprofessionalism of a sexual adventuress.

In contrast with this splintered family, Dilsey maintains a wholeness. Indeed, Dilsey's wholeness constitutes her holiness. (It is well to remember that *whole* and *holy* are related and come from the same root.) In Dilsey the life of the instincts, including the sex drive, the life of the emotions, and the life of ideal values and of rationality are related meaningfully to one another. To say this is to say, of course, that Dilsey is a profoundly religious person. Her life with its round of daily tasks and responsibilities is related to the larger life of eternity and eternal values. Dilsey does not have to strain to make meaningful some particular desire or dream or need. Her world is a solid and meaningful world. It is filled with pain, toil, and difficulty, but it is not wrenched by agonizing doubts and perplexities.

I said a moment ago that Dilsey was sometimes compared to the saint and in what I am going to say I do not mean to deprive her of her properly deserved halo. But we must not allow the term to sentimentalize her. If she treats with compassion the idiot Benjy, saying "You's de Lawd's chile, anyway," she is quite capable of dealing summarily with her own child, Luster, when he needs a rebuke: "Lemme tell you somethin, nigger boy, you got jes es much Compson devilment in you es any of em. Is you right sho you never broke dat window?" Dilsey's earthiness and her human exasperations are very much in evidence in this novel. Because they are, Dilsey's "saintliness" is altogether credible and convincing.

One may say in general of Faulkner's Negroes that they remain close to a concrete world of values—less perverted by abstraction —more honest in recognizing what is essential and elemental than are most of the white people. Faulkner certainly does not assume any inherent virtue in the Negro race. But he does find among his Negro characters less false pride, less false idealism, more seasoned discipline in the elemental human relationships. The Negro virtues which Faulkner praises in "The Bear" are endurance, patience, honesty, courage, and the love of children— white or black. Dilsey, then, is not a primitive figure who through some mystique of race or healthiness of natural impulses is good. Dilsey is unsophisticated and warm-hearted, but she is no noble savage. Her role is in its general dimensions comparable to that of her white sisters such as the matriarchs Aunt Jenny and Mrs. Rosa Millard, fostering and sustaining forces. If she goes beyond them in exemplifying the feminine principle at its best, still hers is no mere goodness by and of nature, if one means by this a goodness that justifies a faith in man as man. Dilsey does not believe in man; she believes in God.

To try for a summary of a very difficult and complicated topic: Evil for Faulkner involves the violation of the natural and the denial of the human. As Isaac's older kinsman says in "The Bear," "Courage and honor and pride, and pity and love of justice and of liberty. They all touch the heart, and what the heart holds to becomes truth, as far as we know truth." A meanness of spirit and coldness of calculation which would deny the virtues that touch the heart is by that very fact proven false. Yet Faulkner is no disciple of Jean-Jacques Rousseau. He has no illusions that man is naturally good or that he can safely trust to his instincts and emotions. Man is capable of evil, and this means that goodness has to be achieved by struggle and discipline and effort. Like T. S. Eliot, Faulkner has small faith in social arrangements so perfectly organized that nobody has to take the trouble to be good. Finally Faulkner's noblest characters are willing to face the fact that most men can learn the deepest truths about themselves and about reality only through sufferings. Hurt and pain and loss are not mere accidents to which the human being is subject; nor are they mere punishments incurred by human error; they can be the means to the deeper knowledge and to the more abundant life.

Faulkner and the Negroes

by Irving Howe

All of the tensions in Faulkner's work reach an extreme in
his presentment of Negro life and character. Problems of value
which in his novels emerge as problems of perception, become
magnified and exacerbated when he writes about Negroes. In
saying this, I would stress that my concern is not with Faulkner's
explicit views about the "racial question," or at least that my
concern with those views extends no further than the way they
condition the novels. In their own right, Faulkner's opinions
are usually the least interesting aspect of his work: they matter
only when absorbed into his art, there to undergo transformations of a kind that justify our speaking of literature as a mode
of creation.

Complex and ambiguous responses to the Negroes are pre-
dictable, almost conventional among sensitive Southern writers;
they stem partly from an inheritance of guilt and uncertainty,
partly from a ripening of heart. But in Faulkner's fiction, beneath
its worried surface of attitude and idea, there is also a remarkable steadiness of feeling toward the Negro. His opinions change,
his early assurance melts away, his sympathies visibly enlarge;
but always there is a return to one central image, an image of
memory and longing.

In *The Unvanquished* the boy, Bayard Sartoris, and his Negro
friend, Ringo, eat, play, and live together. When the two boys
and Granny Rosa Millard begin a long journey, Bayard and
Ringo, to whom Miss Rosa is also "Granny," take turns, in
simple equality, holding a parasol over her head. "That's how
Ringo and I were," Bayard nostalgically recalls. "We were almost
the same age, and Father always said that Ringo was a little

Reprinted with permission from Irving Howe, *William Faulkner: A Critical Study*, 3rd ed. (Chicago: University of Chicago Press, 1975), pp. 116–134.
© 1951 by the American Jewish Committee; © renewed 1979 by Irving Howe.

smarter than I was, but that didn't count with us anymore than
the difference in the color of our skins counted. What counted
was what one of us had done or seen that the other had not,
and ever since that Christmas I had been ahead of Ringo because
I had seen a railroad." Bayard is here expressing an ideal of
boyhood friendship, unaffected by social grade and resting on
that intuitive sense of scruple, that belief in "fairness," common
to boys.

The same vision, or a similar one, appears in other Faulkner
novels. In *The Sound and the Fury* the only happy memories
the Compsons retain are memories of scenes in which white and
Negro children play together. In *Absalom, Absalom!* there are
no glimpses of friendship between boys of the two races, but the
pioneer innocence of young Sutpen is defined as a freedom
from both racial feeling and economic acquisitiveness. In "The
Bear" the boy, Isaac McCaslin, unconsciously—and then with
considered assent—claims as his spiritual parent the old Negro,
Sam Fathers; and a similar claim determines the relationship
between Chick Mallison and Lucas Beauchamp in *Intruder in
the Dust.* In the story "Go Down, Moses" an old white woman,
Miss Worsham, explains her wish to help an old Negro woman,
Mollie Beauchamp, by invoking a childhood friendship of
decades ago: "Mollie and I were born in the same month. We
grew up together as sisters would." By contrast, Joe Christmas
in *Light in August* seems the most deprived of Faulkner's characters precisely because he has no childhood memories to fall
back on.

The most dramatic rendering of this theme occurs in the story,
"The Fire and the Hearth." For the white man Roth Edmonds,
Mollie Beauchamp is "the only mother he ever knew, who had
not only delivered him on that night of rain and flood . . . but
moved into the very house, bringing her own child, the white
child and the black one sleeping in the same room with her so
that she could suckle them both." As a boy, Roth feels that his
home and the home of his Negro friend Henry Beauchamp have
"become interchangeable: himself and his foster-brother sleeping
on the same pallet in the white man's house or in the same bed
in the negro's and eating of the same food at the table in either,
actually preferring the negro house. . . ." And then the moment
of pride: Roth refuses to share his bed with Henry and lies alone

"in a rigid fury of the grief he could not explain, the shame he would not admit." Later he knew "it was grief and was ready to admit it was shame also, wanted to admit it only it was too late then, forever and forever." Forever and forever—the terribleness of this estrangement recurs in Faulkner's work, not simply as a theme, but as a cry of loss and bafflement.

Beneath the white man's racial uneasiness there often beats an impatience with the devices by which men keep themselves apart. Ultimately the whole apparatus of separation must seem too wearisome in its constant call to alertness, too costly in its tax on the emotions, and simply tedious as a brake on spontaneous life. The white man is repeatedly tempted by a memory playing on the rim of his consciousness: a memory of boyhood, when he could live as a brother with his Ringo or Henry Beauchamp—his Nigger Jim or Queequeg—and not yet wince under the needle of self-consciousness. The memory—or a longing in the guise of memory—can be downed by the will and blunted by convention, but it is too lovely and in some final sense too real to be discarded entirely. Beneath the pretense to superiority, the white man reaches for what is true: the time when he could compare bits of knowledge about locomotives with Ringo, share food with Henry Beauchamp, not in equality or out of it—for the mere knowledge of either is a poison—but in a chaste companionship. This is what the white man has lost, forever and forever; and the Negro need not remind him of it, he need only walk past him on the street.

It is a memory fed by guilt. As a confession of failure within society, it shows that status has brought not satisfaction but grief and shame. By questioning the entirety of adult relations, it reveals a hidden weight of despair. Because it glances at the possibilities of life belond society, the writer can imagine it only in a setting of pastoral simplicity or childhood affection. It is a plea to be forgiven for what is and perhaps—but here Faulkner is uncertain—must be. And it is a yearning to find release, to fall away from the burden of one's whiteness.

Touching as this vision of lost fraternity is, it also involves an outrageous naïveté. As Leslie Fielder has remarked, the white man "dreams of his acceptance at the breast he has most utterly offended. It is a dream so sentimental, so outrageous, so desperate that it redeems our concept of boyhood from nostalgia to tragedy." Miss Worsham says of Mollie Beauchamp, "We grew up together as sisters would"—but how many decades of distance have intervened she does not add. It is as though she and Roth Edmonds and all the other whites unconsciously hoped they need but turn again to their childhood companions to find in undiminished purity the love destroyed by caste. How the Negroes themselves might look upon this violated dream they do not think—perhaps they do not dare—to ask.

This image of the white man's longing is not, of course, unique to Faulkner; it appears with astonishing frequency in American writing, and often together with that pastoral impulse so strong among our novelists and poets. Faulkner has rendered it with a particular urgency and sadness, in a setting where at best the races live in quiet rancor. That he has repeatedly turned to this image may be considered a triumph of instinct, but the shape and weight he has given it are a triumph of art.

No such singleness or steadiness can be found in Faulkner's more conscious depiction of the Negro. One finds, instead, a progression from Southern stereotype to personal vision, interrupted by occasional retreats to inherited phobias and to an ideology that is morally inadequate to the vision. These shifting attitudes may be broken into three stages, each symbolized by a major Negro character: Dilsey, Joe Christmas and Lucas Beauchamp.

In *Soldiers' Pay*, Faulkner's first novel, a Negro (George the train porter) briefly appears as a conventional accessory. In *Sartoris* the Negro servants are regarded with truculent condescension, Joby and Simon, the old family retainers who are mere comic stereotypes. When Joby lights a fire on Christmas Day, Faulkner assures us that he feels "the grave and simple pleasures of his race." And when Simon visits some Negro ladies, there follows an uncomfortable moment of low comedy:

> "Ef it ain't Brother Strother," they said in unison. "Come in, Brother Strother. How is you?"
>
> "Po'ly, ladies; po'ly," Simon replied. He doffed his hat and unclamped his cigar stub and stowed it away in the hat. "I'se had a right smart mis'ry in de back."
>
> ". . . . Whut you gwine eat, Brother Strother?" the cook demanded hospitably. "Dey's party fixin's, en day's some col' greens en a little sof' ice cream lef fum dinner."

"I reckon I'll have a little ice cream en some of dem greens, Sis Rachel," Simon replied. "My teef ain't so much on party doin's no mo'. . . ."

Faulkner does this sort of thing skillfully enough, and since the speech of some Negroes may well verge on self-burlesque, the passage cannot simply be dismissed as "unreal." But its reality is of a superficial order, displaying a gift of condescending mimicry rather than the moral sympathy and perception we may expect from a novelist of the first rank.

In *The Unvanquished* a similar stereotyped response to the Negro soon gives way to an awareness that his psychology is not quite so accessible to the white man as the latter would like to believe. Faulkner stresses the free-and-easy relations between white master and Negro slave in the Old South, the peculiar intimacy between a man sure of his command and another who sees no possibility or feels no desire to challenge it; and we know from historical record that, together with brutality, such relationships did once exist. But new voices appear now, particularly the voice of Loosh, a discontented Negro who deserts the Sartoris manor for the Northern lines. "I done been freed," says Loosh, "God's own angel proclamated me free and gonter general me to Jordan. I don't belong to John Sartoris now; I belong to me and God." When asked why he has spirited the Sartoris silver to the Yankees, Loosh replies with vehemence and point: "You ax me that? . . . Where John Sartoris? Whyn't he come and ax me that? Let God ax John Sartoris who the man name that give me to him. Let the man that buried me in the black dark ax that of the man what dug me free."

Loosh's pregnant questions are repeated, in *Sartoris*, by a Negro of a later era. Caspey, home from the First World War, announces: "I don't take nothin' fum no white folks no mo' . . . War done changed all dat. If us cullud folks is good enough ter save France fum de Germans, den us is good enough ter have de same rights de Germans is. French folks think so, anyhow, and ef America don't, dey's ways of learnin' 'um." For such "sullen insolence" Caspey is knocked down by Bayard Sartoris with a stick of stove wood and told by Simon, his father, to "save dat nigger freedom talk fer town-folks."

Neither Loosh nor Caspey is conceived in warmth or developed in depth. Both are singled out for an uneasy kind of ridicule, and their rebelliousness is hardly taken seriously. What is damaging here is not so much Faulkner's laziness of statement as the assumption, throughout his early treatment of Negroes, that they are easily "knowable," particularly by disenchanted Southerners with experience in handling them. Since Faulkner at his weakest, however, remains a writer of some consequence, overtones of doubt and uneasiness shade his portraiture of Negroes even in the minor novels. The discontented ones are seen as loutish or absurd, but this impression is undercut by the power with which their discontent is now and again rendered. One of Faulkner's most admirable qualities as a writer is that even when he wishes to settle into some conventional or trite assumption, a whole side of himself—committed forever to restless inquiry—keeps resisting this desire.

In *Sartoris* there is also a glimpse of another kind of feeling toward the Negro. Visiting the MacCallums, young Bayard instinctively—out of a natural courtesy in abiding by the manners of his hosts—treats their Negro cook with the same rough easiness that the hillsmen do. Bayard does not stop to reflect upon the meaning of this companionship, nor does Faulkner stop to give it any special emphasis: it comes through in a brief ceremony of shaking hands. But in an unfinished way, it points toward a strong motif in Faulkner's work: his conviction that fraternity is morally finer than equality, a fraternity which in his early novels makes the demand for equality seem irrelevant but which in his later ones can come only after equality has been so long secured as to be forgotten.

A gifted artist can salvage significant images of life from the most familiar notions: witness Dilsey in *The Sound and the Fury*. Dilsey is a figure remarkable for her poise, her hard realism, her ability to maintain her selfhood under humiliating conditions. Yet the conception behind Dilsey does not seriously clash with the view of the Negro that could be held by a white man vaguely committed to a benevolent racial superiority. Accepting her inferior status and surviving as a human being despite that acceptance, Dilsey is the last of Faulkner's major Negro characters who can still feel that the South is a "natural" community to which they entirely belong. No sensitive reader would care to deny her strength and moral beauty, but I should like to register a dissent from the effort of certain critics to apotheosize her as the embodiment of Christian resignation and endurance.

The terms in which Dilsey is conceived are thoroughly historical, and by their nature become increasingly unavailable to us: a fact which if it does not lessen our admiration for her as a figure in a novel, does limit our capacity to regard her as a moral archetype or model.[1]

In *The Sound and the Fury* there is an important modulation of attitude toward the Negro. While Dilsey's strength and goodness may be acceptable to traditional paternalism, she gradually assumes a role not quite traditional for the Southern Negro; she becomes, toward the end of the book, an articulate moral critic, the observer with whom the action of the novel is registered and through whom its meanings are amplified. She is not merely the old darky in the kitchen champing at the absurd and evil ways of the folks up front; at the climax of the novel she rises beyond that role, to a concern with universal problems of justice. This is not to suggest that Dilsey is in any way a rebel against the old order of Southern life. She regards most of the Compsons with contempt not because they are white or representative of the ruling social group but because they do not fulfill the obligations that have accrued to their status. Judging the whites in terms of their own proclaimed values, she criticizes not their exploitation of Negroes but their moral mistreatment of each other. This judgment, held with force and purity, leads Dilsey to a principled respect for the human person as such. When the name of the idiot Compson child is changed from Maury to Benjy, she snaps: "He *ain't wore out the name he was born with yet, is he.*" When her daughter whines that "people talk" because Dilsey brings Benjy to the Negro church, the old woman replies: "Tell um the good Lawd don't keer whether he smart or not. Dont nobody but poor white trash keer dat." This sense of honor toward every person in her orbit, this absolute security in her own judgment, is Dilsey's most admirable trait, and a sign, as well, of the more complex treatment of Negroes that is to appear in Faulkner's books.

From traditional paternalism to an awareness of the injustice

[1] But is not Don Quixote, surely a moral archetype, also conceived in historical terms unavailable to us? Yes, he is. Don Quixote, however, survives as a figure "beyond" history, we no longer care about his historical genesis or purpose; while Dilsey, we cannot but remember, is a woman caught up in the recent historical condition of the Southern Negro. Whether time will do for Dilsey what it has done for Don Quixote, no one can say.

suffered by the Negro in Southern society—this, one could say, is the change that now occurs in the Yoknapatawpha novels. But the change is more complicated still, for the growing concern with injustice as a problem flows from an expansion of paternalism to its widest human limits. Dilsey and Joe Christmas are very different kinds of people, but Christmas is possible only because Dilsey already exists.

With *Light in August* the Negro assumes a new role in Faulkner's work. If Dilsey is characterized by an unbreakable sense of "belonging" in a world she knows to be falling apart, Joe Christmas feels that he has no home, that he always has been and must always remain homeless. If in the earlier work the focus of attention is on the white man's feelings toward the Negro, now there is a shock of discovery, a discovery of the Negro "as Negro."

The Faulkner to whom the Looshes and Caspeys and even Dilseys had seemed so accessible now emphasizes that for the whites the Negro often exists not as a distinct person but as a specter or phantasm. He writes brilliantly of what might be called the fetishism of false perception, the kind of false perception that has become systematic and has acquired both a pseudo-religious sanction and an intense emotional stake. Joanna Burden, daughter of abolitionists raised in the south, confesses that "I had seen and known Negroes since I could remember. I just looked at them as I did at rain, or furniture, or food or sleep. But after that I seemed to see them for the first time not as people, but as a thing, a shadow in which I lived, we lived, all white people, all other people. I thought of all the children coming forever and ever into the world, white, with the black shadow falling already upon them before they drew breath. And I seemed to see the black shadow in the shape of a cross." What is so remarkable about this passage—and it seems to me one of the most remarkable in all of Faulkner—is that here the false perception comes from a mixture of humaneness and fright, the two no longer separable but bound together in an apocalyptic image of violation and martyrdom.

In *Light in August* a lynch mob "believed aloud that it was an anonymous negro crime committed not by a negro but by Negro . . . and some of them with pistols already in pockets began to canvass about for someone to crucify." The phrase "not by a negro but by Negro" reflects a deepened understanding;

the reference to men canvassing "for someone to crucify" suggests that Faulkner has been thinking hard about the role of frustration in shaping white behavior. In Percy Grimm, the small-town boy who has absorbed sadism from the very air, Faulkner gives form to his pained awareness that a society of inequality can lead only to abuse of status and arbitrary violence. This idea is expressed more abstractly in *The Wild Palms* when Faulkner describes the "indelible mark of ten thousand Southern deputy sheriffs, urban and suburban—the snapped hatbrim, the sadist's eyes, the slightly and unmistakably bulged coat, the air not swaggering exactly but of a formally pre-absolved brutality." Precise in each detail, this description opens to brilliance in the final phrase, "a formally pre-absolved brutality"—a phrase that epitomizes a vision of society.

That the white man has been calloused by status and the fear and guilt inevitable to status is not a novel insight; but to a writer wrestling with the pieties of the Southern tradition the price of such knowledge can hardly come low. For it is not, after all, the "South," that convenient abstraction of geography or history, about which Faulkner sees this; it is his own immediate cut of land, the place where he will spend his remaining time and die. Consider, then, the significance of the scene in *Light in August* where a sheriff, preparing to sweat some information out of a Negro, tells his deputy, "Get me a nigger"—get me a nigger, no matter which, they are indistinguishable.

We witness in Faulkner's novels a quick and steep ascent: from benevolence to recognition of injustice, from amusement over idiosyncrasies to a principled concern with status, from cozy familiarity to a discovery of the estrangement of the races. Realizing that despite their physical nearness Negroes must coil large parts of themselves beyond the vision of white society, Faulkner remarks in the story "The Old People" upon "that impenetrable wall of ready and easy mirth which negroes sustain between themselves and white men." Instead of being easily reached, the Negro is now locked behind suspicion; and while he may be, as Quentin Compson has said, "a form of behavior . . . [an] obverse reflection of the white people he lives among," he is also and more importantly something else: a human being whom the whites can seldom know. (One of Faulkner's later stories, "Pantaloon in Black," dramatizes this idea: after the death of his wife, a Negro runs berserk with grief while the whites, blind to the way he expresses it, sneer at his apparent insensitivity.) As Faulkner discovers the difficulty of approaching Negroes, he also develops an admirable sense of reserve, a blend of shyness and respect; trusting few of his preconceptions he must look at everything afresh.

A curious result of this growth in perception is, occasionally, a loss of concreteness in the presentation of character. Faulkner's discovery of the power of abstraction as it corrupts the dealings men have with one another, can lead him to portray Negroes in abstract terms. If the mob in *Light in August* looks upon black men as "Negro" in order to brutalize them, Faulkner sometimes looks upon them as "Negro" in order to release his sympathy. Joe Christmas and Charles Bon are sharply individualized figures, but there also hangs over them a racial aura, a halo of cursed blackness. In an early story, "Dry September," this tendency toward the abstraction of character is still clearer; like a paradigm of all lynching stories, it is populated not with men but with Murderer and Victim.

Nor is it accidental that those Negroes whom Faulkner most readily imagines in the posture of the victim should be mulattoes. Trapped between the demarcated races, the mulatto is an unavoidable candidate for the role of victim. Velery Bon in *Absalom, Absalom!* is a man adrift. The Negroes "thought he was a white man and believed it only the more strongly when he denied it," while the whites, "when he said he was a negro, believed that he lied in order to save his skin." Joe Christmas is cursed by "that stain on his white blood or his black blood, whichever you will." Whether he actually has Negro blood is never clear, and this uncertainty points a finger of irony at the whole racial scheme.

Such symbolic uses of the mulatto do not exhaust the reasons for his prominence in Faulkner's novels. Mulattoes are living agents of the "threat" of miscegenation, a "threat" which seems most to disturb Faulkner whenever he is most sympathetic to the Negro. All rationalizations for prejudice having crumbled, there remains only an inherited fear of blood-mixture. The more Faulkner abandons the "ideas" of the folk mind in relation to Negroes, the more does he find himself struggling with the deeper phobias of the folk mind. In two of the novels where miscegenation is a major theme, *Light in August* and *Absalom, Absalom!*, it arouses a painfully twisted response. Miscegenation releases the fears of the white unconscious but also suggests, as Faulkner will hint in a later book, an ultimate solution to the racial problem. Even as it excites a last defense for the dogma of superiority, the thought of miscegenation opens a vision of a distant time when distinctions of blood and barriers of caste will be removed. In *Absalom, Absalom!* there is a whole range of responses to miscegenation, from the strongly-articulated sympathy for its victims to the conventional prophecy that it will lead to a corruption of the races; and it is quite impossible to say with any assurance where Faulkner's final sympathy, or the final stress of the novel itself, lies. Because of this ambivalent response, the mulatto occasions some of Faulkner's most intense, involuted and hysterical writing. As a victim the mulatto must be shown in all his suffering, and as a reminder of the ancestral phobia, must be made once or twice to suffer extravagantly. But since Faulkner is trying to free himself from both phobia and the injustice it sustains, the mulatto also excites in him his greatest pity, a pity so extreme as often to break past the limits of speech. On the mulatto's frail being descends the whole crushing weight of Faulkner's world.

With the appearance of Lucas Beauchamp, most of Faulkner's previous attitudes toward the Negro are transcended. Lucas is neither at home in the South, like Dilsey, nor homeless, like Joe Christmas; he exists in himself. He is well enough aware of white society and he knows exactly what it is; in "The Fire and the Hearth" he does not hesitate to express his bitterness. But as he strides into sight in *Intruder in the Dust,* powerful and complete, he is entirely on his own: he has put society behind him. Too proud to acquiesce in submission, too self-contained to be either outcast or rebel, Lucas has transformed the stigma of alienation into a mark of dignity and assurance. He is truly a character who has "made" himself, who has worked through to his own kind of authenticity. The gain is high, so too the price; for Lucas is friendless, and his grandeur is a crotchety grandeur. Apparently meant by Faulkner as a tribute to the strength and endurance of the Negroes, Lucas is something better still: a member of an oppressed group who appears not as a catalogue of disabilities or even virtues, but as a human being in his own right. He is not a form of behavior but a person, not "Negro" but a Negro.

Occasionally Faulkner lets him slip into the stubborn old nigger who grumbles and bumbles his way to domination over the delightfully helpless whites. This may be justifiable, for, to an extent difficult to specify, the "stubborn old nigger" is Lucas' social mask—and Faulkner realizes now that in white society Negroes must often use a social mask. Because he is so aware that they can seldom risk spontaneity in the company of whites, Faulkner, like the boy Chick Mallison, circles about Lucas with humor and a shy respect, never daring to come close lest the old Negro growl at him. He feels about Lucas somewhat as Chick and Stevens do, sharing the boy's irritated awe and the man's uneasy admiration. Toward no other character in any of his books does Faulkner show quite the same uncomfortable deference; of none other can it be said that Faulkner looks up to him with so boyish and pleading an air, as if he wishes to gain from the old man a measure of forgiveness or acceptance, perhaps finally even love.

By indirection, Lucas challenges a good many of the notions Faulkner has previously expressed about the Negroes. In the final scene of *Intruder in the Dust* Lucas shows himself unyielding and unforgiving; he insists upon taking the white man's gesture of equality as if it came from condescension—and who will dare bluntly to contradict him? In an earlier scene Lucas stares up at Stevens from his jail cell, refusing to speak to him openly because he senses that the white lawyer believes him guilty. Completely dramatized and without any intruding comment, this scene suggests the insight that even the best whites are full of ambiguous feelings toward the Negroes and hence not to be trusted by them.

This insight acknowledged, one is tempted to speculate about certain of Faulkner's attitudes toward the Negroes. Throughout his work there is an admiring emphasis on their patience and "endurance." Negroes are "better than we" because "they will endure." In the Appendix to *The Sound and the Fury* Faulkner honors Dilsey and her kin with a bare sentence, "They endured." Such sentiments, fondly quoted by traditionalist critics, have their obvious bearing when advanced as statements about the past; but if, as Faulkner intimates, they are also meant as prescription and prediction, they invite a measure of doubt.

How Negroes "really" feel about Southern, or American, society is terribly hard for any white man to say. Serious whites, as they learn more about the hidden, the true life of Negroes, grow hesitant to generalize: they discover how little they know. Yet one may wonder whether Negroes are quite as ready to "endure" as Faulkner suggests—a question that has a decided relevance to his work, since a fixed idea about Negro "endurance" can limit his capacity to see Negro life freshly.

Faulkner wishes to dramatize his admiration for their ability to survive injustice, and he is right to do so. Nor is his respect for the power and virtues of passivity confined to his treatment of Negro figures; it comes through with great assurance in his portraits of Lena Grove and Ike McCaslin; and indeed, it forms one of his deepest personal feelings toward human existence. But it may still be suggested that Faulkner, like any other man of his color, has less "right" to admire the posture of passivity in the Negroes than he does in the whites. And we must also suppose that those human beings, like the Negroes, who have long been subjected to humiliation will probably resent it, no matter how much they may be required to veil their more intimate responses. Is this not exactly what Faulkner begins so brilliantly to show in his treatment of Lucas Beauchamp, a man whose irascible desire for justice—he demands nothing else from society —is quite distant from the style of "endurance"? May it not be that the patient willingness to "endure," far from being a root attitude among Negroes, is another of the masks they assume in order to find their way through a hostile world? Again I add that this is not merely a question concerning the social order of the South: it arises repeatedly and with growing urgency in some of Faulkner's later novels.

Though he has given us a wider range and taken a deeper sounding of Negro character than any other American writer, Faulkner has not yet presented in his novels an articulate Negro who speaks for his people. No one has the right to demand that he do so, but it is a legitimate problem in literary criticism to ask why he has not. That such a Negro may not be within Faulkner's range of personal experience is unimportant, unless one accepts the naïve assumption that fictional characters must always be drawn from a writer's immediate knowledge. Faulkner's honesty, his continuous moral growth, but above all, the inner logic of his own work—all these would seem to require that he confront the kind of Negro who is in serious, if covert, rebellion against the structure of the South.

To present such a character, Faulkner would have to take the risk of examining Negro consciousness from within, rather than as it is seen or surmised by white characters. It may be said that precisely Faulkner's awareness of the distance between the races and of the ultimate inaccessibility of the Negroes makes him hesitate to use a Negro as his center of consciousness. Such scruples deserve to be honored, yet the fact is that great writers, including Faulkner himself, are always coming up with characters "they do not know"—surely this must be part of what is meant when we say they are using their imagination. To portray Negro consciousness from the inside would be a hazard for Faulkner, as it must be for any white novelist, but the possibility, perhaps the need, for such an attempt arises from his own achievement. And he has never been a writer to avoid risks.

Such speculations apart, Faulkner's most recent books testify to the almost obsessive role the Negro continues to play in his imaginative life. *Requiem for a Nun* casts a Negro prostitute and dope addict, Nancy, as scourge and saviour of white society. Nancy's murder of a white child is traced back to the earlier guilt of the child's parents; and even as she prepares to die in her repentance and piety, she becomes a nemesis calling them back to their moral obligations. In assigning this role to Nancy, Faulkner is perhaps placing too heavy a weight of responsibility on the Negroes, and in a way opposite to the harangues of *Intruder in the Dust* he may even be doing them a certain injustice. For it is a little unreasonable—though surely also desperate—to burden the Negroes with the salvation of the whites. Whatever the whites will be able to manage in this latter department, they will have to do for themselves.

One suspects that the difficulties behind the creation of Nancy reflect a charge of emotion, a surging mixture of guilt and impatience, which Faulkner cannot objectify in conduct or character and which, therefore, forces him toward a kind of Dostoevskian apocalypse. Because of this ideological weight, Nancy figures in the novel more as an abstract intention than as a blooded human being. Lacking the rich particularity of a Lucas Beauchamp, she is "Negro" rather than a Negro, and "Negro" put to very special and unclarified uses. Still, the novel shows that Faulkner continues to brood over the Negroes, passionately and erratically; and as long as these questions remain alive for him, there is reason to hope they will take on fresh embodiment in future novels.

The shift of response toward the Negro forms a moral history, a record of growth from early work to last. But it would be a grave distortion to suppose that this history is entirely reckoned once attitudes and underlying themes have been traced—these are only the raw materials from which literature is made or, perhaps more accurately, the abstractions critics like to draw from or impose upon literature. Despite the ideological passages in *Intruder in the Dust,* Faulkner is not, and should not be considered, a systematic thinker; he has no strictly formulated views on the "Negro question," and as a novelist he is under no obligation to have them. In the more than two decades of his literary career he has taken a painful journey of self-education, beginning with an almost uncritical acceptance of the more benevolent Southern notions and ending with a brooding sympathy and humane respect for the Negroes. His recent books indicate that no other social problem troubles him so greatly, and that his mind is constantly driven to confront it. What counts in his work is not the occasional splinter of program that can be scratched out of it—whoever wants a precise platform or a coherent sociology for the Negroes had better look elsewhere. Faulkner's triumph is of another kind, the novelist's triumph: a body of dramatic actions, a group of realized characters. No other American novelist has watched the Negroes so carefully and patiently; none other has listened with such fidelity to the nuances of their speech and recorded them with such skill; none other has exposed his imagination so freely, to discover, at whatever pain or discomfort, their meaning for American life.

Faulkner and the Avant-Garde

by Hugh Kenner

Faulkner is clearly part of something modern: we have no difficulty thinking of whole pages and chapters of *The Sound and the Fury* or *Absalom, Absalom!* which it is inconceivable that anyone could have written before the complex revolution of verbal and narrative techniques we associate with the early twentieth century. Yet avant-garde is a metaphor of which we sense the wrongness as soon as we apply it. It is a military metaphor; the avant-garde is the forward edge of an army, or perhaps a scouting party, or a clutch of purposeful dynamiters —in any case a coherent group under discipline. Applied to the arts, this metaphor reflects a bourgeois fear of being plotted against, and a plot entails a group. Faulkner wasn't a group man. No other major twentieth-century writer was so isolated from his peers. The list of men he admired but never met would astonish by its length. In Paris, in 1925, he seems to have glimpsed Joyce once, at a cafe. They did not meet; nor did Faulkner meet Pound, nor Hemingway, nor Gertrude Stein, nor even Sylvia Beach.

Poets, it may be, congregate more than novelists, perhaps because, putting fewer words on fewer pages, they have more time to spare from driving the pen. Though Joyce seems to have met nearly everybody, it was because they sought him out, during the nearly twenty years he lived in Paris, and revolutionaries of the word had more reasons for coming to Paris than to Oxford, Mississippi. Still, allowing for the fact that professional gregariousness has not been a conspicuous trait of novelists, there is something idiosyncratic about Faulkner's isolation. He did not even talk much about his reading—his equivocation

Reprinted with permission from Evans Harrington and Ann J. Abadie, eds., *Faulkner, Modernism, and Film: Faulkner and Yoknapatawpha, 1978* (Jackson: University Press of Mississippi, 1979), pp. 182–196.

about his knowledge of *Ulysses* is famous—and when, in late years, confronting undergraduate audiences, he was asked about his peers he tended to answer in lists: "Wolfe, John Dos Passos, Hemingway, Willa Cather, John Steinbeck" ran one such list; and as for detailed comment, he would merely rank them according to what he called "the splendor of the failure": that ranking ran "Wolfe, Faulkner, Dos Passos, Hemingway and Steinbeck." [1]

Such evasiveness seems meant to create a presumption: that the heart of writing is ultimately moral, that each writer confronts his aspiration and his failure alone, and that what writers learn from one another is either private or trivial. But avant-garde by definition professes a community of aim. It is held together by what its members profess in common, by interchange, by an emphasis on the part of the craft that is learned, shared, exchanged, sharpened in the phrasing and the exchanging. Manifestoes are its staple, and cafe talk; and if Joyce for example signed no manifestoes, he is nonetheless legitimately claimed by a modernism that learned from his example, in part because he had so clearly thought out his methods that his example could teach them, and teach the attitudes behind them.

Faulkner clearly wanted no part of pedagogy, nor of literary politics. But in talking as he did about the intensities of solitary aspiration and failure, he seemed to disavow the other face of avant-gardism as well, its emphasis on what can be defined as a community of aim and means: the deliberate craft, the statable grounds of self-criticism. Faulkner, it seems, did not mind anyone's believing that the hard work he did came from his gut: that there was nothing to talk about save the sense of dedicated effort.

This proposition may be conveniently illustrated from the history of one twentieth-century group, the imagists, who were united, insofar as anything united them save mutual acquaintance, by a program with three points. (1) "Direct treatment of the 'thing,' whether subjective or objective"; (2) no unnecessary word; (3) a metric obeying the phrase rather than the metronome. We may think of this program under either of two aspects, the public and the technical. One part of its intent—and the purpose of publishing it rather than confining it to talk

---

[1] Joseph Blotner, *Faulkner: A Biography* (New York: Random House, 1974), II, 1232.

and private circulation—was pedagogic: to alter public taste, to
define criteria that will exclude much that gets readily admired,
and focus attention on much that gets forgotten, or admired
without perception. For it does not describe only future poems:
it isolates certain past ones. Sappho meets these criteria; so does
Catullus; so does Villon. Swinburne does not, running riot
with unnecessary words; and if many Greek writers were, as
Pound said, "rather Swinburnian," the effect of the imagist
canon is to isolate Sappho and the epigrammatists of the Greek
anthology from what is inertly celebrated as "Greek Literature."
So a manifesto that seems phrased for the use of poets can alter
the perceptions of a reader of poetry who has no ambition to
write a line.

The other aspect of the program is technical; it gives a poet
criteria for revision. Have I worked for direct presentation, or
contented myself with abstraction? Have I admitted nonfunc-
tioning words, words maybe that swarm out of habit, or that fill
out a rhythm and do nothing else? Have I permitted my rhythm
to sway mechanically?

We may add that in redefining a tradition, and in isolating
technical matters from it, the imagist canon allowed poets to
admire Sappho or Catullus, and aspire to emulate their excel-
lence, without imitating them directly, thus saving your writers
much time they might otherwise lose executing pastiche. In this
respect it defines prose canons too; Stendhal for instance is by
extension an imagist, Stendhal who based his style, he said, on
that of the *Code Napoleon.* So is Jane Austen, so is the Joyce
of *Dubliners,* but not Dickens, nor Walter Scott.

Now clearly William Faulkner would not have subscribed to
this particular set of criteria, beyond perhaps agreeing, through
a cloud of pipe smoke, that in some ways what was proposed
was a pretty good thing. The famous description of Popeye in
the opening paragraphs of *Sanctuary* might pass for the writing
of a writer of imagist prose: "His face had a queer, bloodless
color, as though seen by electric light; against the sunny silence,
in his slanted straw hat and his slightly akimbo arms, he had
that vicious depthless quality of stamped tin." "Sunny silence"
looks like a mannered synaesthesia, but "sunny" is needed to
offset "electric light": under the sky, this face is unnatural in
color. And the superb "stamped tin," with its clanked dull
rhythm—how much contempt resonates in the sound of the words,

a "musical phrase" indeed if we eschew the sentimental connotations of "musical," to reinforce the absolute finality of the image. Still, no manifesto would have made Faulkner forego his love of many words, superfluous if we examine them one by one but defensible as contributing to a copiousness, a garrulousness, a quality of psychic overflowing he discerned in the tradition of oral storytelling and prized above any satisfactions to be obtained from erasure, paring, spareness.

But the real point is not an incompatibility between Faulkner's practice and any particular set of modernist criteria. The real point is that he had no special use for either of the two aspects of any program. He had no special ambition to reform public taste, none of the pedagogical fervor of the born avant-gardist. And he had no desire, by any commitment now, to limit the scope of his operations in the future.

We have already glanced at one reason for this temperamental aversion. The base of Faulkner's storytelling was oral, and every twentieth-century avant-garde movement one can think of was dedicated to canons not oral but literary, canons which if they admit copiousness require even it to seem a little synthetic, like the lists in *Ulysses*, every item of which Joyce means us to feel can be justified on deliberated and specifiable grounds. The assumption that we are free to weigh and question every word is an assumption peculiar to written literature, where the words stay still for inspection as they do not when someone is talking; to written literature, moreover, which has accepted and come to terms with its status as writing, in fact as writing for a printing press, and envisions a reader silent before printed pages. In this sense the entire thrust of twentieth-century modernism—the Revolution of the Word which commenced in English about 1910, inheriting French developments that date from 1880 and before; the complex eponymous movement that gave us *Ulysses, The Waste Land,* the *Cantos,* the *Paterson* of Williams, and the poems of Marianne Moore—its thrust was toward a consolidation of all that printed paper implies: the well-wrought artifact, the tireless revision, the skilled reader, the habitual rereader, in an economy of typescripts, numbered pages, typographic cues for which a speaking voice has no equivalent, etymologies, dictionaries. (Shakespeare had no dictionary.) Questioned about his relationship to this context of creativity, questioned moreover by questioners in classrooms who had no idea that any other context was pertinent, Faulkner was understandably either brusque or evasively polite, feeling perhaps like a shaman who has wandered into a conference of brain surgeons, knowing that he commands skills of incantation incompatible with their discourse of subtle instruments.

A narrative passage from *The Hamlet* runs like this:

> And after that, not nothing to do until morning except to stay close enough where Henry can call her until it's light enough to chop the wood to cook breakfast and then help Mrs. Littlejohn wash the dishes and make the beds and sweep while watching the road. Because likely any time now Flem Snopes will get back from wherever he has been since the auction, which of course is to town naturally to see about his cousin that's got into a little legal trouble and so get that five dollars. "Only maybe he won't give it back to me," she says, and maybe that's what Mrs. Little-john thought too, because she never said nothing.

Though written, this is not *writing*, not by the criteria Stendhal taught us, or Flaubert, or Conrad, or Joyce. Not merely are its sentence rhythms those of oral narrative (rhythms Conrad eschewed despite his fondness for oral narrators; rhythms Joyce in synthesizing them beautifully in "Cyclops" nevertheless interrupted thirty-two times with interpolations from the domain of print): not only that, but it requires the reader to play the role of hearer, participating in the "now" of "any time now" and in the speculation about where Flem had been. Not the sentence rhythms but the role forced on the reader will serve to discriminate what is radically written from what is radically oral. The reader-as-listener must pretend as listeners do that he does not confront anonymously the anonymity of print, that he is acquainted with time and place and genealogy, that he knows people who are barely named, that characters and their pasts need not be cunningly "introduced" because knowledge of all that attaches to a name is part of the communal stock which includes the storyteller and of which the bounds are indefinite.

This is of course a radically unreal supposition, but we brave it out and pick up such knowledge the way a tactful stranger does, never impeding nor embarrassing the storyteller. We pick it up from clues, which means close reading: which means, since reading despite the oral convention is what we are after all doing, that we approach the Faulkner text very like New Critics, as if it had been written by James Joyce. Hence a curious strain at the heart of anyone's confrontation with a Faulkner novel. For ideal comprehension we must take notes, turn back to an earlier page, keep track of time schemes and family trees; we must simultaneously pretend that we need do none of this, need only listen to a voice we ourselves supply. The puzzle we are put to, making out what really did happen, is exactly the trouble we incur with a difficult written text in which the paring away of unnecessary words has been carried perhaps excessively far.

What Faulkner tended to pare away, or perhaps didn't think of supplying in the first place, isn't the verbiage which both imagism and the more general canons of international modernism have interdicted, but information, the sort of information a storyteller's hearers take for granted because they are part of his community. Take, for a brief and amusing illustration, the story "An Error in Chemistry," an unimportant potboiler nine editors rejected before *Ellery Queen's Mystery Magazine* paid $300 for it in 1945. The story turns on a mystery writer's gimmick: an imposter exposes himself by not knowing how a Mississippian would make a cold toddy. He spoons sugar into raw whiskey, which won't dissolve it, instead of into water to which the whiskey will then be added, and everybody in the room is aghast at this violation not only of chemistry but of an immutable folkway. As the narrator tells us, "I had not only watched Uncle Gavin, and the sheriff when he would come to play chess with Uncle Gavin, but Uncle Gavin's father too who was my grandfather, and my own father before he died, and all the other men who would come to Grandfather's house who drank cold toddies": that is how you acquire that sort of information; any member of the storyteller's community has acquired it likewise; the northern impostor hasn't. And in the first version of the story, the one his agent tried in vain to place for five years, Faulkner apparently forgot that most of his readers would be in the position of the northern impostor: failed at the very climax of his tale to specify what error the impostor made: forgot in short to tell us outlanders what any Mississippian would know.[2] The incident illuminates his principle of omission, which isn't that of a disciplined imagist at all.

So he makes the modernist demand that we read slowly and

[2] Blotner, *Faulkner*, II, 1189n.

closely for reasons diametrically opposite to those that govern modernist orthodoxy. The modernist assumption, arising from the economy of print, is that to tell your story, secure your effect, there exists a discoverable combination of just the right words, a minimal set of words, not to be exceeded, and to be arranged in exactly the right order. The James Joyce of a famous anecdote spent all day on two sentences, not seeking the exact word—he had his words already—but seeking the perfect order of fifteen words in two sentences. "There is an order in every way appropriate. I think I have it." [3] But the storyteller confronting a living audience hasn't time for that order of research; if he began to fumble over two sentences he would rapidly lose his audience. He is apt to tell his story over and over again, never twice in quite the same way. His unit of attention is not the word but the event, and the practice that shapes the tale toward its definitive ordering is likely to experiment as Faulkner often did, rearranging whole blocks of narrative, placing this incident now before, now after that one, until the most satisfying version is certified by communal agreement and embedded in his repertoire. But even the "final" version will not be told twice in quite the same words.

Being engaged with his audience, the storyteller (or the bardic singer of tales) is little tempted to be engaged with himself. Walter Ong, our prime theorist of these matters, remarks that "You cannot find Homer's personality in the *Iliad,* although you might find the personality of an entire culture there." [4] Nor can you find Faulkner's personality in *Light in August*—not because, like Joyce, he took conscious steps to keep it out, playing "the God of creation . . . within or behind or beyond or above his handiwork, invisible, refined out of existence, indifferent, paring his fingernails," but because his absorption with tale and audience make it unlikely that self-consciousness will creep in. It is the writer who is conscious of being alone with a sheet of paper, making word-by-word decisions and revisions, hesitating all day over two sentences, who is apt to find a self-absorption invading his work unless he makes deliberate resolves to keep it out.

[3] Frank Budgen, *James Joyce and the Making of Ulysses,* 20.
[4] Walter J. Ong, *Interfaces of the Word* (Ithaca, New York: Cornell University Press, 1977), 221.

Faulkner's oral storytelling mode, it is commonplace to observe, is that of a provincial culture with its small towns, its agriculture, its still living religion, its implicit norms of conduct. Drawing an analogy between Faulkner and Yeats, Cleanth Brooks has quoted the Irishman Sean O'Faolain, who thought that life in Mississippi sounded very like life in County Cork:

> There is the same passionate provincialism; the same local patriotism; the same southern nationalism—those long explicit speeches of Gavin Stevens in *Intruder in the Dust* might, *mutatis mutandis,* be uttered by a southern Irishman—the same feeling that whatever happens in Ballydehob or in Jefferson has never happened anywhere else before, and is more important than anything that happened in any period of history in any part of the cosmos; there is the same vanity of an old race; the same gnawing sense of old defeat; the same capacity for intense hatred; a good deal of the same harsh folk-humor; the same acidity; the same oscillation between unbounded self-confidence and total despair; the same escape through sport and drink.[5]

We may next note that of the two great writers born in nineteenth-century Ireland, the elder, W. B. Yeats, was excited by collections of folk narratives and even helped Lady Gregory collect them, while the younger, James Joyce, affected a bored contempt for such materials though he put them to covert use in *Finnegans Wake.* Yeats (who like Faulkner went on to win the Nobel Prize, bestowed by a committee with a demonstrable predilection for regional writers) argued memorably that

> All that we did, all that we said or sang
> Must come from contact with the soil, from that
> Contact everything Antaeus-like grew strong.

Joyce (whom the Nobel committee overlooked, omitting as it did so to honor the greatest man of letters of the twentieth century) called Ireland "the afterthought of Europe" and spent his last decades in Europe's most cosmopolitan capital, Paris.

One cannot imagine modern letters without Joyce, one cannot imagine modern Ireland without Yeats. To say that is not to

---

[5] Sean O'Faolain, *The Vanishing Hero,* as quoted in Cleanth Brooks, *William Faulkner: The Yoknapatawpha Country* (New Haven: Yale University Press, 1963), 2.

confine the interest of Yeats to the Irish; without Yeats we
should all be deprived of a memorable, an irreplaceable body
of work. (Many curricula moreover would be impoverished, so
great is his pedagogical usefulness.) But it is difficult to specify
the difference Yeats made to any other major writer, whatever
moral difference his existence assuredly made to the next generation in Ireland; whereas Joyce was so great an innovator his
mark is on all prose narrative since the publication of *Ulysses*.

In making this distinction we are preparing for a clarification
of twentieth-century modernism which in turn will help clarify
Faulkner's relationship to it. One way of describing what happened to English in the twentieth century is this: English ceased
to be the language of a country and its former colonies; it became instead simply an available language, regarded differently
by writers in England, in the United States, in Ireland. Three
regional literatures arose: the English, the American, the Irish,
writers in each country bringing different social assumptions to
their common dictionary. Take the word "accurate." An Englishman, guided by the Latin *cura*, "care," in an etymology he may
not even know, feels *trouble* in accuracy; it is achieved by taking
care. William Carlos Williams said of something he was writing,
"As far as I have gone it is accurate"; "it," not "I"; the emphasis
is not on the trouble but on the close tolerances of the result.
An American senses in accuracy a technological *precision*. James
Joyce in *Ulysses* presents Mr. Philip Beaufoy "in accurate morning dress"; we may be tempted to say that an Englishman who
invokes accuracy is being troubled, an American is being precise,
and an Irishman is being funny. Such examples could be multi-
plied by the thousand. James Joyce wrote of an English priest,
"How different are the words *home, Christ, ale, master,* on his
lips and on mine! . . . His language, so familiar and so foreign,
will always be for me an acquired speech." Yet Joyce had grown
up speaking no language save what everyone called "English."

Three languages then, drawn from the same dictionary; three
social experiences likewise; and by the mid-twentieth century,
for the first time, three literatures. Earlier Irish writers had won
their fame in England, earlier American ones had hoped to. We
may speak now of the literatures of the three provinces, England
too a province like the others. For the twentieth century also
gave birth to a fourth English, that of international modernism.
It seems clear, for instance, that *Ulysses* is in no meaningful

way a part of Irish literature; nor is *Waiting for Godot* (which is not part of French literature either, though the first version was written, by an Irishman, in French). Is *The Waste Land* part of English literature? Probably not; not the way *The Vanity of Human Wishes* is, or *Mrs. Dalloway*. It is easier to assign these works, and others, to a new international tradition, the language of which is to be found in an English dictionary; much as it is easier to assign the oeuvre of Picasso to something analogously international than to the history of Spanish art, or the history of French. Virginia Woolf's work on the other hand, despite certain avant-garde mannerisms, is simply English; Sean O'Casey's is Irish; Ernest Hemingway's is American; and so is Scott Fitzgerald's and most of Faulkner's.

Such a taxonomy is not a means of assigning value but a way of assessing relationships. The masters of international modernism were the century's great innovators, on whose innovations the writers of the three provinces habitually drew. They pay for their grandeur, though, with a certain abstractness—an attenuation of the richness and power that is available to a novelist or poet who is working within a culture, with the culture's norms and its minute signals. Little that is specifically Irish, except the precision of speech rhythm and a taste for the comedy of logic, has survived the process by which Samuel Beckett's novels and plays were extracted from the language he learned in Dublin. Joyce bent his intention not on being Irish but on being a pupil of the Jesuits who chanced to have grown up in Ireland. But remove his southernness from Faulkner, or remove Sligo and the Anglo-Irish pride from Yeats, and nothing much is left.

We have in Faulkner, then, a distinguished and powerful instance of the sort of local literary tradition the modernism of the twentieth century has made possible: a way of being intensely local which profits from a range of expressive devices not local at all but developed by several great contemporary innovators whose intention was to see their native region from afar, with cosmopolitan eyes. Joyce could not have written in Dublin, nor Eliot in St. Louis, nor Pound in either Idaho (where he was born) or Pennsylvania (where he grew up). They went to the great capitals, never forgetting their roots, always looking back.

But Faulkner could not have written *The Sound and the Fury* in Paris, nor could William Carlos Williams have carried his Jersey materials there. And yet every page of theirs bespeaks their contemporaneity with Joyce and with Pound, but for whom neither could have written as he did.

We may want to ask, finally, what all this implies about Faulkner's reader. We have employed, for expository convenience, the model of the communal storyteller, who tells tall tales, tales his hearers already half know, and tells them over and over, he and those who hear knit in a web of comprehension a great deal of which need not even entail what is spoken. Such a man enjoys extraordinary intimacy with the hearers he knows, and may be half-incomprehensible fifty miles away, where certain names have no potency.

Moving such a model from folklorists' Platonism toward reality, we obtain for instance Faulkner's V. K. Ratliff, with his perfect assurance of how to enter a store "on the gallery of which apparently the same men who had been there when he saw it last a year ago were still sitting," and his sense of how to obtain an audience by dropping the impenetrable phrase "Goat-rancher." People who feign indifference to Ratliff's presence absorb every word he says, as a story perfectly shaped to pique curiosity winds from a teasing opener to a climax that restates the opening in new light. He is like the bard Demodokos in the *Odyssey*, a portrait within the work of the shaper of the work itself.

But this too is Platonized. Demodokos may give us Homer's sense of himself, but Faulkner, a man in a study with a pen, is no V. K. Ratliff, nor do his readers sit on the gallery of even an ideal store. Faulkner's fame did not start in Oxford and spread outward. It started in places like Paris and New York, and eventually reached Mississippi. "Mr. Faulkner a great writer?" ran an Oxford comment on the 1939 cover story in *Time*; "Well, they sure wouldn't hire him to write a Chamber of Commerce booklet for the town." [6]

Print is perilous stuff, like electricity. They read print as far away as New York, and stories should be kept in the family. And Dublin, by the way, contains dozens of raconteurs who will tell you that the city contained and still contains a host of storytellers more gifted than Joyce. As it may; he was more than a storyteller. And they say his great gift was for taking in Americans.

No, the ideal Faulkner reader is not the ideal listener the

[6] Blotner, *Faulkner*, II, 1016.

communal storyteller supposes. Nor is he that "ideal reader suffering from an ideal insomnia" whom Joyce presupposed and did so much to train: the patient correlator of clues and looker-up of stray facts. The ideal Faulkner reader must combine New-Critical skills of textual response with an imaginative flexibility that can bend salmon-supple in and out of the Yoknapatawpha community: for if you read him as if he were Joyce you are repeatedly snagged by what seem like hundreds of running feet of lazily coiled rusty rhetoric and thickets of unregarded narrative gestures, whereas if you read him as if he were a comfortable old-fashioned novelist the coinages, the neologisms, the inner monologues and resonant italics—all the contrivances of literary technology—betray you. And if you read him as if he were an awkward amalgam of both you get no satisfaction at all. It is a unique role that the reader must play, seeing folk material imitated, synthesized, by the devices of the twentieth-century avant-garde, being aware that that is what is going on and yet responding as if he were what he cannot be, a sympathetic member of a vanished community. Our role demands tact and resourcefulness, an ability to adjust repeatedly to altered focus, and we may be years learning it. The avant-garde created Faulkner's techniques but did not train his reader. We must acquire our training from his books.

Repetition and Revenge

by John T. Irwin

In the story of the Sutpens the threat of miscegenation between Bon and Judith is also a threat of brother-sister incest,
and it is another brother, Henry, who acts to stop these threats.
This archetype of the brother who must kill to protect or avenge
the honor of his sister pervades *Absalom, Absalom!* It occurs,
first of all, in the very title of the novel. In the Old Testament
(2 Sam. 13), Absalom, one of David's sons, kills his brother
Amnon for raping their sister Tamar. The archetype presents
itself again in Quentin Compson, the principal narrator of
Absalom. From *The Sound and the Fury* we know that Quentin
is in love with his own sister Candace and that he is tormented
by his inability to play the role of the avenging brother and
kill her seducer. Of the many levels of meaning in *Absalom*,
the deepest level is to be found in the symbolic identification
of incest and miscegenation and in the relationship of this symbolic identification both to Quentin Compson's personal history
in *The Sound and the Fury* and to the story that Quentin narrates in *Absalom, Absalom!*

There are, of course, four narrators in the novel—Quentin, his
father, his roommate Shreve, and Miss Rosa Coldfield—but of
these four certainly Quentin is the central narrator, not just
because he ends up knowing more of the story than do the other
three, but because the other three only function as narrators in
relation to Quentin. When Mr. Compson or Shreve or Miss Rosa
Coldfield tell what they know or conjecture of the Sutpens'
story, they are talking, either actually or imaginatively, to Quentin. One reason that the voices of the different narrators sound
so much alike is that we hear those voices filtered through the

Reprinted with permission from John T. Irwin, *Doubling and Incest/
Repetition and Revenge* (Baltimore: The Johns Hopkins University Press,
1975), pp. 25–28, 95–107, 109–122.

mind of a single listener: Quentin's consciousness is the fixed point of view from which the reader *overhears* the various narrators, Quentin included. Since Quentin is the principal narrative consciousness in *Absalom,* and since the story of the Sutpens contains numerous gaps that must be filled by conjecture on the part of the narrators, it is not surprising that the narrative bears a striking resemblance to Quentin's own personal history and that of his family. Quentin uses his own experience of family life in a small Southern town to try to understand the motives for events in the story of Thomas Sutpen and his children, particularly that central enigmatic event to which the narration continually returns—the murder of Charles Bon by his best friend, Henry Sutpen. This is not to imply that the factual similarities between the stories of the Sutpen and Compson families are a product of Quentin's imagination, but to point out that, given these similarities of fact, Quentin as creative narrator could easily presume similarity of motivation. It is a mutual process in which what Quentin knows of the motivations in his own family life illuminates the story of the Sutpens and, in turn, the events in the Sutpens' story help Quentin to understand his own experiences. . . .

To what extent, then, does the story that Quentin tells in *Absalom* resemble his own life story in *The Sound and the Fury*? We noted first of all that Quentin's failure to kill Candace's seducer and thus fulfill the role of protective brother has its reverse image in Henry's murder of Bon to safeguard the honor of their sister. Also, Quentin's incestuous love for Candace is mirrored by Bon's love for Judith. That Quentin identifies with both Henry, the brother as protector, and Bon, the brother as seducer, is not extraordinary, for in Quentin's narrative they are not so much two separate figures as two aspects of the same figure. Quentin projects onto the characters of Bon and Henry opposing elements in his own personality—Bon represents Quentin's unconsciously motivated desires for his sister Candace, while Henry represents the conscious repression or punishment of that desire. . . .

In the story of the Sutpens, Quentin also finds a reenactment of the way that the fate of a father is passed on to a son. When Sutpen was a child, he received an affront from the black servant of a rich plantation owner. He was told that he could not come to the front door of the planter's house, he had to go around to the back because he was white trash, because he and his family were not as good as the plantation owner. Comparing the plantation owner with his own father, Sutpen rejects his father as a model and adopts the plantation owner as his surrogate father, as his model for what a man should be. And Sutpen feels the same ambivalence toward him that a son would feel for a father. At first, he considers killing him, but then he realizes that he doesn't want to do away with the plantation owner, he wants to become the plantation owner. The ruthless odyssey on which Sutpen embarks is a quest for revenge for the affront that he suffered as a boy—not revenge against a system in which the rich and powerful can affront the poor and powerless but against the luck of birth that made him one of the poor when he should have been one of the rich. Like Gatsby, Sutpen distinguishes between the "Platonic" and the "merely personal." Ideally, he accepts the justice of that mastery which the powerful have over the powerless, which the rich planter has over the poor boy, a father over his son. The fact that circumstance happened to start Sutpen off by casting him in the role of the powerless, poor boy is merely personal. A mere stroke of chance does not invalidate that hierarchy—or rather, patriarchy—of power. Sutpen seeks revenge within the rules of patriarchal power for the affront that he suffered; he does not try to show the injustice of the system, but rather to show that he is as good as any man in the system. If the planter is powerful because he is rich, then Sutpen will have his revenge by becoming richer and more powerful than the planter. And he will pass that wealth and power on to his son, doing for his son what his own father could not do for him. Sutpen comes to terms with the traumatic affront that he suffered as a boy by accepting the impersonal justice of it even though he feels its personal inappropriateness. He incorporates into himself the patriarchal ideal from which that affront sprang in much the same way that a son comes to terms with the image of his father as a figure of mastery and power by impersonalizing and internalizing that image as the superego, accepting the justice of the father's mastery even though that mastery has been exercised against the son. It is a mechanism by which the son tries to overcome the mastery of the personal father while maintaining the mastery of fatherhood—a mechanism in which the personal father dies without the son's having to kill him. Accepting this idea of patriarchal power, Sutpen determines his fate—to repeat periodically that traumatic affront but in a different role. Henceforth, he will no longer receive the affront, he will deliver it. Thus, he rejects his first wife and son because they are not good enough to share the position to which he aspires. And he passes that fated repetition on to his sons—to Charles Bon, who returns thirty years later seeking admittance to the rich plantation owner's "house" (and thereby represents the return of that repressed traumatic affront of Sutpen's boyhood) and to Henry, who, acting as his father's surrogate, delivers the final affront to Bon, killing him at the gates of the house to prevent his entering.

In his interviews at the University of Virginia, Faulkner repeatedly pointed out that *Absalom* is a revenge story—indeed, a double revenge story: Sutpen's revenge for the affront that he suffered as a boy and Bon's revenge for the affront that he and his mother suffered at Sutpen's hands during Sutpen's quest for revenge. Faulkner said of Sutpen: "He wanted revenge as he saw it, but also he wanted to establish the fact that man is immortal, that man, if he is man, cannot be inferior to another man through artificial standards or circumstances. What he was trying to do—when he was a boy, he had gone to the front door of a big house and somebody, a servant, said, Go around to the back door. He said, I'm going to be the one that lives in the big house, I'm going to establish a dynasty, I don't care how, and he violated all the rules of decency and honor and pity and compassion, and the fates took revenge on him." [1] Sutpen wants revenge not against the injustice of that mastery which the powerful have over the powerless, but against those "artificial standards or circumstances" that determine who are the powerful and who the powerless, against the artificial standard of inherited wealth and the circumstances of one's birth. Faulkner says that Sutpen in his quest for revenge violated all the rules of decency and honor and pity and compassion. But there is one rule that Sutpen does not violate, and that is the rule of power. For the rule that Sutpen follows is that real power springs not from the external, artificial advantages of birth and inherited wealth but from something internal: for Sutpen the source of real power

---

[1] Frederick L. Gwynn and Joseph L. Blotner, eds., *Faulkner in the University* (New York: Vintage Books reprint, 1959), p. 71.

is the force of the individual will. In any group of men, power belongs to the man whose will is strong enough to seize that power and hold it against his fellow men. But that brings us face to face with the central paradox of Sutpen's quest—that he seeks revenge on the artificial standards of birth and inherited wealth as the determinants of power by setting out to establish a dynasty—that is, by trying to confer those very same artificial advantages on his son. Faulkner gives us the key to this paradox when he says that Sutpen "wanted revenge as he saw it, but also he wanted to establish the fact that man is immortal, that man, if he is man, cannot be inferior to another man through artificial standards or circumstances." It is a puzzling statement. First of all, what does it mean to equate Sutpen's attempt to establish that man is immortal with his effort to prove that one man cannot be inferior to another through artificial standards or circumstances? And then, what does it mean to link these two with the quest for revenge?

The idea that lies behind Faulkner's statement is what Nietzsche called "the revenge against time." [2] To understand what this idea involves, let us compare for a moment the careers of Jay Gatsby and Thomas Sutpen. Clearly, what Gatsby and Sutpen both seek in their quests is to alter the past—to repeat the past and correct it. As Sutpen in the role of the poor boy suffered an affront from the rich plantation owner, so Gatsby as the poor boy was rejected by the rich girl Daisy Buchanan, and as the former affront initiated Sutpen's grand design to get land, build a mansion, and establish a dynasty, that is, to repeat the past situation but with Sutpen now in the role of the affronter rather than the affronted and to pass on to his son the rich man's power to affront the poor and powerless, so Daisy's rejection of Gatsby initiates Gatsby's dream of acquiring a fortune, owning a great house, and winning Daisy back, his dream of repeating the past by marrying Daisy this time and obliterating everything that occurred between that rejection and his winning her back. When Nick Carraway realizes the enormity of Gatsby's dream, he tells him, "You can't repeat the past," and Gatsby with his Sutpen-like innocence replies, "Why of course you can." As Sutpen rejected his powerless, real father as a model in favor

---

[2] Friedrich Nietzsche, *Thus Spoke Zarathustra*, in *The Portable Nietzsche*, trans. Walter Kaufman (New York: Viking Press, 1954), pp. 249–54. All subsequent quotations from *Zarathustra* are taken from this edition.

of the powerful plantation owner, so Gatsby rejected his father who was a failure, changed his name from Gatz to Gatsby, and adopted the self-made man Dan Cody as his surrogate father. But now the question arises, Why does the attempt to repeat the past and correct it turn into the revenge against time? Nietzsche's answer is worth quoting at length:

> "To redeem those who lived in the past and to recreate all 'it was' into a 'thus I willed it'—that alone should I call redemption. Will—that is the name of the liberator and joy-bringer; thus I taught you, my friends. But now learn this too: the will itself is still a prisoner. Willing liberates; but what is it that puts even the liberator himself in fetters? 'It was'—that is the name of the will's gnashing of teeth and most secret melancholy. Powerless against what has been done, he is an angry spectator of all that is past. The will cannot will backwards; and that he cannot break time and time's covetousness, that is the will's loneliest melancholy.
>
> "Willing liberates; what means does the will devise for himself to get rid of his melancholy and to mock his dungeon? Alas, every prisoner becomes a fool; and the imprisoned will redeems himself foolishly. That time does not run backwards, that is his wrath; 'that which was' is the name of the stone he cannot move. And so he moves stones out of wrath and displeasure, and he wreaks revenge on whatever does not feel wrath and displeasure as he does. Thus the will, the liberator, took to hurting; and on all who can suffer he wreaks revenge for his inability to go backwards. This, indeed this alone, is what *revenge* is: the will's ill will against time and its 'it was.' "   (pp. 251–52)

Since the will operates in the temporal world and since time moves only in one direction, the will can never really get at the past. The will's titanic, foredoomed struggle to repeat the past and alter it is simply the revenge that the will seeks for its own impotence in the face of what Nietzsche calls the "it was" of time. Nietzsche connects this revenge against time with the envy that a son feels for his father. In a passage on the equality of men, Zarathustra says,

> "What justice means to us is precisely that the world be filled with the storms of our revenge"—thus they speak to each other. "We shall wreak vengeance and abuse on all whose equals we are not"—thus do the tarantula-hearts vow. "And 'will to equality'

shall henceforth be the name of virtue; and against all that has
power we want to raise our clamor!"

You preachers of equality, the tyrannomania of impotence
clamors thus out of you for equality: your most secret ambitions
to be tyrants thus shroud themselves in words of virtue. Aggrieved
conceit, repressed envy—perhaps the conceit and envy of your
fathers—erupt from you as a flame and as the frenzy of revenge.

What was silent in the father speaks in the son; and often I
found the son the unveiled secret of the father.

They are like enthusiasts, yet it is not the heart that fires them
—but revenge.   (p.212)

Clearly, the doctrine of the equality of men is at odds with
the patriarchal principle that fathers are inherently superior to
sons, for obviously the doctrine of equality is the doctrine of a
son. The son, finding himself powerless in relation to the father,
yet desiring power, admits that mastery inheres in the role of
the father but disputes the criteria that determine who occupies
that role. The doctrine of the son is simply the doctrine of the
son's equality of opportunity to assume the role of the father
through a combat with the father that will show who is the better
man. But that doctrine of equality the father must reject, for
from the father's point of view the authority which he holds as
the father is not open to dispute; it is not subject to trial by
combat because that authority is not something that the father
could ever lose, it is not accidental to fatherhood, it inheres in
its very nature. That authority is something which has been
irrevocably conferred on the father by the very nature of time,
for the essence of the authority, the mastery, that a father has
over his son is simply priority in time—the fact that in time the
father always comes first. And against that patriarchal authority
whose basis is priority in time, the son's will is impotent, for
the will cannot move backwards in time, it cannot alter the past.
In his rivalry with the father for the love of the mother, the son
realizes that no matter how much the mother loves him, she
loved the father *first.* Indeed, the son carries with him in the
very fact of his own existence inescapable proof that she loved
the father first and that the son comes second. Any power that
the son has, he has not in his own right, but by inheritance from
the father, by being a copy of the father, who has supreme
authority because he comes first, who has power because of the

very nature of time. No wonder, then, that the envy of the son for the father takes the form of the revenge against time.

When Nietzsche speaks of the "envy of your fathers," the phrase is intentionally ambiguous, for it is not just the envy that a son feels for his father, it is as well the envy that the son inherits from his father, who was himself a son once. The targets of Sutpen's revenge for the affront that he suffered as a boy are the artificial advantages of high birth and inherited wealth (or the artificial disadvantages of low birth and inherited poverty), that is, generation and patrimony—those modes of the son's dependence on his father, those expressions of the fact that whatever the son is or has, he has received from his father and holds at the sufferance of the father. But again we confront the paradox of Sutpen's solution—that he seeks revenge on the artificial standards that make one man inferior to another, not by trying to do away with those standards, but rather by founding a dynasty, by establishing that same artificial standard of superiority for his family and bequeathing it to his son. Put in that way, the paradox seems clearer: it is the paradox that sons turn into fathers by trying to forget (albeit unsuccessfully) that they were once sons. When Sutpen began his quest for revenge, his quest to supplant the father, his attitude was that of a son: that the authority and power of the father obey the rule of power, that they are subject to a trial by combat, and if the son's will proves the stronger, belong to the son not as a gift or inheritance (which would entail his dependence on the father) but as a right, a mark of his independence. Yet (and here is the paradoxical shift) the proof of the son's success in his attempt to become the father will be the son's denial of the attitude of the son (the rule of power) in favor of the attitude of the father. The proof that Sutpen has achieved his revenge, that he has become the father, will be his affirmation that the authority and power of the father obey not the rule of power but the rule of authority, that is, that they are not subject to dispute or trial by combat since they belong irrevocably to the father through priority in time, that to oppose the father is to oppose time, that authority and power cannot be taken from the father by the son but can only be given as a gift or inheritance by the father to the son. We see why Sutpen's revenge requires that he found a dynasty, for the proof that he has succeeded in becoming the father will finally be achieved only when he bequeaths his authority and power to his son as an inheritance (a gift, not a right), thereby establishing the son's dependence on his father and thus the father's mastery. That proof, of course, Sutpen never achieves, though he dies trying. . . .

When Sutpen returns from the Civil War to find one son dead and the other gone, he starts over a third time in his design to found a dynasty, to get the son who will inherit his land and thereby prove, through dependence, that Sutpen has succeeded in his quest to be the son who seized the power of the father and then, as the father, kept that power from being seized by his own son in turn. For Sutpen can only prove that he is a better man than his father if he proves that he is a better man than his son, since Sutpen's father would have been defeated by his son in that very act. In Sutpen's final attempt to achieve his design, the battle against time receives its most explicit statement: "He was home again where his problem now was haste, passing time, the need to hurry. *He was not concerned,* Mr. Compson said, *about the courage and the will, nor even about the shrewdness now. He was not for one moment concerned about his ability to start the third time. All that he was concerned about was the possibility that he might not have time sufficient to do it in, regain his lost ground in.*" [3] But then, *"he realized that there was more in his problem than just lack of time, that the problem contained some super-distillation of this lack: that he was now past sixty and that possibly he could get but one more son, had at best but one more son in his loins, as the old cannon might know when it had just one more shot in its corporeality"* (p. 279). The problem is not just too little time; it is also the physical impotence that time brings, a physical impotence symbolic of Sutpen's "old impotent logic" (p. 279), of the impotence of the son's will in the face of the "it was" of time. Rosa says that when Sutpen gave her her dead sister's wedding ring as a sign of their engagement it was "as though in the restoration of that ring to a living finger he had turned all time back twenty years and stopped it, froze it" (p. 165).

Sutpen's concern that he might be able to get only one more son leads him to suggest to Rosa that they try it first, and if the child is a male, that they marry. That suggestion drives Rosa

---

[3] William Faulkner, *Absalom, Absalom!* (New York: Random House, Modern Library College Edition, 1964), p. 278. All subsequent quotations from *Absalom, Absalom!* are taken from this edition.

from Sutpen's home and leads Sutpen to choose for his partner in the last effort to accomplish his design the only other available woman on his land, Milly Jones, the granddaughter of the poor-white Wash Jones, and that choice brings Sutpen to the final repetition of the traumatic affront. In fact, Sutpen had reenacted that affront from the very start of his relationship with Wash Jones, never allowing Jones to approach the front of the mansion. When Sutpen seduces Milly and when her child is a daughter rather than the required son, Sutpen rejects mother and child as he had rejected his first wife and child. He tells Milly that if she were a mare he could give her a decent stall in his stable—a remark that Wash Jones overhears and that makes Jones realize for the first time Sutpen's attitude toward him and his family. Jones confronts the seducer of his granddaughter and kills him with a scythe. The irony of Sutpen's final repetition of the affront is that, though he delivers the affront in the role of a father rejecting his child, in order to get that child he had to assume the role of the son, he had to become the seducer; and Wash Jones, the poor white who had been the object of Sutpen's paternalism, now assumes the role of outraged father in relation to Sutpen. It is emblematic of the fate of the son in his battle against time that Sutpen, struggling in his old age to achieve his revenge, must again become the son and in that role be struck down by an old man with a scythe. . . .

The struggle between Quentin and his father that runs through the stream-of-consciousness narrative of Quentin's last day is primarily a dispute about time. The narrative begins with Quentin's waking in the morning ("I was in time again," [4] to the ticking of his grandfather's watch, the watch that his father had presented to him, saying, "I give it to you not that you may remember time, but that you may forget it now and then for a moment and not spend all your breath trying to conquer it" (p. 95). Quentin twists the hands off his grandfather's watch on the morning of the day when he forever frees himself and his posterity from the cycles of time and generation. When Quentin is out walking that morning, he passes the shopwindow of a watch store and turns away so as not to see what time it is, but there is a clock on a building and Quentin sees the time in spite

[4] William Faulkner, *The Sound and the Fury* (New York: Random House, 1946), p. 95. All subsequent quotations from *The Sound and the Fury* are taken from this edition.

of himself: he says, "I thought about how, when you dont want to do a thing, your body will try to trick you into doing it, sort of unawares" (p. 102). And that, of course, is precisely Quentin's sense of time—that it is a compulsion, a fate. For his father has told him that a man is the sum of his misfortunes and that time is his misfortune like "a gull on an invisible wire attached through space dragged" (p. 123). In his struggle against his father and thus against time, Quentin must confront the same problem that he faces in the story of Sutpen and his sons—whether a man's father is his fate. In *Absalom* when Shreve begins to sound like Quentin's father, Quentin thinks, *"Am I going to have to hear it all again. . . . I am going to have to hear it all over again I am already hearing it all over again I am listening to it all over again I shall have to never listen to anything else but this again forever so apparently not only a man never outlives his father but not even his friends and acquaintances do"* (p. 277).

When Quentin demands that his father act against the seducer Dalton Ames, Quentin, by taking this initiative, is in effect trying to supplant his father, to seize his authority. But Quentin's father refuses to act, and the sense of Mr. Compson's refusal is that Quentin cannot seize his father's authority because there is no authority to seize. Quentin's alcoholic, nihilistic father presents himself as an emasculated son, ruined by General Compson's failure. Mr. Compson psychologically castrates Quentin by confronting him with a father figure, a model for manhood, who is himself a castrated son. Mr. Compson possesses no authority that Quentin could seize because what Mr. Compson inherited from the General was not power but impotence. If Quentin is a son struggling in the grip of Father Time, so is his father. And it is exactly that argument that Mr. Compson uses against Quentin. When Quentin demands that they act against the seducer, Mr. Compson answers in essence, "Do you realize how many times this has happened before and how many times it will happen again? You are seeking a once-and-for-all solution to this problem, but there are no once-and-for-all solutions. One has no force, no authority to act in this matter because one has no originality. The very repetitive nature of time precludes the existence of originality within its cycles. You cannot be the father because I am not the father—only Time is the father." When Quentin demands that they avenge Candace's virginity, his father replies, "Women are never virgins. Purity is a negative state and therefore contrary to nature. It's nature is hurting you not Caddy and I said That's just words and he said So is virginity and I said you dont know. You cant know and he said Yes. On the instant when we come to realize that tragedy is second-hand" (p. 135). In essence Quentin's father says, "We cannot act because there exists no virginity to avenge and because there exists no authority by which we could avenge since we have no originality. We are second-hand. You are a copy of a copy. To you, a son who has only been a son, it might seem that a father has authority because he comes first, but to one who has been both a father and a son, it is clear that to come before is not necessarily to come first, that priority is not necessarily originality. My fate was determined by my father as your fate is determined by yours." Quentin's attempt to avenge his sister's lost virginity (proving thereby that it had once existed) and maintain the family honor is an attempt to maintain the possibility of "virginity" in a larger sense, the possibility of the existence of a virgin space within which one can still be first, within which one can have authority through originality. . . .

Mr. Compson's denial of the existence of an authority by which he could act necessarily entails his denial of virginity, for there is no possibility of that originality from which authority springs if there is no virgin within which one can be first. And for the same reason Quentin's obsession with Candace's loss of virginity is necessarily an obsession with his own impotence, since the absence of the virgin space renders him powerless. When Mr. Compson refuses to act against Dalton Ames, Quentin tries to force him to take some action by claiming that he and Candace have committed incest—that primal affront to the authority of the father. But where there is no authority there can be no affront, and where the father feels his own inherited impotence, he cannot believe that his son has power. Mr. Compson tells Quentin that he doesn't believe that he and Candace committed incest, and Quentin says, "If we could have just done something so dreadful and Father said That's sad too, people cannot do anything that dreadful they cannot do anything very dreadful at all they cannot even remember tomorrow what seemed dreadful today and I said, You can shirk all things and he said, Ah can you" (p. 99). Since Mr. Compson believes that man is helpless in the grip of time, that everything is fated, there is no question of shirking or not shirking, for there is no question of willing. In discussing the revenge against time, Nietzsche speaks of those preachers of despair who say, "Alas, the stone *It was* cannot be moved" (p. 252), and Mr. Compson's last words in Quentin's narrative are "was the saddest word of all there is nothing else in the world its not despair until time its not even time until it was" (p. 197).

Is there no virgin space in which one can be first, in which one can have authority through originality? This is the question that Quentin must face in trying to decide whether his father is right, whether he is doomed to be an impotent failure like his father and grandfather. And it is in light of this question that we can gain an insight into Quentin's act of narration in *Absalom,* for what is at work in Quentin's struggle to bring the story of the Sutpens under control is the question of whether narration itself constitutes a space in which one can be original, whether an "author" possesses "authority," whether that repetition which in life Quentin has experienced as a compulsive fate can be transformed in narration, through an act of the will, into a power, a mastery of time. Indeed, Rosa Coldfield suggests to Quentin when she first involves him in the story of the Sutpens that becoming an author represents an alternative to repeating his father's life in the decayed world of the postwar South: " 'Because you are going away to attend the college at Harvard they tell me,' Miss Coldfield said. 'So I dont imagine you will ever come back here and settle down as a country lawyer in a little town like Jefferson, since Northern people have already seen to it that there is little left in the South for a young man. So maybe you will enter the literary profession as so many Southern gentlemen and gentlewomen too are doing now and maybe some day you will remember this and write about it' " (pp. 9–10). We noted earlier that the dialogue between Quentin and his father about virginity that runs through the first part of *Absalom* appears to be a continuation of their discussions of Candace's loss of virginity and Quentin's inability to lose his virginity contained in Quentin's section of *The Sound and the Fury.* Thus, the struggle between father and son that marked their dialogue in *The Sound and the Fury* is continued in their narration of *Absalom.* For Quentin, the act of narrating Sutpen's story, of bringing that story under authorial control, becomes a struggle in which he tries to best his father, a struggle to seize "authority" by achieving temporal priority to his father in the narrative act. At the beginning of the novel, Quentin is a passive narrator. The story seems to choose him. Rosa involves him in the narrative against his will, and he spends the first half of the book listening to Rosa and his father tell what they know or surmise. But in the second half, when he and Shreve begin their imaginative reconstruction of the story, Quentin seems to move from a passive role to an active role in the narrative repetition of the past.

So far I have mainly discussed the experience of repetition as a compulsion, as a fate, using Freud's analysis of the mechanism of the repetition compulsion in *Beyond the Pleasure Principle* as the basis for my remarks. But in that same text, Freud also examines the experience of repetition as a power—repetition as a means of achieving mastery. He points out that in children's play an event that the child originally experienced as something unpleasant will be repeated and now experienced as a source of pleasure, as a game. He describes the game of *fort/da* that he had observed being played by a little boy of one and a half. The infant would throw away a toy and as he did, utter a sound that Freud took to be the German word *fort*—"gone." The child would then recover the toy and say the word *da*—"there." Freud surmised that the child had created a game by which he had mastered the traumatic event of seeing his mother leave him and into which he had incorporated the joyful event of her return. Freud points out that the mechanism of this game in which one actively repeats an unpleasant occurrence as a source of pleasure can be interpreted in various ways. First of all, he remarks that at the outset the child "was in a *passive* situation—he was overpowered by the experience; but, by repeating it, unpleasurable though it was, as a game, he took on an *active* part. These efforts might be put down to an instinct for mastery that was acting independently of whether the memory was in itself pleasurable or not. But still another interpretation may be attempted. Throwing away the object so that it was 'gone' might satisfy an impulse of the child's, which was suppressed in his actual life, to revenge himself on his mother for going away from him. In that case it would have a defiant meaning: 'All right, then, go away! I don't need you. I'm sending you away myself.' " [5]

[5] Sigmund Freud, *The Standard Edition of the Complete Psychological Works of Sigmund Freud,* trans. and ed. James Strachey, et al. (London: Hogarth Press, 1953), 18:16. All subsequent quotations from Freud are taken from this edition, which will be cited hereafter as S.E.

Freud makes a further point about the nature of children's games that has a direct bearing on our interest in the son's effort to become his father: ". . . it is obvious that all their play is influenced by a wish that dominates them the whole time—the wish to be grown-up and to be able to do what grown-up people do. It can also be observed that the unpleasurable nature of an experience does not always unsuit it for play. If the doctor looks down a child's throat or carries out some small operation on him, we may be quite sure that these frightening experiences will be the subject of the next game; but we must not in that connection overlook the fact that there is a yield of pleasure from another source. As the child passes over from the passivity of the experience to the activity of the game, he hands on the disagreeable experience to one of his playmates and in this way revenges himself on a substitute" (S.E., 18:17). Significantly, Freud refers to this mastery through repetition as "revenge," and his remarks suggest that this revenge has two major elements —repetition and reversal. In the game of *fort/da* the child repeats the traumatic situation but reverses the roles. Instead of passively suffering rejection when his mother leaves, he actively rejects her by symbolically sending her away. And in the other case, the child repeats the unpleasant incident that he experienced but now inflicts on a playmate, on a substitute, what was formerly inflicted on him.

In this mechanism of a repetition in which the active and passive roles are reversed, we have the very essence of revenge. But we must distinguish between two different situations: in the ideal situation, the revenge is inflicted on the same person who originally delivered the affront—the person who was originally active is now forced to assume the passive role in the same scenario; in the other situation, the revenge is inflicted on a substitute. This second situation sheds light on Sutpen's attempt to master the traumatic affront that he suffered as a boy from the man who became his surrogate father, to master it by repeating that affront in reverse, inflicting it on his own son Charles Bon. This scenario of revenge on a substitute sheds light as well on the connection between repetition and the fantasy of the reversal of generations and on the psychological mechanism of generation itself. The primal affront that the son suffers at the hands of the father and for which the son seeks revenge throughout his life is the very fact of being a son—of being the generated in relation to the generator, the passive in relation to the active, the effect in relation to the cause. He seeks revenge on his father for the generation of an existence which the son, in relation to the father, must always experience as a dependency. But if revenge involves a repetition in which the active and passive roles are reversed, then the very nature of time precludes the son's taking revenge on his father, for since time is irreversible, the son can never really effect that reversal by which he would become his father's father. The son's only alternative is to take revenge on a substitute—that is, to become a father himself and thus repeat the generative situation as a reversal in which he now inflicts on his own son, who is a substitute for the grandfather, the affront of being a son, that affront that the father had previously suffered from his own father. We can see now why Nietzsche, in connecting the revenge against time with the "envy of your fathers" (that envy which the son feels for his father and which the son has inherited from his father, who was himself a son), says, "What was silent in the father speaks in the son; and often I found the son the unveiled secret of the father."

When Sutpen takes revenge on a substitute for the affront that he received as a boy, he takes revenge not just on Charles Bon but on Henry as well. For if the primal affront is the very fact of being a son, then acknowledgment and rejection, inheritance and disinheritance are simply the positive and negative modes of delivering the affront of the son's dependency on the father. . . .

Keeping in mind this notion of revenge on a substitute, we can now understand how Quentin's act of narration in *Absalom* is an attempt to seize his father's authority by gaining temporal priority. In the struggle with his father, Quentin will prove that he is a better man by being a better narrator—he will assume the authority of an author because his father does not know the whole story, does not know the true reason for Bon's murder, while Quentin does. Instead of listening passively while his father talks, Quentin will assume the active role, and his father will listen while Quentin talks. And the basis of Quentin's authority to tell the story to his father is that Quentin, by a journey into the dark, womblike Sutpen mansion, a journey back into the past, has learned more about events that occurred before he was born than either his father or grandfather knew:

"Your father," Shreve said. "He seems to have got an awful lot of delayed information awful quick, after having waited forty-five years. If he knew all this, what was his reason for telling you that the trouble between Henry and Bon was the octoroon woman?"

"He didn't know it then. Grandfather didn't tell him all of it either, like Sutpen never told Grandfather quite all of it."

"Then who did tell him?"

"I did." Quentin did not move, did not look up while Shreve watched him. "The day after we—after that night when we—"

"Oh," Shreve said. "After you and the old aunt. I see. Go on. . . ."   (p. 266)

In terms of the narrative act, Quentin achieves temporal priority over his father, and within the narrative Quentin takes revenge against his father, against time, through a substitute—his roommate Shreve. As Quentin had to listen to his father tell the story in the first half of the novel, so in the second half Shreve must listen while Quentin tells the story. But what begins as Shreve listening to Quentin talk soon turns into a struggle between them for control of the narration with Shreve frequently interrupting Quentin to say, "Let me tell it now." That struggle, which is a repetition in reverse of the struggle between Mr. Compson and Quentin, makes Quentin realize the truth of his father's argument in *The Sound and the Fury*—that priority is not necessarily originality, that to come before is not necessarily to come first. For Quentin realizes that by taking revenge against his father through a substitute, by assuming the role of active teller (father) and making Shreve be the passive listener (son), he thereby passes on to Shreve the affront of sonship, the affront of dependency, and thus ensures that Shreve will try to take revenge on him by seizing "authority," by taking control of the narrative. What Quentin realizes is that generation as revenge on a substitute is an endless cycle of reversibility in which revenge only means passing on the affront to another who, seeking revenge in turn, passes on the affront, so that the affront and the revenge are self-perpetuating. Indeed, the word "revenge," as opposed to the word "vengeance," suggests this self-perpetuating quality—*re-*, again + *venger*, to take vengeance—to take vengeance again and again and again, because the very taking of revenge is the passing on of an affront that must be revenged. . . .

In his narrative struggle with Shreve, Quentin directly experiences the cyclic reversibility involved in revenge on a substitute— he experiences the maddening paradox of generation in time. At the beginning of their narrative, Quentin talks and Shreve listens, and in their imaginative reenactment of the story of the Sutpens, Quentin identifies with Henry, the father-surrogate, and Shreve identifies with Charles Bon, the son, the outsider. But as the roles of brother avenger and brother seducer are reversible (precisely because the roles for which they are substitutes—father and son— are reversible through substitution), so Quentin and Shreve begin to alternate in their identifications with Henry and Bon, and Quentin finds that Shreve is narrating and that he (Quentin) is listening and that Shreve sounds like Quentin's father. Quentin not only learns that *"a man never outlives his father"* and that he is going to have to listen to this same story over and over again for the rest of his life, but he realizes as well that in their narration he and Shreve *"are both Father"—"Maybe nothing ever happens once and is finished. . . . Yes, we are both Father. Or maybe Father and I are both Shreve, maybe it took Father and me both to make Shreve or Shreve and me both to make Father or maybe Thomas Sutpen to make all of us."* In terms of a generative sequence of narrators, Mr. Compson, Quentin, and Shreve are father, son, and grandson (reincarnation of the father). Confronting that cyclic reversibility, Quentin realizes that if sons seek revenge on their fathers for the affront of sonship by a repetition in reverse, if they seek to supplant their fathers, then the very fathers whom the sons wish to become are themselves nothing but sons who had sons in order to take that same revenge on their own fathers. Generation as revenge against the father, as revenge against time, is a circular labyrinth; it only establishes time's mastery all the more, for generation establishes the rule that a man never outlives his father, simply because a man's son will be the reincarnation of that father. And if for Quentin the act of narration is an analogue of this revenge on a substitute, then narration does not achieve mastery over time; rather, it traps the narrator more surely within the coils of time. What Quentin realizes is that the solution he seeks must be one that frees him alike from time and generation, from fate and revenge: he must die childless, he must free himself from time without having passed on the self-perpetuating affront of sonship.

Faulkner and the Burdens of the Past

by David M. Wyatt

Folks dont have no luck, changing names.—Dilsey

The Burdens

In the middle of Chapter 11 of *Light in August,* Faulkner inter-rupts the violent affair between Joe and Joanna to relate the Burden family history. The story focuses upon three generations of Burdens: Calvin the grandfather, Nathaniel the father, and Calvin the brother. Thirty-four years younger than the second Calvin, Joanna experiences her family more as a fourth-generation heir than as a third-generation participant. Faulkner underscores her distance from her family history by telling most of it for her:

> Calvin Burden was the son of a minister named Nathaniel Bur-rington. The youngest of ten children, he ran away from home at the age of twelve, before he could write his name (or would write it, his father believed) on a ship. He made the voyage around the Horn to California and turned Catholic; he lived for a year in a monastery. Ten years later he reached Missouri from the west. Three weeks after he arrived he was married, to the daughter of a family of Huguenot stock which had emigrated from Carolina by way of Kentucky.[1]

Fanatically opposed to slaveholding and always on the move, the Burden family wanders around the plains until its three gen-erations make the fatal decision to settle in Jefferson. Here their

Reprinted with permission from David M. Wyatt, *Prodigal Sons: A Study in Authorship and Authority* (Baltimore: The Johns Hopkins University Press, 1980), pp. 72–76, 77–80, and 94–100.

[1] William Faulkner, *Light in August* (New York: Random House, 1932), p. 228. Subsequent references are to this edition.

confused migrations assume tragic shape when the first and second Calvin are shot in the town square "by an ex-slaveholder and Confederate soldier named Sartoris, over a question of negro voting" (p. 235). Nathaniel spirits the bodies away for burial in a cedar grove, remains to father Joanna, and contents himself with passing on the legacy of revenge to her: "The only time I can remember him as somebody, a person, was when he took me and showed me Calvin's and grandpa's graves" (p. 238). Nathaniel's one moment of presence seems to turn upon this uncanny scene of instruction: "I didn't want to go into the cedars. . . . I think it was something about father, something that came from the cedar grove to me, through him. A something that I felt that he had put on the cedar grove, and that when I went into it, the grove would put on me so that I would never be able to forget it" (pp. 238–39). With Joanna reiterating the lasting effects of this trauma, her story ends.

Joe's immediate response is to reduce the Burden family history to one unanswered question: "Why your father never killed that fellow—what's his name? Sartoris" (p. 240). Joe here raises the largest possible issue in Faulkner—the problem of unconsummated revenge. How to live with a past that has not been avenged proves the most consistent threat to the stability of the Faulknerian present. Joanna resorts to genetic determinism as a way of explaining Nathaniel's failure to act. "I think that it was because of his French blood." Joe proposes a more conventional answer: "I guess your father must have got religion" (p. 241). Joe is probably closer to the truth. Getting religion could obviate the need for revenge. Based as it is upon the trope of sacrifice, or substitution, religion proposes that what is owed one, or what one owes, can be paid for by a mediator. In taking revenge upon a substitute (a ram, Christ), religion guarantees a displacement of wrath away from a human victim and onto an intercessor that has assimilated guilt. Art is the other great form of human mediation, as Faulkner was fond of reminding us: "those who can, do, those who cannot and suffer enough because they can't, write about it." [2] This is perhaps his most famous formula for the way in which words can take the place of deeds. Art intercedes between the artist and his experience, the artist and his audience, as a vehicle that expresses and even partially resolves those desires and

[2] *The Unvanquished* (New York: Random House, 1938), p. 262.

grievances that cannot be confronted through action. To Joe, anything but a man of words, such displaced revenge can only look like surrender. As he prepares to listen to the Burden chronicle, Joe sardonically observes that "when they [women] finally come to surrender completely, it's going to be in words" (p. 227). But what Joe registers as surrender Faulkner himself may experience as something like victory. In telling Joanna's story he achieves one more figurative revenge through language against the past that provoked him into writing. The actual shape of this past can be sketched in after giving closer attention to the way the past returns in *Light in August*. If we look at *how* Faulkner treats this material, we can better understand why he finds it so compelling.

Joanna finally does go beyond words in her attempt to escape the burden of her forefathers. No other woman in Faulkner seems to achieve so violent a break with her past. Her "wild throes of nymphomania" (p. 245) attempt at once to repudiate past time and to recover lost time. Yet as her quest for a release from Puritan self-consciousness and the debt of revenge she owes it proves increasingly obsessive, her promiscuity looks more like the return of the repressed. As a product of three generations of violent release and stubborn restraint, Joanna can find no middle ground between the two. Her apparent rupture with the past proves to be just one more repetition, and one that even fails to take revenge.

So Joanna begins to crave resolution through begetting a new generation. "She began to talk about a child, as though instinct had warned her that now was the time when she must either justify or expiate" (p. 248). A child would act both as a revenge against a repressive past and as a potential avenger of it. It would compensate for the "frustrate and irrevocable years" (p. 244) and assert the survival of the line. Above all, Joanna wishes her ancestors could see it: "A full measure. Even to a bastard negro child. I would like to see father's and Calvin's faces" (p. 251). The child, she knows, would rebuke them in complex ways; as the objectification of the Burden belief in the merging of the races, it would also be the product of a union they could not abide. Once Joanna discovers that she cannot carry her revenge forward into the future, she regresses into a mere woman of words. As Joe listens to the "calm enormity which her cold, still voice unfolded" (p. 261), he witnesses a retreat to a position where all that will be left to Joanna is prayer. In the severe economy of Faulkner's fiction, those who live by words die by words: Joe kills Joanna while refusing her entreaty to kneel.

The split in Joanna's experience between restitution through deeds and restitution through words is fundamental to Faulkner's perception of his own situation. His profound mistrust of words is only slightly exceeded by his indebtedness to them. Faulkner was not inclined to take solace in the paradox that words become deeds through the alchemy of the creative "act." Words remain words; they can never actually "do" anything. Yet they can register a shift in attitude toward the past to which they refer, and hence, if not a change in those antecedents, a change in what they mean for their inheritor. The very way in which Faulkner presents Joanna's family history indicates the changing significance for him of its highly charged material.

The sheer fact of the Burden chronicle requires explanation. Why is it even there? Do we need this much background about this character? Joanna's ambivalent attitude toward Joe's blackness could be explained without all the invention of three generations and a fatal shoot-out in the town square. The excessive detail and length of the story is no more suspicious than its form. The mode is epic chronicle, full of messengers, flights, heroic deeds. The third person narration (which Joanna's voice only partially recovers as it proceeds) is a throwback to a more traditional form of presentation than the elliptical flashbacks through which much of the novel unfolds. Even the revisions in the manuscript reflect Faulkner's attempts, once he had invented the Burdens, to elaborate their story within a linear framework. As Regina Fadiman has shown, the Burden history was "composed independently" of, and probably before, the developing affair between Joanna and Joe.[3] The manuscripts at the University of Virginia indicate that the story underwent two major revisions. The story originally began with Joanna's father: "Her father, Calvin Burden, was a stocky, dark man with black eyes and hair and a pale beak of a nose."[4] Faulkner then cut up this version

[3] Regina K. Fadiman, *Faulkner's "Light in August": A Description and Interpretation of the Revisions* (Charlottesville: University Press of Virginia, 1975), p. 87.

[4] The manuscript of *Light in August*, in the William Faulkner Collections, University of Virginia Library, p. 93.

and inserted a flashback dealing with the "older Calvin," [5] Joanna's grandfather. In the second and final revision Faulkner
rewrote the story as we have it, starting with the grandfather and
changing the father's name to Nathaniel. The linked fate of the
first and third generation is emphasized and clarified through the
final name change: Calvin—Nathaniel—Calvin rather than Calvin
—Calvin—Calvin. The final emphasis is upon genealogy and
chronology, upon an orderly disposition of Joanna's legacy.

We witness here a fulfilled will to digress, one bent upon dom-
inating material hardly necessary to the successful development
of the novel. Faulkner's novels are full of material unassimilated
to any obvious formal purpose, and the generosity of the digres-
sive style is often invoked as a convenient way of justifying such
excesses. Here Faulkner's purpose seems very likely beyond the
control of his creative will. The mode of presentation conveys
the sense that life is simple enough to be *told;* the telling is of a
pattern of repetition and revenge. As John Irwin has shown, this is
a pattern Faulkner continually rehearses. In *Light in August* the
pattern insinuates itself where we might least expect it. As outsiders, the Burdens are unlikely candidates for a genealogy developed to express the uniquely repetitive nature of Southern doom.
In *Light in August* Faulkner tries to master this doom through
his own voice rather than allowing it to emerge through the multiple soliloquies of clearly obsessed speakers. But the sheer fact
that such mastery proves gratuitous in view of the larger purposes
of the novel leaves open the question whether Faulkner has full
control of the material this chronicle is meant to order.

If the Burdens embody a story Faulkner cannot seem to forget,
his treatment of Hightower reveals his attitude toward such a
story. With the Burdens, Faulkner works from cause to effect.
Joanna's "revenge" directly follows and is meant to be understood
as the inevitable result of a family history she at once rejects and
extends. With Hightower, Faulkner works from effect to cause.
He presents Hightower as paralyzed by a memory of his grandfather before filling in the history which would make his behavior
explicable. Since Faulkner does not locate any objective correlative for Hightower's obsessive behavior in the present, we are left
to assume that Hightower's grandfather is himself the cause of

[5] *Ibid.*

Hightower's obsession with his grandfather. Richard Chase accuses Faulkner of being an implausible psychologist here:

> Hightower has projected his sexual and spiritual impotence back upon a myth of his grandfather. Faulkner goes along with Hightower on this point, assuming too that a fantasy projected from some center of real causation is the cause itself. He nearly allows Hightower to determine the quality of his (Faulkner's) consciousness.[6]

This is a curious charge. What does Chase mean by the phrase "goes along with Hightower?" How does a character one has created turn upon one "to determine" one's consciousness? Only if the character himself originates from material unavailable to introspection. If we take Chase's analysis as a point of departure, the largely unconscious workings of Faulkner's creative mind can be thrown into relief. By the logic of Chase's argument, what is not true of the character (determination of ancestry) may well be true of his author: Faulkner risks psychological implausibility with Hightower because Hightower allows him to express a fantasy he is determined by. Faulkner apparently has little choice but to create fictions in which an imaginative relation to one's past proves as formative as any "center of real causation" in the present. He displaces onto Hightower his predicament of being determined by "a myth of his grandfather." Hightower is a symptom of the very symptom he falsely diagnoses in himself. Faulkner's statements about him thus reveal as much about Faulkner as about Hightower. It is Faulkner who "produces" stories "out of his subconscious . . . without volition" (p. 346). It is Faulkner who, in confronting his own past, "skipped a generation" (p. 452). And it is Faulkner who discovers that his "only salvation must be to return to the place to die where my life had already ceased before it began" (p. 452). How he survives that return is the drama of his career.

The Burden

Faulkner's imagination performed an extreme abbreviation of the stories handed down to him about his ancestors. He seems to have reduced this legacy to one episode, its "repetition," and the re-

[6] *William Faulkner: Two Decades of Criticism*, ed. Frederick J. Hoffman and Olga W. Vickery (East Lansing: Michigan State University Press, 1951), p. 251.

sponse to the first and second event by a figure caught up between the two. The pattern centers on three figures in Faulkner's male line: the Old Colonel, William's great-grandfather; John W. T. Falkner, his grandfather; and Murry, his father. It is tempting to linger over the details of the Old Colonel's turbulent life—his flight from Missouri to Mississippi at fourteen, his mysterious wounding in the Mexican War, his two acquittals for murder, his short tenure as commander of "The Magnolia Rifles," his career as a novelist, railroad builder, and aspirant to the state legislature. But for William, the essence of the Old Colonel is summed up in his end. For all that happened to his great-grandfather—much of which Faulkner repeatedly incorporates—it was the way he died that made it necessary to *write* about him. It was an end that had to be written about, as we shall see, because it was unfinished, unresolved, unrevenged.

Even William's brother John, writing in *My Brother Bill,* feels it appropriate to introduce the Old Colonel at the moment of his death. John has been talking about the difficulty he had as a child grasping the age difference between himself and William. His thoughts suddenly shift:

> Mother finally explained it to me one day and after that Bill left me alone about it.
>
> The Old Colonel was killed by a man named Thurmond. Their differences had extended back over the years. They had grown more bitter with time. The final edge was reached when the Old Colonel defeated Thurmond for a seat in the state legislature in 1892. When the Old Colonel came back from Jackson, Thurmond shot him down on the street when he walked up to the Square from the depot. He died three days later.[7]

The very abruptness of this transition testifies to the familiarity (despite a number of inaccuracies) of the facts it introduces. They were familiar to William as well. After reminding Robert Cantwell that "he wasn't armed the day Thurmond shot him," Faulkner stresses the lasting effects of the Old Colonel's murder. "The feeling in Ripley did not die out with Colonel Falkner's death and Thurmond's leaving. I can remember myself, when I was a boy in Ripley, there were some people who would pass on the

---

[7] John Faulkner, *My Brother Bill: An Affectionate Reminiscence* (New York: Trident Press, 1963), p. 11.

other side of the street to avoid speaking—that sort of thing." [8]
Yet William (writing in 1945) could be remarkably forgetful
about a story of which he must have heard, like Quentin, all
"too much." [9] In a letter to Malcolm Cowley he casually ticks off
the Old Colonel's achievements and ends with this sentence: "He
built the first railroad in our country, wrote a few books, made
grand European tour of his time, died in a duel and the county
raised a marble effigy which still stands in Tippah County." [10]
There was no duel, and the marble effigy, an eight-foot statue of
Carrara marble, had been purchased for the eventuality by the
Colonel himself. His death was an episode about which the great-
grandson remained at once intensely concerned and curiously
vague. The facts are as follows:

THE MURDER: In 1886 Colonel Falkner assumed control of the
Ship Island, Ripley & Kentucky Railroad by buying out his business partner, Dick Thurmond. The two men had long since
become hardened rivals, fond of competing with each other by
expanding the dimensions of their palatial estates. When Falkner
declared for the Mississippi legislature, Thurmond tried unsuccessfully to finance his defeat. Two weeks before the election,
Falkner arranged his affairs with his lawyer, who warned him to
arm himself against the aggrieved Thurmond. On election day
the apparently victorious Falkner walked down to the Ripley
town square. He stood directly in front of Thurmond's office,
talking with a friend, Thomas Rucker. "Suddenly," as Blotner
tells it,

> Thurmond was there beside him, and Falkner turned to see a
> .44 pistol pointed at his head. "Dick, what are you doing?" he
> said. "Don't shoot!" But the pistol roared and Falkner fell, his
> pipe clattering on the pavement. He looked up at Thurmond.
> "Why did you do it, Dick?" he asked. Then he lost conscious-
> ness.[11]

[8] *William Faulkner: Three Decades of Criticism,* ed. Frederick J. Hoffman
and Olga W. Vickery (East Lansing: Michigan State University Press, 1960),
p. 56.

[9] *Absalom, Absalom!* (New York: Random House, 1936), p. 207.

[10] *Selected Letters of William Faulkner,* ed. Joseph Blotner (New York:
Random House, 1977), pp. 211–12.

[11] Joseph Blotner, *Faulkner: A Biography* (New York: Random House,
1974), p. 47.

The bullet had hit Falkner in the mouth, knocked out teeth, and lodged in the right side of the neck under the ear. The Colonel regained consciousness on Wednesday morning, bequeathed his affairs to his son John W. T., and died at 10:40 that evening. THE REACTION: John W. T. Falkner was forty-one when his father was shot. Thirty miles away in Oxford at the time, it took him over a day to reach the Colonel's bedside. In the meantime, two of Thurmond's men had secured the services of Judge Stephens—a widely respected barrister—for the defense. Apparently John W. T. had decided against taking the law into his own hands. When the trial began in February, the defense managed to secure a charge of manslaughter. John W. T. Falkner served as one of the assistants to the district attorney. Two days after the trial began it was finished: Thurmond had been acquitted. John W. T.'s friends talked him out of taking revenge against Thurmond, but he did experience the minor satisfaction of assaulting Joe Brown, one of the men who had pumped a handcar to Judge Stephens's on the night of the shooting.

THE REPETITION: About a year after his grandfather's murder, Murry Falkner became embroiled in an ugly feud. His sweetheart, Miss Pat Fontaine, enlisted Murry's aid in suppressing gossip being spread about her by a seamstress named Mollie Walker. Murry approached Mollie's brother, Elias, with the blunt command, "Tell your sister to stop making remarks about Miss Fontaine." Elias protested; Murry knocked him down twice. Later in the day Murry stopped in at Herron's drugstore to get a powder for his headache. "A moment later," Blotner relates,

> the door swung open and Herron dropped to the floor. Falkner turned his head to find himself looking at the barrel of 'Lias Walker's twelve-gauge shotgun. The blast hit him in the back and knocked him off the stool. In two quick strides Walker was standing over him, a pistol in his hand.
>
> "Don't shoot any more," Falkner groaned, "you've already killed me."
>
> "I want to be damned sure," Walker said, and pulled the trigger. The slug hit Falkner in the mouth, knocking out teeth, damaging his jaw, and lodging against bone near the roof of his mouth.[12]

[12] Blotner, *Faulkner*, pp. 53–54.

John W. T.'s response to the shooting of his son was more precipitous. He pumped a handcar thirty miles from Oxford and cornered Walker behind a hardware store. Armed with his big Navy revolver, standing at point blank range, John W. T. took aim at the would-be murderer of his son. The gun failed to fire. It proceeded to misfire six times. In the meantime Elias had pulled his own gun and shot John W. T. in the hand. "If it had hit me in the stomach it wouldn't have hurt so much."[13]

Back at Nelson's Boarding House Murry lay in critical condition. Sallie Murry, his mother, undaunted by the failure of the doctors to extract the bullet from Murry's mouth, tried an expedient of her own. She poured liquid gum resin in his mouth, Murry began to vomit, and the bullet popped out into the basin. Six years later Murry fathered William Cuthbert Faulkner.

What conclusion can we draw from this chain of events? In his abstract of the biography, Blotner omits important similarities between the two shootings while obscuring the pivotal role played in both by John W. T. "Looking at the eldest sons in the four Falkner generations, one notes that all of them except the author had been shot at least once, two of them twice. And if his father had not killed anyone, his grandfather had tried his best, and his great-grandfather had succeeded at least twice."[14] Here being "shot at least once" is advanced as a connecting link between three generations of Falkners. But surely what matters here is *how* one was shot, and *whether* one was revenged. Blotner misses the woods for the trees. John W. T. is shot not as a heroic victim but as a failed avenger. The shootings of his father and son are linked not only by the similarity of their wounds * and the exact repetition of the plea "Don't shoot," but, in each case, by the ineffectuality of John W. T.'s response. It was a pattern such as this, in which three generations are brought together in an ordeal of suffering and unfulfilled obligation, which made the generations an obsessive subject for fiction. The pattern is at once

---

[13] *Ibid.*

[14] Joseph Blotner, "The Falkners and the Fictional Families," *Georgia Review* 30 (Fall 1976), p. 585.

* Donald Duclos, who interviewed uncles and aunts along with Faulkner himself, emphasizes their awareness of this pattern: "The bullet (and this is what amazes the family) struck Murry in the face, doing the same physical damage to him as had been done to his grandfather by Thurmond's bullet." Donald Philip Duclos, *Son of Sorrow: The Life, Works, and Influence of Col. William C. Falkner, 1825–1889* (Ann Arbor: University Microfilms), p. 50.

repetitive and unfulfilled; while two generations, in the act of flaunting their courage, suffer a remarkably similar act of revenge, the intervening generation proves unable to achieve requital. Thus a fourth generation is bound to feel adumbrated by a pattern of repetition that exercises sway over the family destiny, as well as by the more painful fact that the logic of the pattern (similar fates befall alternating generations) links it with a figure who has contributed to the pattern by failing decisively to alter it. Out of such an inheritance may very likely have been born the recurring feeling in Faulkner "that an ancestor's actions can determine the actions of his descendants for generations to come by compelling them periodically to repeat his deeds." [15] The saddest word in Faulkner is not "was" but "again." He is threatened less by a past that is unrecapturable than by a past which continually recaptures him. . . .

The particular affront to Faulkner's psychic apparatus inflicted by his past was that time had taken revenge against him, leaving him a fourth generation heir of a pattern he could well feel powerless to reverse and even compelled to extend. His response was, in Irwin's words, "an oblique attempt to get even with that irreversibility of time that has rendered the original affront immune to direct action." [16] He became a storyteller.

In the course of trying to rewrite his family history, and thus his place in it, Faulkner came to understand and embrace the impossibility of his task. Irwin argues that it was the very nature of narration itself—its foredoomed attempt to get even—that led Faulkner deeper into the conflicts narration was meant to resolve. Thus his works become at once self-perpetuating and self-defeating, eventuating wholly out of themselves. Since Irwin views the entire process of Faulkner's career as so circular and self-reflexive —"to use narration to get even with the very mode of narration's existence"—he treats the novels as occupying "a multidimensional imaginative space . . . in which every element could be simultaneously folded into every other element." [17] The great strength of this method is in its tyrannizing unity. It can endlessly multiply examples of the elements which bind the works together in a set of mutually constitutive relationships. But it implies that

[15] John T. Irwin, *Doubling and Incest/Repetition and Revenge* (Baltimore: Johns Hopkins University Press, 1975), p. 61.
[16] Ibid., p. 3.
[17] Ibid., pp. 4 and 7.

Faulkner did not develop, and it obscures the relationship of the work to anything beyond the logic of its internal struggle against belatedness. Irwin brilliantly establishes Faulkner's career as the ultimate example of the anxiety of influence. In the course of proving this, however, he generalizes Faulkner's predicament into one so prevalent as to make it uninteresting. Such anxiety derived as much from deeply personal sources as from the paradox of creation itself. It was thus subject to a kind of resolution, since these sources stood in a dialectical (rather than a self-reflexive) relationship to the activity of creation. The meaning of Faulkner's work is not only to be found *among* the texts (in what Irwin calls "interstitial" space) but *between* the texts and the life. As Faulkner's understanding of his inheritance grew, his works changed. In the following pages I intend to show that Faulkner's struggle for a revenge against time was also an ambition which changed through time.

Starting with John W. T.

The central human act in Faulkner is the act of listening. Joe listens to Joanna, Quentin to Rosa, Ike to the hunters, Chick to Gavin Stevens. A relentless voice pours forth into an inevitable ear: narration typically preempts conversation. People relate by telling stories. The test of a good listener is his ability to retell with a difference. Verbal mastery of a verbal inheritance becomes the sign of maturity. Ike celebrates his majority by wresting the narration of his life away from the third person: "then he was twenty-one. He could say it, himself." [18] Development comes to be measured by the growing authority and autonomy of voice. One has grown up when one has learned to resist being entrapped by the "rhetoric of retellings" [19] into a mere repetition of the past.

Since Faulkner was born into a world of stories, it is perhaps no accident that the book he called his first "personal" [20] novel begins with one man listening to another. The immediate impact

---

[18] *Go Down, Moses* (New York: Random House, 1942), p. 254.

[19] Lawrance Thompson, "Afterword" in *Sartoris* (New York: Signet—Harcourt Brace, 1964), p. 310.

[20] "William Faulkner's Essay on the Composition of *Sartoris,*" *Yale University Library Gazette* 47 (January 1973), p. 123.

of *Sartoris* flows directly from being in the felt presence of ancestors. The "spirit of the dead man" [21] John Sartoris has been fetched by old Falls, the custodian of his life story. It is the *influence* of this spirit which interests Faulkner; throughout, Colonel John Sartoris is a figure mediated by the subjectivity of his son old Bayard. (*Flags in the Dust,* the first version of *Sartoris,* opens with the story and largely dispenses with its effects. Whoever revised this opening, its final form, in which we move from effect to cause, has proven more characteristically Faulknerian). On the opening page we witness only the effects of the father's presence; as with Hightower, Faulkner gives us the burden of the past before the past itself.

Old Bayard is deaf. This ailment seems perfectly tuned to his predicament—having heard too much. (He will later protest against old man Falls's interrogations "every time you tell me this damn story" [p. 20].) As if to emphasize the deafness as a defense against a burden passed on by the mouth, Faulkner ushers in the spirit of Colonel John through the transfer of his pipe from old man Falls to Bayard: "The bowl of the pipe was ornately carved, and it was charred with much usage, and on it were the prints of his father's teeth, where he had left the very print of his ineradicable bones as though in enduring stone" (p. 2). The bequest of the pipe suggests the bathetic conceit of Old Bayard following less in his father's footsteps than in his toothprints. (This transfer acquires more resonance when we remember that William inherited the very pipe his great-grandfather had been smoking when he was shot.[22]) The passing on of family identity will prove, for the Sartorises, a burden passed on from mouth to mouth.

The mere sight of the pipe a few pages later can thus function as a *petite madeleine* to conjure up the story which precipitates the opening scene:

> Through the cloth of his pocket his hand had touched the pipe there, and he took it out and looked at it again, and it seemed to him that he could still hear old man Falls' voice in roaring recapitulation: "Cunnel was settin' thar in a cheer, his sock feet propped on the po'ch railin', smokin' this hyer very pipe. . . ." (pp. 19–20)

[21] *Sartoris* (1929; rpt. New York: Random House, 1956), p. 1. Subsequent references are to this edition.

[22] See Duclos, *Son of Sorrow,* pp. 352–53.

This recollection begins with Colonel Sartoris's narrow escape from the Yankees and ends with the circumstances of his death:

> "That 'us when it changed. When he had to start killin' folks. Them two cyarpetbaggers stirrin' up niggers, that he walked right into the room whar they was a-settin' behind a table with they pistols layin' on the table, and that robber and that other feller he kilt, all with the same dang der'nger. When a feller has to start killin' folks, he 'most always has to keep on killin' 'em. And when he does, he's already dead hisself."

> It showed on John Sartoris' brow, the dark shadow of fatality and doom, that night when he sat beneath the candles in the dining-room and turned a wineglass in his fingers while he talked to his son. The railroad was finished, and that day he had been elected to the state legislature after a hard and bitter fight, and doom lay on his brow, and weariness.

> "And so," he said, "Redlaw'll kill me tomorrow, for I shall be unarmed. I'm tired of killing men. . . . Pass the wine Bayard (pp. 22–23).

The similarities between the death of Colonel Falkner and the death of Colonel Sartoris do not again need to be emphasized. The central issue here for our purposes is the first intersection of the Sartoris family fate with that of the as yet unnamed Burdens.

In order to understand the curious symmetries between these fatally linked families, consider the following genealogies:

Falkner	*Sartoris*	*Burden*
Col. William Clark Falkner (1825–89)	Col. John Sartoris (1823–73) Bayard Sartoris (1838–62)	Calvin Burden (1804–65)
John W. T. Falkner (1848–1922)	Bayard Sartoris ("old Bayard") (1849–1919)	Nathaniel Burden (1827–?)
Murry C. Falkner (1870–1932)	John Sartoris (d. 1901)	Calvin Burden (1845–65)
William Cuthbert Faulkner (1897–1962)	Bayard Sartoris ("young Bayard") (1893–1920) John Sartoris (1893–1918)	Joanna Burden (1879–1932)

The relevant incidents in the Sartoris genealogy can best be understood in light of old man Falls's theory that people can be made "kin" not only by the way they come into but by the way they go out of the world. " 'Bayard,' old man Falls said, 'I sort of envied them two Nawthuners, be damned ef I didn't. A feller kin take a wife and live with her fer a long time, but after all they ain't no kin. But the feller that brings you into the world or sends you outen hit . . .' " (p. 236). Given this theory of kinship, blood ties can be reinforced—even created—by intervening in the process of death. Intervention is precisely what old Bayard forgoes when John Sartoris is shot by Redlaw. He lives out a long and peaceful life punctuated only by the death of his son, the second John, from "yellow fever and an old Spanish bullet wound" (p. 90). After his grandson John is killed in aerial combat, old Bayard's namesake returns home as a guilty survivor. If old Bayard had failed to assert his kinship with his father by not avenging the way he was sent out of the world, young Bayard insists upon assuming responsibility for the way in which his brother died. Young Bayard's relentlessly suicidal behavior culminates in the automobile crash in which old Bayard is killed, directly under the figure of "John Sartoris' effigy" (p. 304). A few months later young Bayard finally destroys himself in a plane crash on the very day that his son, the fourth John, is born. This is the child Narcissa tries to unname.

Perhaps the most striking aspect of this story is the inconsequence of the third generation. In every account of the Sartoris family, the second John Sartoris is the man left out. William's "melancholy excision" of Murry Falkner's "opposite number" leads Blotner to this conclusion: "There seems to have been almost no rapport between these two Falkners, father and son." [23] Very likely so, but an interpretation more useful for our purposes has been suggested by Faulkner himself. "The twins' father didn't have a story. He came at a period in history which, in this country, people thought of and think of now as a peaceful one. That it was an optimistic one, nothing was happening. There would be little brush-fire wars that nobody paid much attention to, the country was growing, the time of travail and struggle where the hero came into his own had passed. From '70 on to 1912–14, noth-

---

[23] Blotner, "The Falkners and the Fictional Families," p. 583.

ing happened to Americans to speak of. This John Sartoris, the father, lived in that time when there was nothing that brought the issue to him to be brave and strong or dramatic—well, call it dramatic, not brave, but dramatic, nothing happened to him. But he had to be there for the simple continuity of the family." [24] If the second John Sartoris was conceived as Murry's "opposite number," the one happening Faulkner had to draw upon was Murry's youthful wounding. John Sartoris dies, in fact, from a wound of the sort that Murry survived. The major similarity between these two fathers still resides, however, in the utter uneventfulness of their lives as compared to the other males in their line. (Even William had fabricated the story of surviving a plane crash so as to acquire his share of vainglory.) Murry's wound at the hand of Elias Walker may have been enough to fulfill a pattern of repetition and to raise the issue of revenge, but the specific episode is apparently not one Faulkner feels the need to recapitulate in *Sartoris*. Only in the Burden genealogy does Faulkner link the third generation more dramatically to the family history through the one repetition which confirms Calvin's (as it did Murry's) place in the line.

Taken together then, the Sartoris and Burden genealogies reveal the ways in which Faulkner incorporates the patterns of repetition and revenge derived from his family history. In both families we find the device of the skipped generation: Calvin and Calvin shot by the same gun, Bayard and Bayard linked in their quest for self-destruction. The Sartorises especially display the pattern of spatial doubling within, and temporal doubling across, generations singled out by Irwin. Seen from the perspective of the present, both families contain a second generation which has avoided a clear call to revenge the first. These similarities become more remarkable when we consider that the fates of these two families intersect *because* of their mortal differences. Why should Faulkner, who so self-consciously patterned the Sartoris family after his own, bequeath such a similar genealogy to the Burdens? According to old man Falls's logic, the Burdens become "kin" to the Sartorises once the two Calvins are murdered by the Colonel. But their "kinship" antedates this episode; both families were

[24] *Faulkner in the University*, ed. Frederick L. Gwynn and Joseph L. Blotner (1959; rpt. New York: Vintage, 1965), p. 251.

grafted, as we have seen, from the same family tree. It is as if Faulkner cannot imagine a genealogy without relying upon *his* genealogy.

Perhaps we can now put the importance of old Bayard's development into clearer perspective. A generalized passivity shadows Bayard throughout *Sartoris*. This can be explained less by his old age than by his having failed to commit a purgative act of revenge. Revenge is continually held up by this novel as a means of resolving obligations and relieving guilt. It becomes a primary mode of releasing tension: Horace seeks "revenge on perfection" (p. 178) (meaning the sister to whom he is incestuously bound); women, Miss Jenny admits, "take our revenge wherever and whenever we can get it" (p. 56); young Bayard takes revenge against the future, "the long, long span of man's natural life" (p. 160), through suicide. If the constant reiteration of stories (old man Falls's revenge?) keeps Colonel John alive, they are kept lively for old Bayard by his not having imposed closure upon his father's end. Bayard's one attempt to do so is reminiscent of the ineffectuality of John W. T.'s. His father's tombstone had originally borne the words

> For man's enlightenment he lived
> By man's ingratitude he died
>
> Pause here, son of sorrow; remember death (p. 375)

"This inscription," Faulkner relates, "had caused some furore on the part of the slayer's family, and a formal protest had followed. But in complying with popular opinion, old Bayard had had his revenge: he caused the line 'By man's ingratitude he died' to be chiseled crudely out, and added beneath it: 'Fell at the hand of —— Redlaw, Sept. 4, 1876' " (pp. 375–76). But this is a revenge of words, not deeds. It leaves old Bayard unfulfilled, as Aunt Jenny's meditation by his grave clearly shows:

> Old Bayard's headstone was simple too, having been born, as he had, too late for one war and too soon for the next, and she thought what a joke They had played on him—forbidding him opportunities for swashbuckling and then denying him the privilege of being buried by men, who would have invented vainglory for him (p. 374).

That Faulkner felt Bayard's history to be an unresolved dimension of the novel becomes abundantly clear when we consider his

major revision of its plot. *The Unvanquished* not only gives old
Bayard a childhood, but grants him the opportunity to fashion
his unique and triumphant "revenge." . . .

Redeeming John W. T.

Faulkner's solution to the problem of old Bayard's passivity is
not to invent for him a catharsis through action, but to arrive at
a more generous interpretation of what Bayard "failed" to do.
In the same way that Quentin supplies his dark double (Henry)
with stronger and stronger motives, Faulkner learns to invent for
his (John W. T.) a usable past. The issue in both cases of identification is one of failed revenge, and how not to repeat the failure
without becoming entrapped in the cycle of revenge itself. By
1937 Faulkner had discovered that deeds are little help at all in
response to deeds. When committing an act, one can neither
truly imitate nor entirely avoid imitation. The challenge becomes
to find some means of participating in one's family destiny without simply reconfirming that destiny as an unavoidable fate.

Little in the first six stories of *The Unvanquished* would have
predicted the resolution achieved in the seventh, "An Odor of
Verbena." Almost three years separate the completion of the last
story from the composition of those which precede it, years which
Faulkner spent finishing *Absalom, Absalom!* Like "Big Two-
Hearted River," "An Odor of Verbena" can be read alone. But
also like Hemingway's story, it gathers together and fulfills a book
of stories which would not be a book without it. Faulkner admits
this when he writes to Morton Goldman about "the Civil War
Stories we sold the Post. . . . They needed one more story to
finish them, which I have just completed, named 'An Odor of
Verbena.' " [25] While the seventh story beautifully completes the
first six, it does so by utterly reversing the direction in which they
seem to move.

Bayard narrates the whole of *The Unvanquished*. Twelve at
the beginning, in "Ambuscade," he is twenty-four at the end. Just
as *The Unvanquished* was a book allowed to mature, so Bayard
is one of the few Faulkner narrators allowed to age. While the
entire narration is retrospective, Bayard's voice actually seems to
grow younger as he gets older. He begins with the melodramatic

[25] *Letters*, p. 100.

impatience of a Quentin Compson, a boy grown old before his time. Thus his miniature Vicksburg can provoke "a prolonged and wellnigh hopeless ordeal in which we ran, panting and interminable, with the leaking bucket between wellhouse and battlefield, the two of us needing first to join forces and spend ourselves against a common enemy, time, before we could engender between us and hold intact the pattern of recapitulant mimic furious victory like a cloth, a shield between ourselves and reality, between us and fact and doom." [26] He ends with a tone of resolution and calm unsurpassed in Faulkner, less knowing, more hopeful. One can hear, in the quiet phrases which close the book, the acceptance of a whole life coming forward to meet Bayard. Faulkner allows him a farewell beautifully understated in its promise of a new start:

> As I passed down the hall the light came up in the diningroom and I could hear Louvinia laying the table for supper. So the stairs were lighted quite well. But the upper hall was dark. I saw her open door (that unmistakable way in which an open door stands open when nobody lives in the room any more) and I realised I had not believed that she was really gone. So I didn't look into the room. I went on to mine and entered. And then for a long moment I thought it was the verbena in my lapel which I still smelled. I thought that until I had crossed the room and looked down at the pillow on which it lay—the single sprig of it (without looking she would pinch off a half dozen of them and they would be all of a size, almost all of a shape, as if a machine had stamped them out) filling the room, the dusk, the evening with that odor which she said you could smell alone above the smell of horses (pp. 292–93).

Bayard's voice changes because he has come to terms with his place in time.

The overriding emotion provoked by the first six stories is the desire to get back at an enemy. The reader is lured into a series of comic acts of revenge which gradually darken into tragedy. Granny turns the tables on the Yankees only to die at Grumby's nervous hand. While she claims that "I did not sin for revenge" (p. 167), her mule-swapping has the effect of drawing her sixteen-year-old grandson into a fatal quest after it. The book is struc-

---

[26] *The Unvanquished* (New York: Random House, 1938), p. 4. Subsequent references are to this edition.

tured in so linear a fashion—one thing simply leads to another—
that the reader never has a chance to question the direction he
finds his allegiances carrying him. The one thing we want to do
is give back, as we do in "Vendée." The pleasure we take in Bayard's tracking and killing Grumby may strike us as ominous, but
is not felt as objectionable. Faulkner successfully manipulates
the reader's impatience for closure into an acceptance of every
aspect of the grisly hunt, even up to pegging the mutilated "mur-
dering scoundrel" (p. 213) against the old compress door.

So Bayard proves his place in the line by revenging affronts to
that line. The supreme conclusion Uncle Buck can draw from
his triumph over Grumby is a genealogical one: "Ain't I told you
he is John Sartoris' boy? Hey? Ain't I told you?" (p. 213). (The
ascendancy of names later forces itself upon Bayard once his
father is shot: "I was now The Sartoris" [p. 247].) The Sartorises
are unquestioning of the code of *lex talionis*. It is perhaps therefore not surprising that the one warning against revenge in the
first six stories is expressed by someone else. On the note Grumby
leaves to frighten the boys off his trail, a postscript in another
hand offers the boys *"one more chance,"* the chance to quit before they are killed. *"Take it, and some day become a man. Refuse it, and cease even to be a child"* (p. 203). It is just this advice
which Bayard unwittingly follows in "An Odor of Verbena." He
becomes a man on the day he declines the further pursuit of
revenge.

The external events of this climactic story are easily sum-
marized, although the internal ones hold the key to the action.
"Skirmish at Sartoris" ends with Colonel John Sartoris murder-
ing the Burdens and marrying cousin Drusilla on the same day.
"An Odor of Verbena" opens eight years later as Bayard, a law
student in Oxford, receives news of his father's murder at the
hands of Ben Redmond. Bayard immediately rides the forty miles
back to Jefferson, musing upon all that his father has now "re-
linquished along with the pipe which Ringo said he was smoking,
which slipped from his hand as he fell" (p. 252). A flashback then
intrudes in which Bayard recalls an argument with Drusilla over
Sutpen's "dream" (p. 255). This memory merges with one of the
preceding August, in which Drusilla had challenged Bayard to
hate Redmond and to kiss her. Bayard kisses her twice and immediately tries to confess to his father. The story then returns to
the present with Bayard's arrival home and refusal of help from

his father's friends. That night Drusilla confronts him with her offer of two duelling pistols. Bayard refuses them, Drusilla collapses in hysteria, while Aunt Jenny, once she has packed Drusilla upstairs, assures Bayard that "I know you are not afraid" (p. 276). The next morning Bayard walks to the town square, unarmed, and enters Redmond's office. Redmond, seated behind his desk, fires two shots to the side of Bayard, staggers out of the room, and flees Jefferson forever. Bayard returns home to find Drusilla gone.

The one thing this story lacks is suspense. As he departs from Oxford, Bayard makes his first refusal of a pistol and betrays his intention not to kill by speaking of himself as "one still young enough to have his youth supplied him gratis as a reason (not an excuse) for cowardice" (p. 250). The question then becomes not will Bayard shoot Redmond, but what will support him in his resolve not to? *The Unvanquished* is a novel which turns upon itself, Faulkner's revenge against revenge. The common reader's surprise—even frustration—at this reversal finds expression in George Wyatt, who grudgingly accepts Bayard's unique solution:

> "You ain't done anything to be ashamed of. I wouldn't have done it that way, myself. I'd a shot him once, anyway. But that's your way or you wouldn't have done it."
>
> "Yes," I said. "I would do it again (p. 289).

The Unvanquished is a novel of education, and of no one more than the vengeful reader himself.

Bayard's solution is to refuse to repeat. By not killing again as his father had killed, by not killing for his father's sake, Bayard asserts his originality within his society and his indebtedness to a code older than the Southern tradition of honor which surrounds him. His reliance upon the wisdom of "the Book" expresses itself in the form of proverbs. *"Who lives by the sword shall die by it"* (p. 246) is perhaps the central proverb in Faulkner, positing as it does the repetitive fate of all those who seek revenge. An unspoken proverb dominates the story, as Drusilla reminds us when she tells Bayard that "you will remember me who put into your hands what they say is an attribute only of God's" (p. 273). "Vengeance is mine, saith the Lord." We may balk at experience reduced to proverb, even if the proverb is right. Proverbs beg, rather than answer, the question of Bayard's motivation. His willingness to repeat proverbs which express his decision not to repeat suggests that he has passed through analysis of his dilemma and on to resolve. But what has made this resolution possible? As Bayard rides back to Jefferson, Drusilla rises to the surface of his memory. She returns almost as if in response to his father's death, as if thinking about her will in some way help Bayard to decide upon the course of action he should take. Yet by this point in the story we are already aware that Bayard has decided. Remembering Drusilla gives Bayard access to the process which freed him to make such a decision. His recollection centers about the kiss:

> . . . "Kiss me, Bayard."
>
> "No. You are Father's wife."
>
> "And eight years older than you are. And your fourth cousin. And I have black hair. Kiss me, Bayard."
>
> "No."
>
> "Kiss me, Bayard." So I leaned my face down to her. But she didn't move, standing so, bent lightly back from me from the waist, looking at me; now it was she who said, "No." So I put my arms around her. Then she came to me, melted as women will and can, the arms with the wrist- and elbow-power to control horses about my shoulders, using the wrists to hold my face to hers until there was no longer need for the wrists; I thought then of the woman of thirty, the symbol of the ancient and eternal Snake and of the men who have written of her, and I realised then the immitigable chasm between all life and all print—that those who can, do, those who cannot and suffer enough because they can't, write about it. Then I was free . . . (p. 262).

Bayard will kiss her again, but not before insisting that "I must tell Father" (p. 263). His father's reply is a scene out of *The Sound and the Fury,* and also very likely reconstructs what once passed between Colonel William and John W. T.:

> You are doing well in the law, Judge Wilkins tells me. . . . I acted as the land and the time demanded and you were too young for that, I wished to shield you. But now the land and the time too are changing; what will follow will be a matter of consolidation, of pettifogging and doubtless chicanery in which I would be a babe in arms but in which you, trained in the law, can hold your own—our own. Yes, I have accomplished my aim, and now

> I shall do a litttle moral housecleaning. I am tired of killing
> men, no matter what the necessity nor the end. Tomorrow, when
> I go to town and meet Ben Redmond, I shall be unarmed (p.266).

The next day John Sartoris is shot, and that night Bayard sets
out to return to the home he had ridden away from so soon
before.

The basic genius of "An Odor of Verbena" lies in its overt
linkage of the Oedipal conflict with revenge tragedy. Eliot might
have puzzled over Hamlet's inaction as an aggrieved son, but
Faulkner is careful that we will not lack an objective correlative
for Bayard's motives. Bayard is Hamlet with insight. In the kiss
scene he and the reader are made to acknowledge that wishes for
a mother lead to ambivalence toward the father. Bayard at once
commits and refuses incest; the kiss is a measure of how far he
will not go. (His subsequent refusal of the duelling pistols confirms his resolve to take nothing more from Drusilla than two
kisses, least of all his father's pistols.) His immediate response is
"Now I must tell Father." Here he openly admits and renounces
his claim to his (step)mother. If he has done so, he should feel
no further need to pursue that claim through a revenge upon
the father, or even (as Irwin has it) through a revenge upon
his father's killer that really acts as a symbolic revenge upon the
father. (Of course Bayard "unmans" Redmond, but through an
act of the imagination which only he fully understands.) It is as
if Hamlet were relieved of his conflict over revenging his father's
murder by being made to confront (by Gertrude) and accept *and*
forgo his wish to do what the murderer had done. Bayard "for-
gives" Redmond because he has been given the chance to forgive
himself.

Bayard does not speak for himself alone in the kiss scene. He
speaks for Faulkner as well. If we examine the progression of his
thoughts, we see that they move swiftly from sexual and physical
to verbal conquest. Taking the "woman" in the flesh is precisely
what Bayard will not "do," just as revenging his father's murder
is something he will not "do." His not "doing" seems to be expressed as a limitation, as something he "cannot" do. "Those who
can, do, those who cannot and suffer enough because they can't,
write about it." Yet Bayard's not doing, however despairing his
tone here, ultimately affects the reader as anything but a display
of impotence. Taken out of context, the quote means what it

says; writing, like all *not* acting, is a mere substitute for doing, a weak man's way out. But within the context of the story, an entirely new attitude is encouraged toward the admittedly still "immitigable chasm" between life and print. The story posits substitution—of passive for active resistance, of the words of the Book for the deeds of the code—as the only truly adaptive solution open to Bayard. Unlike Quentin, Bayard understands and can articulate the difference between literal and symbolic action, and this allows him to substitute the one for the other. To all outer appearances, Bayard does no more to avenge his father than did John W. T. He does *not* kill for him. But for the first time Faulkner fully embraces the belief that symbolic or internalized actions can be made to take the place of literal ones, and so redeems, not only his hero, but the grandfather for whom he stands.

This triumph over the literal finds oblique confirmation in Bayard's meditation upon his dead father's hands:

> the empty hands still now beneath the invisible stain of what had been (once, surely) needless blood, the hands now appearing clumsy in their very inertness, too clumsy to have performed the fatal actions which forever afterward he must have waked and slept with and maybe was glad to lay down at last—those curious appendages clumsily conceived to begin with yet with which man has taught himself to do so much, so much more than they were intended to do or could be forgiven for doing (p. 272).

Faulkner here redefines the verb "do." He implies that hands were at best intended to "do" something on paper, that they should bear, if anything, not the "invisible stain" of blood, but the visible one of ink. Writing and killing are both works of the hands, but Faulkner learned better than Hemingway the difference between picking up a pen and picking up a gun. When you pick up a gun with resolution in mind, he could have warned his great rival, you turn your hand against no one as surely as yourself.

In revising the stories he had inherited about his grandfather, Faulkner completed his quest for authority as an artist. *Not* doing is finally made good, in the history of the ancestor, in the life of his grandson. *The Unvanquished* displays a fully conscious grasp of the conflicts which had possessed Faulkner since the writing of *Flags in the Dust*. If the conflict was not resolved, it had at least been understood. The decade of the great formal experiments was over. Faulkner had made the one discovery which he had to make—that understanding *is* forgiveness. . . . After *The Unvanquished* the familiar patterns may recur, but within a context which reduces them more and more to objects of inquiry.

Faulkner's distance from material which would previously have led him into extreme technical innovation can be felt, for instance, in *Go Down, Moses,* which makes rather clear its scorn for Ike's premature unburdening of the weight of the past. When Ike, a budding genealogist, turns upon his family to relinquish it, he reenacts the familiar revenge against time. Ike has tried to compose a History which will serve him as a platform from which he can view history, but this is too ambitious a substitute of imagination for experience. The book's qualifying ironies—especially Ike's "salvation" of his son by refusing to beget him—everywhere suggest that his is a project which his author sees as evasive and self-destructive. *Go Down, Moses* is a reprise of Faulkner's entire career in which he finally lays to rest his quarrel with genealogy. Thus the novel can invent a new kind of hero, Lucas Beauchamp, who has *"fathered himself."* He can never be convicted of a sense of belatedness. He is "durable, ancestryless." [27] He moves through a world filling up with Snopeses, equally durable, equally ancestryless. The problem to which Faulkner turns himself in the second phase of his career is not the past and its burdens but the lack of one.

Being fathered proves less oppressive than being unable to father for Harry, Flem, Ike, Lucas, and Gavin. By the time Faulkner writes *A Fable,* he can imagine a world of fathers unable to make any legitimate claim upon sons. No longer does the Corporal need the acknowledgment which Quentin, Henry, Charles, and Bayard once craved. Thus he can refuse what would have been, twenty years earlier, the ultimate gift, the final triumph. In a single phrase of promise, Faulkner's "magnum o" [28] at once sums up the deepest yearning of a career and reminds us of how long since it has been requited, so much so that a son no longer listens to or answers a father as he speaks the wished for words, "I will acknowledge you as my son." [29]

[27] *Go Down, Moses,* p. 118.
[28] *Letters,* p. 233.
[29] *A Fable* (New York: Random House, 1954), p. 348.

Faulkner, Childhood, and the Making of
The Sound and the Fury

by David Minter

Early in 1928, while he was still trying to recover from
Horace Liveright's rejection of *Flags in the Dust*, William Faulkner began writing stories about four children named Compson.
A few months earlier, his spirits had been high. Confident that
he had just finished the best book any publisher would see that
year, he had begun designing a dust jacket for his third novel.
His first book, *The Marble Faun*, had sold few copies, and
neither of his previous novels, *Soldiers' Pay* and *Mosquitoes*, had
done very well. But *Flags in the Dust* had given him a sense of
great discovery, and he was counting on it to make his name for
him as a writer. Following Liveright's letter, which described
the novel as "diffuse and non-integral," lacking "plot, dimension
and projection," Faulkner's mood became not only bitter but
morbid. For several weeks he moved back and forth between
threats to give up writing and take a job, and efforts to revise
his manuscript or even re-write the whole thing. Yet nothing
seemed to help—neither the threats, which he probably knew
to be empty, nor the efforts, which left him feeling confused and
even hopeless. Finally, he decided to re-type his manuscript and
send it to Ben Wasson, a friend who had agreed to act as his
agent.[1]

From David Minter, "Faulkner, Childhood, and the Making of *The Sound
and the Fury*," *American Literature* [1979], 51, 376–393. Copyright © 1979,
Duke University Press (Durham, N.C.).

[1] See Faulkner to Liveright, Sunday,—October [16 Oct. 1927]; 30 Novem-
ber [1927]; and [mid or late Feb. 1928] in Joseph Blotner, ed., *Selected
Letters of William Faulkner* (New York: Random House, 1977), pp. 38–39.
For Liveright's letter of rejection, see Joseph Blotner, *Faulkner: A Biography*
(New York: Random House, 1974), pp. 559–560.

The disappointment Faulkner experienced in the aftermath of Liveright's blunt rejection was intensified by the solitude it imposed. He had enjoyed sharing the modest success of his earlier books, particularly with his mother, with old friends like Phil Stone, and with his childhood sweetheart, Estelle Oldham Franklin. But he found it impossible to share failure. "Don't Complain —Don't Explain" was the motto his mother had hung in the family kitchen and imprinted on the minds of her sons.[2] To her eldest son the experience of failure proved not only more painful but more solitary than any anticipation of it. Soon he also found himself immersed in a deep personal crisis, the contours of which remain a mystery. Several years later he spoke to Maurice Coindreau of a severe strain imposed by "difficulties of an intimate kind" ("des difficultes d'order intime").[3] To no one was he more specific. In a letter to his favorite aunt, he refers to a charming, shallow woman, "Like a lovely vase." "Thank God I've no money," he added, "or I'd marry her." [4] But what if anything his intimate difficulties had to do with his new love, we do not know. What we know is that the difficulties touched much. "You know, after all," he said to an acquaintance, "they put you in a pine box and in a few days the worms have you. Someone might cry for a day or two and after that they've forgotten all about you." [5]

As his depression deepened, Faulkner began reviewing his commitment to his vocation. Unable to throw it over, he determined to alter his attitude toward it—specifically by relinquishing hope of great recognition and reward. For several years, he had written in order to publish. After *Soldiers' Pay* that had meant writing with Horace Liveright before him. Yet, as his work had become more satisfying to him, it had become less acceptable to Liveright. Refusing to go back to writing things he now

[2] Murry C. Falkner, *The Falkners of Mississippi: A Memoir* (Baton Rouge: Louisiana State University Press, 1967), pp. 9–10.

[3] Maurice Coindreau, Introduction, *Le bruit et la fureur* (Paris: Gallimard, 1938), p. 14. See also James B. Meriwether, "Notes on the Textual History of *The Sound and the Fury*," *Papers of the Bibliographical Society of America*, LVI (1962), 288.

[4] See Faulkner to Mrs. Walter B. McLean, quoted in Blotner, *Faulkner*, pp. 562–563.

[5] J. W. Harmon in *William Faulkner of Oxford*, ed. James W. Webb and A. Wigfall Green, Baton Rouge: Louisiana State University Press, 1965), pp. 93–94.

thought "youngly glamorous," like *Soldiers' Pay,* or "trashily smart," like *Mosquitoes,* he decided to go on even if it meant relinquishing his dream of success.[6]

His hope faded slowly, he recalled, but fade it did. "One day I seemed to shut a door between me and all publishers' addresses and book lists. I said to myself, Now I can write"—by which he meant that he could write for himself alone. Almost immediately he felt free. Writing "without any accompanying feeling of drive or effort, or any following feeling of exhaustion or relief or distaste," he began with no plan at all. He did not even think of his manuscript as a book. "I was thinking of books, publication, only in . . . reverse, in saying to myself, I wont have to worry about publishers liking or not liking this at all." [7]

More immediately, however, what going on and feeling free to write for himself meant was going back—not only to stories about children but to experiences from his own childhood and to characters he associated with himself and his brothers. Taking a line from "St. Louis Blues," which he had heard W. C. Handy play years before, he called the first Compson story "That Evening Sun Go Down." The second he called "A Justice." In both stories children face dark, foreboding experiences without adequate support. At the end of "A Justice" they move through a "strange, faintly sinister suspension of twilight"—an image which provided the title for another story, which Faulkner began in early spring.

Called "Twilight," the third of the Compson stories engaged him for several months, and became *The Sound and the Fury,* his first great novel. Through the earlier stories he had come to see the Compson children poised at the end of childhood and the beginning of awareness, facing scenes that lie beyond their powers of understanding and feeling emotions that lie beyond their powers of expression. In the second story, as twilight descends and their world begins to fade, loss, consternation, and bafflement become almost all they know.

This moment, which the stories discovered and the novel ex-

---

[6] Faulkner to Liveright, [mid or late Feb. 1928], *Selected Letters,* pp. 39–40.

[7] See both versions of Faulkner's Introduction to *The Sound and the Fury,* one in *The Southern Review,* VIII (Autumn 1972), 705–710; and one in *The Mississippi Quarterly,* XXVI (Summer 1973), 410–415. [Both introductions are reprinted in this volume.—Ed.] For the quoted phrases, see the first of these [p. 20 of this volume].

plores, possessed particular poignancy for Faulkner—a fact confirmed by scattered comments as well as by the deep resonance of the novel and the story of its making. "Art reminds us of our youth," Fairchild says in *Mosquitoes,* "of that age when life don't need to have her face lifted every so often for you to consider her beautiful."[8] "It's over very soon," Faulkner remarked as he observed his daughter nearing the end of her youth. "This is the end of it. She'll grow into a woman."[9] During the creation of the Compson children, he became not merely private but secretive. Even the people to whom he had talked and written most freely while working on *Flags in the Dust*—his mother and his aunt, Phil Stone and Estelle Franklin—knew nothing about his new work until it was finished.[10] Although he was capable, as he once remarked, of saying almost anything in an interview, and on some subjects enjoyed contradicting himself, his comments on *The Sound and the Fury* remained basically consistent for more than thirty years. Even when the emotion they express is muted and the information they convey is limited, they show that the novel occupied a special place in his experience and in his memory. The brooding nostalgia which informs the novel also survived it: it entered interviews for years to come, and it dominated the "introduction" he wrote to *The Sound and the Fury* in the early thirties, both as emotion recalled and as emotion shared. Looking back on the painful yet splendid months of crisis during which he wrote *The Sound and the Fury,* Faulkner was able to discover emotions similar to those which that crisis enabled him to discover in childhood.

Like *Flags in the Dust, The Sound and the Fury* is set in Jefferson and recalls family history. The Compson family, like the Sartoris family, mirrors Faulkner's deepest sense of his family's story as a story of declension. But *The Sound and the Fury* is more bleak and more compelling. It is also more personal, primarily because the third or parental generation, which in *Flags in the Dust* is virtually deleted as having no story, plays a major role in *The Sound and the Fury*.[11] Despite its pathos, *Flags* re-

---

[8] *Mosquitoes* (New York: Boni and Liveright, 1927), p. 319.

[9] See Faulkner as quoted in Blotner, *Faulkner,* p. 1169.

[10] See both versions of the Introduction to *The Sound and the Fury* cited in note 7; and Blotner, *Faulkner,* pp. 570–571 and 578–580.

[11] See Faulkner's explanation of his deletion of the parental generation from *Flags in the Dust* in *Faulkner in the University,* ed. Frederick L. Gwynn

mains almost exuberant; and despite its use of family legends, it remains open, accessible. Faulkner's changed mood, his new attitude and needs, altered not only his way of working but his way of writing. A moving story of four children and their inadequate parents, *The Sound and the Fury* is thematically regressive, stylistically and formally innovative. If being free to write for himself implied freedom to recover more personal materials, being free of concern about publishers' addresses implied freedom to become more experimental. The novel thus represented a move back toward home, family, childhood, and a move toward the interior; but it also represented an astonishing breakthrough.[12] Furthermore, both of its fundamental principles, the regressive and the innovative, possessed several corollaries. Its regressive principle we see, first, in the presence of the three Compson brothers, who recall Faulkner's own family configuration, and second, in the use of memory and repetition as formal principles.[13] Faulkner possessed the three Compson brothers, as he later put it, almost before he put pen to paper. He took a central event and several germinating images from the death of the grandmother he and his brothers called Damuddy, after whose lingering illness and funeral they were sent from home so that it could be fumigated. For Faulkner, as for Gertrude Stein, memory is always repetition, being and living never repetition. *The Sound and the Fury,* he was fond of remarking, was a single story several times told. But memory was never for him simple repetition. He used the remembered as he used the actual: less to denominate lived events, relationships, and configurations, with their attendant attributes and emotions, than to objectify them and so be free to analyze and play with them. To place the past under the aspect of the present, the present under the aspect of

---

and Joseph Blotner, (Charlottesville, Va.: University Press of Virginia, 1959), p. 251.

[12] See Conrad Aiken, "William Faulkner: The Novel as Form," in *Faulkner: A Collection of Critical Essays,* ed. R. P. Warren (Englewood Cliffs, N.J.: Prentice-Hall, 1966), p. 51.

[13] Faulkner had three brothers, of course, but during the crucial years to which his memory turned in *The Sound and the Fury,* he had only two. Leila Dean Swift, the grandmother whom the first three Falkner boys called Damuddy, died on June 1, 1907. The youngest of the four Falkner boys, Dean Swift Falkner, was born August 15, 1907. Also, see Faulkner as quoted in the statement cited in note 28.

the past, was to start from the regressive toward the innovative. Like the novel's regressive principle, its innovative principle possessed several corollaries, as we see, for example, in its gradual evocation of Caddy, the sister he added to memory, and in its slow progression from private toward more public worlds.[14]

The parental generation, which exists in *Flags in the Dust* only for sake of family continuity, is crucial in *The Sound and the Fury*. Jason is aggressive in expressing the contempt he feels for his mother and especially his father. Although Benjy shares neither Jason's contempt nor the preoccupations it inspires, he does feel the vacancies his parents' inadequacies have created in his life. Although Quentin disguises his resentment, it surfaces. Like Benjy's and Quentin's obsessive attachments to Caddy, Jason's animosity toward her originates in wounds inflicted by Mr. and Mrs. Compson. In short, it is in Caddy that each brother's discontent finds its focus, as we see in their various evocations of her.

To the end of his life, Faulkner spoke of Caddy with deep devotion. She was, he suggested, both the sister of his imagination and "the daughter of his mind." [15] Born of his own discontent, she was for him "the beautiful one," his "heart's darling." [16] It was Caddy, or more precisely, Faulkner's feeling for the emerging Caddy, that turned a story called "Twilight" into a novel called *The Sound and the Fury*: "I loved her so much," he said, that "I couldn't decide to give her life just for the duration of a short story. She deserved more that that. So my novel was created, almost in spite of myself." [17]

In the same statements in which Faulkner stressed the quality of his love for Caddy, he emphasized the extent to which his novel grew as he worked on it. One source of that growth derived from Faulkner's discovery of repetition as a technical principle. Having presented Benjy's experience, he found that it was so

---

[14] See Aiken as cited in note 12.

[15] See the discussions of Caddy in the Introduction cited in note 7; *Mosquitoes*, p. 339; and "Books and Things: Joseph Hergesheimer," in *William Faulkner: Early Prose and Poetry*, ed. Carvel Collins, (Boston: Little, Brown, 1962), pp. 101–103. The quoted phrase is a translation of an Italian phrase quoted in the last of these pieces, p. 102.

[16] *Faulkner in the University*, p. 6.

[17] See Faulkner as quoted in the translation of Maurice Coindreau's Introduction to *The Sound and the Fury*, in *The Mississippi Quarterly*, XIX (Summer 1966), 109.

"incomprehensible, even I could not have told what was going on then, so I had to write another chapter." The second section accordingly became both a clarification and a counterpoint to the first, just as the third became both of these to the second.[18] The story moves from the remote and strange world of Benjy's idiocy and innocence, where sensations and basic responses are all we have; through the intensely subjective as well as private world of Quentin's bizarre idealism, where thought shapes sensation and feeling into a kind of decadent poetic prose full of idiosyncratic allusions and patterns; to the more familiar, even commonsensical meanness of Jason's materialism, where rage and self-pity find expression in colloquialisms and clichés. Because it is more conventional, Jason's section is more accessible, even more public. Yet it too describes a circle of its own.[19] Wanting to move from three peculiar and private worlds toward a more public and social one, Faulkner adopted a more detached voice. The fourth section comes to us as though from "an outsider." The story, as it finally emerged, tells not only of four children and their family, but of a larger world, itself at twilight. "And that's how that book grew. That is, I wrote that same story four times. . . . That was not a deliberate *tour de force* at all, the book just grew that way. . . . I was still trying to tell one story which moved me very much and each time I failed. . . ." [20]

Given the novel's technical brilliance, it is easy to forget how simple and how moving its basic story is. In it we observe four children come of age amid the decay and dissolution of their family. It began, Faulkner recalled, with "a brother and a sister splashing one another in the brook" where they had been sent to play during the funeral of a grandmother they called Damuddy. From the play in the brook came what Faulkner several times referred to as the central image in the novel—Caddy's muddy drawers. As she clambers up a tree outside the Compson home to observe the funeral inside, we and her brothers see them from below. From these episodes, Faulkner got several things: his sense of the branch as "the dark, harsh flowing of time" which was sweeping Caddy away from her brothers; his sense that the

<hr />

[18] Robert A. Jelliffe, ed., *Faulkner at Nagano* (Tokyo: Kenkyusha, 1956), p. 104.

[19] See F. H. Bradley, *Appearance and Reality* (New York: Macmillan, 1908), p. 346; and T. S. Eliot's note to line 142 of *The Waste Land.*

[20] *Faulkner at Nagano,* pp. 103–105.

girl who had the courage to climb the tree would also find
the courage to face change and loss; and his sense that the brothers who waited below would respond very differently—that Benjy
would feel but never understand his loss; that Quentin would
seek oblivion rather than face his; and that Jason would meet
his with vindictive rage and terrible ambition.[21] The novel thus
focuses not only on the three brothers Faulkner possessed when
he began, but also on Caddy, the figure he added to memory—
which is to say, on the child whose story he never directly told
as well as on those whose stories he directly tells. His decision
to approach Caddy only by indirection, through the needs and
demands of her brothers, was in part technical, as he repeatedly
insisted. By the time he came to the fourth telling, he wanted a
more detached, public voice. In addition, he thought indirection
more "passionate." It was, he said, more moving to present "the
shadow of the branch, and let the [reader's] mind create the
tree." [22]

But in fact Caddy grew as she is presented, by indirection—
in response to needs shared by Faulkner and his characters.
Having discovered Benjy, in whose idiocy he saw "the blind,
self-centeredness of innocence, typified by children," he "became
interested in the relationship of the idiot to the world that he
was in but would never be able to cope with. . . ." What particularly agitated him was where such a one as Benjy could find
"the tenderness, the help, to shield him. . . ." [23] The answer he
hit upon had nothing to do with Mr. and Mrs. Compson, and
only a little to do with Dilsey. Mr. Compson is a weak, nihilistic
alcoholic who toys with the emotions and needs of his children.
Even when he feels sympathy and compassion, he fails to show
it effectively. Mrs. Compson is a cold, self-involved woman who
expends her energies worrying about her ailments, complaining
about her life, and clinging to her notions of respectability. "If

[21] See both versions of Faulkner's Introduction, cited in note 7; and compare *Faulkner in the University*, pp. 31–32.

[22] *Faulkner at Nagano*, p. 72. Compare this statement with Mallarmé's
assertion: "Nommer un objet, c'est supprimer les trois-quarts de la jouissance
du poeme. . . ." See also A. G. Lehmann, *The Symbolist Aesthetic in France,
1885–1895* (Oxford: Blackwell, 1950), particularly chapters 1, 2, and 6.

[23] James B. Meriwether and Michael Millgate, eds., *Lion in the Garden:
Interviews with William Faulkner, 1926–1962* (New York: Random House,
1968), p. 146.

I could say Mother. Mother," Quentin says to himself. Dilsey, who distinctly recalls Mammy Caroline Barr, to whom Faulkner later dedicated *Go Down, Moses,* epitomizes the kind of Christian Faulkner most deeply admired. She is saved by a minimum of theology. Though her understanding is small, her wisdom and love are large. Living in the world of the Compsons, she commits herself to the immediate; she "does de bes' " she can to fill the vacancies left in the lives of the children around her by their loveless and faithless parents. Since, by virtue of her love and faith she is part of a larger world, she is able not only to help the children but "to stand above the fallen ruins of the family. . . ." [24] She has seen, she says, the first and the last. But Dilsey's life combines a measure of effective action with a measure of pathetic resignation. Most of Benjy's needs for tenderness and comfort, if not help and protection, he takes to his sister. And it was thus, Faulkner said, that "the character of his sister began to emerge. . . ." [25] Like Benjy, Quentin and Jason also turn toward Caddy, seeking to find in her some way of meeting needs ignored or thwarted by their parents. Treasuring some concept of family honor his parents seem to him to have forfeited, Quentin seeks to turn his fair and beautiful sister into a fair, unravished, and unravishable maiden. Lusting after an inheritance, and believing his parents to have sold his birthright, Jason tries to make Caddy the instrument of a substitute fortune.

The parental generation, which exists in *Flags in the Dust* only for the sake of continuity, thus plays a crucial if destructive role in *The Sound and the Fury.* Several readers have felt that Faulkner's sympathies as a fictionist lay more with men than with women.[26] But his fathers, at least, rarely fare better than his mothers, the decisive direction of his sympathy being toward children, as we see most clearly in *The Sound and the Fury,* but clearly too in works that followed it. Jewel Bundren must live without a visible father, while Darl discovers that in some fundamental sense he "never had a mother." Thomas Sutpen's children live and die without an adequate father. Rosa Coldfield lives a long life only to discover that she had lost childhood before she

---

[24] See p. 414 of the second version of Faulkner's Introduction to *The Sound and the Fury,* cited in note 7.

[25] See *Lion in the Garden,* pp. 146–147.

[26] See Albert J. Guerard, *The Triumph of the Novel* (New York: Oxford University Press, 1976), pp. 109–135.

possessed it. Yet, even as they resemble the deprived and often deserted or orphaned children of Charles Dickens, Faulkner's children also resemble Hawthorne's Pyncheons. Held without gentleness, they are still held fast. Suffering from a malady that resembles claustrophobia no less than from fear of desertion, they find repetition easy, independence and innovation almost impossible.

Although he is aggressive in expressing the hostility he feels for his parents, Jason is never able satisfactorily to avenge himself on them. Accordingly, he takes his victims where he finds them, his preference being for those who are most helpless, like Benjy and Luster, or most desperate, like Caddy. Enlarged, the contempt he feels for his family enables him to reject the past and embrace the New South, which he does without recognizing in himself vulgar versions of the materialism and self-pity that we associate with his mother. Left without sufficient tenderness and love, Quentin, Caddy, and Benjy turn toward Dilsey and each other. Without becoming aggressive, Benjy feels the vacancies his parents create in his life. All instinctively, he tries to hold fast to those moments in which Caddy meets his need for tenderness. In Quentin, we observe a very different desire: he wants to possess moments only as he would have them. Like the hero of Pound's *Cantos,* Quentin lives wondering whether any sight can be worth the beauty of his thought. His dis-ease with the immediate, which becomes a desire to escape time itself, accounts for the strange convolutions of his mind and the strange transformations of his emotions. In the end it leads him to a still harbor, where he fastidiously completes the logic of his father's life. Unlike her brothers, Caddy establishes her independence and achieves freedom. But her flight severs ties, making it impossible for her to help Quentin, comfort Benjy, or protect her daughter. Finally, freedom sweeps "her into dishonor and shame. . . ." [27] Deserted by her mother, Miss Quentin is left no one with whom to learn love, and so repeats her mother's dishonor and flight without ever knowing her tenderness. If in the story of Jason we observe the near-triumph of all that is repugnant, in the stories of Caddy and Miss Quentin we observe the degradation of all that is beautiful. No modern story has done

[27] See p. 413 of the second version of Faulkner's Introduction to *The Sound and the Fury,* cited in note 7.

more than theirs to explore Yeats's terrible vision of modernity in "The Second Coming," where the "best lack all conviction," while the "worst are full of passionate intensity."

Faulkner thus seems to have discovered Caddy as he presents her—through the felt needs of her brothers. Only later did he realize that he had also been trying to meet needs of his own: that in Caddy he had created the sister he had wanted but never had and the daughter he was fated to lose, "though the former might have been apparent," he added, "from the fact that Caddy had three brothers almost before I wrote her name on paper." [28] Taken together, the Compson brothers body forth the needs Faulkner expressed through his creation of Caddy. In Benjy's need for tenderness we see something of the emotional confluence which precipitated the writing of *The Sound and the Fury*. The ecstasy and relief Faulkner associated with the writing of the novel as a whole, he associated particularly with the writing of Benjy's section.[29] In Jason's preoccupation with making a fortune, we see a vulgar version of the hope Faulkner was trying to relinquish. In Quentin's Manichaean revulsion toward all things material and physical, we see both a version of the imagination Allen Tate called "angelic" and a version of the moral sensibility that Faulkner associated with the fastidious aesthete.[30] It is more than an accident of imagery that Quentin, another of Faulkner's poets *manqués*, seeks refuge, first, in the frail "vessel" he calls Caddy, and then, in something very like the "still harbor" in which Faulkner had earlier imagined Joseph Hergesheimer submerging himself—"where the age cannot hurt him and where rumor of the world reaches him only as a far faint sound of rain." [31]

In one of his more elaborate as well as more suggestive descriptions of what the creation of Caddy meant to him, Faulkner associated her with one of his favorite images.

> I said to myself, Now I can write. Now I can make myself a vase like that which the old Roman kept at his bedside and wore the rim slowly away with kissing it. So I, who had never had a

---

[28] Ibid.

[29] Ibid., p. 414.

[30] See Allen Tate, "The Angelic Imagination," *The Man of Letters in the Modern World* (New York: Noonday Press, 1955), pp. 113–131; and Robert M. Slabey, "The 'Romanticism' of *The Sound and the Fury*," *The Mississippi Quarterly*, XVI, (Summer 1963), 152–157.

[31] "Books and Things: Joseph Hergesheimer," *Early Prose and Poetry*, p. 102.

sister and was fated to lose my daughter in infancy, set out to make myself a beautiful and tragic little girl.[32]

The image of the urn or vase had turned up earlier in a review of Hergesheimer's fiction; in Faulkner's unpublished novel about Elmer Hodge; in *Mosquitoes;* and in *Flags in the Dust.* It had made a recent appearance in the letter to Aunt Bama describing his new love, and it would make several later appearances. It was an image, we may fairly assume, which possessed special force for Faulkner, and several connotations, at least three of which are of crucial significance.

The simplest of these, stressing desire for shelter or escape, Faulkner first associated with Hergesheimer's "still harbor" and later with "the classic and serene vase" which shelters Gail Hightower "from the harsh gale of living." [33] In *The Sound and the Fury* Benjy comes to us as a wholly dependent creature seeking shelter. Sentenced to stillness and silence—"like something eyeless and voiceless which . . . existed merely because of its ability to suffer" [34]—he is all need and all helplessness. What loss of Caddy means to him is a life of unrelieved, and for him meaningless, suffering. For Quentin, on the other hand, it means despair. In him the desire for relief and shelter becomes desire for escape. In one of the New Orleans sketches, Faulkner introduces a girl who presents herself to her lover as "Little sister Death." In an allegory written in 1926 for Helen Baird, who was busy rejecting his love, he reintroduces the figure called Little sister Death, this time in the company of a courtly knight and lover—which is, of course, one of the roles Quentin seeks to play.[35] At first all of

---

[32] See p. 710 of the first version of Faulkner's Introduction to *The Sound and the Fury,* cited in note 7.

[33] See the works cited in note 15; compare *Light in August* (New York: Harrison Smith and Robert Haas, 1932), p. 453.

[34] See p. 414 of the second version of Faulkner's Introduction to *The Sound and the Fury,* cited in note 7.

[35] See "The Kid Learns," in *William Faulkner: New Orleans Sketches,* ed. Carvel Collins, (New York: Random House, 1958), p. 91. See also "Mayday," the allegory Faulkner wrote for Helen Baird, as discussed by Blotner, *Faulkner,* pp. 510–511; by Cleanth Brooks, "The Image of Helen Baird in Faulkner's Early Poetry and Fiction," *The Sewance Review,* LXXXV (Spring 1977), 220–222; and by Cleanth Brooks, *William Faulkner, Toward Yoknapatawpha and Beyond* (New Haven, Conn.: Yale University Press, 1978), pp. 47–52. A facsimile of *Mayday* edited by Carvel Collins, has recently been published by

Quentin's desire seems to focus on Caddy as the maiden of his dreams. But as his desire becomes associated with "night and unrest," Caddy begins to merge with "Little sister Death"—that is, with an incestuous love forbidden on threat of death. Rendered impotent by that threat, Quentin comes to love, not the body of his sister, nor even some concept of Compson honor, but death itself. In the end, he ceremoniously gives himself, not to Caddy, but to the river. "The saddest thing about love," says a character in *Soldiers' Pay,* "is that not only the love cannot last forever, but even the heartbreak is soon forgotten." Quentin kills himself in part as punishment for his forbidden desires; in part because Caddy proves corruptible; in part, perhaps, because he decides "that even she was not quite worth despair." But he also kills himself because he fears his own inconstancy. What he discovers in himself is deep psychological impotence. He is unable to play either of the heroic roles—as seducer or as avenger—that he deems appropriate to his fiction of himself as a gallant, chivalric lover. What he fears is that he will ultimately fail, too, in the role of the despairing lover. What he cannot abide is the prospect of a moment when Caddy's corruption no longer matters to him.[36]

Never before had Faulkner expressed anxiety so deep and diverse. In Quentin it is not only immediate failure that we observe; it is the prospect of ultimate failure. Later, Faulkner associated the writing of *The Sound and the Fury* specifically with anxiety about a moment "when not only the ecstasy of writing would be gone, but the unreluctance and the something worth saying too."[37] Coming and going throughout his life, that anxiety came finally to haunt him. But as early as his creation of Quentin he saw clearly the destructive potential of the desire to escape it. If he wrote *The Sound and the Fury* in part to find shelter, he also wrote it knowing that he would have to emerge from it. "I had made myself a vase," he said, though "I suppose I

---

the University of Notre Dame Press (1977). See also Collins, Introduction, *New Orleans Sketches,* pp. xxiv–xxv.

[36] See *Soldiers' Pay* (New York: Boni and Liveright, 1926), p. 318. Compare Faulkner's statement, years later, to Meta Carpenter: "what is valuable is what you have lost, since then you never had the chance to wear out and so lose it shabbily. . . ." Quoted in Meta Carpenter Wilde and Orin Borsten, *A Loving Gentleman* (New York: Simon and Schuster, 1976), p. 317.

[37] See p. 415 of the second version of Faulkner's Introduction to *The Sound and the Fury* cited in note 7.

knew all the time that I could not live forever inside of it. . . ." [38]
Having finished *The Sound and the Fury*, he in fact found
emergence traumatic. Still, it is probably fair to say that he knew
all along what awaited him. Certainly his novel possessed other
possibilities than shelter and escape for him, just as the image
through which he sought to convey his sense of it possessed other
connotations, including one that is clearly erotic and one that is
clearly aesthetic.

The place to begin untangling the erotic is the relation between
the old Roman who kept the vase at his bedside so that he could
kiss it and "the withered cuckold husband that took the De-
cameron to bed with him every night. . . ." [39] These two figures
are not only committed to a kind of substitution; they practice a
kind of auto-eroticism. The old Roman is superior only if we
assume that he is the maker of his vase—in which case he resembles Horace Benbow, who in *Flags in the Dust* makes an "almost
perfect vase" which he keeps by his bedside and calls by his sister's
name. With Horace and his vase, we might seem to have come
full circle, back to Faulkner and his "heart's darling." [40] In *The
Sound and the Fury* affection of brother for sister and sister for
brother becomes the archetype of love; and with Caddy and
Quentin, the incestuous potential of that love clearly surfaces—
as it had in *Elmer, Mosquitoes*, and *Flags in the Dust*, and as it
would in *Absalom, Absalom!*.

The circle, however, is less perfect than it might at first appear,
since at least one difference between Horace Benbow and William Faulkner is both obvious and crucial. Whereas Horace's
amber vase is a substitute for a sister he has but is forbidden and
fears to possess, Faulkner's is a substitute for the sister he never
had. In this regard Horace Benbow is closer to Elmer Hodge,
Faulkner to the sculptor named Gordon in *Mosquitoes*. Elmer is
in fact a more timid as well as an earlier version of Horace. Working with his paints—"thick-bodied and female and at the same
time phallic: hermaphroditic"—Elmer creates figures he associates
with something "that he dreaded yet longed for." The thing he
both seeks and shuns is a "vague shape" he holds in his mind; its
origins are his mother and a sister named Jo-Addie. Like Hor-

---

[38] Ibid.

[39] *Mosquitoes*, p. 210.

[40] Compare *Flags in the Dust* (New York: Random House, 1973), pp. 153–
154, 162; and *Faulkner in the University*, p. 6.

ace's, Elmer's art is devoted to imaginative possession of figures he is forbidden and fears sexually to possess.[41] When Horace calls his amber vase by his sister's name, he articulates what Elmer merely feels. Like Elmer, however, Horace makes indirect or imaginative possession a means of avoiding the fate Quentin enacts. Through their art, Elmer and Horace are able to achieve satisfaction that soothes one kind of despair without arousing guilt that might lead to another.[42]

In *Mosquitoes,* the origins of Gordon's "feminine ideal" remain obscure, though his art is quite clearly devoted to creation and possession of her. For Gordon as for Elmer and Horace, the erotic and the aesthetic are inseparable. A man is always writing, Dawson Fairchild remarks, for "some woman"; if she is not "a flesh and blood creature," she is at least "the symbol of a desire," and "she is feminine." [43] In their art Elmer and Horace work toward a figure that is actual, making art a substitute for love of a real woman. Gordon, on the other hand, associates art with an ideal whose identity remains vague. We know of it two things—that it is feminine and that it represents what Henry James called the beautiful circuit and subterfuge of thought and desire. Whereas Horace expresses his love for a real woman through his art, Gordon expresses his devotion to his sculpted ideal by pursuing, temporarily, a woman named Patricia who interests him only because she happens to resemble "the virginal breastless torso of a girl" he has already sculpted.[44] Whereas Horace is a failed, inconstant artist, Gordon is a consecrated one, the difference being that Gordon devotes his life as well as his art to pursuing the figure which exists perfectly only in thought and imagination.

On a voyage to Europe, shortly after finishing *Soldiers' Pay* and before beginning *Elmer* and *Mosquitoes,* Faulkner told William Spratling that he thought love and death the "only two basic

---

[41] The *Elmer* manuscripts are in the William Faulkner Collections, University of Virginia Library. For a valuable discussion of them, see Thomas L. McHaney, "The Elmer Papers: Faulkner's Comic Portraits of the Artist," *The Mississippi Quarterly,* XXVI (Summer 1973), 281–311.

[42] See the manuscripts cited in note 41 and compare *Flags in the Dust,* pp. 153–154, 162.

[43] *Mosquitoes,* p. 250.

[44] See John Irwin, *Doubling & Incest, Repetition & Revenge* (Baltimore: Johns Hopkins University Press, 1975), pp. 160–161; and *Mosquitoes,* pp. 11, 24, 28, 47–48.

compulsions on earth. . . ." [45] What engaged his imagination as much as either of these compulsions, however, was his sense of the relation of each to the other and of both to art. The amber vase Horace calls Narcissa, he also addresses "as Thou still unravished bride of quietude." [46] "There is a story somewhere," Faulkner said,

> about an old Roman who kept at his bedside a Tyrrhenian vase which he loved and the rim of which he wore slowly away with kissing it. I had made myself a vase, but I suppose I knew all the time that I could not live forever inside of it, that perhaps to have it so that I too could lie in bed and look at it would be better; surely so when that day should come when not only the ecstasy of writing would be gone, but the unreluctance and the something worth saying too. It's fine to think that you will leave something behind you when you die, but it's better to have made something you can die with.[47]

In this brief statement, the vase becomes both Caddy and *The Sound and the Fury;* both "the beautiful one" for whom he created the novel as a commodious space, and the novel in which she found protection, even privacy, as well as expression. Through its basic doubleness, the vase becomes many things: a haven or shelter into which the artist may retreat; a feminine ideal to which he gives his devotion; a work of art which he can leave behind when he is dead; and a burial urn which will contain one expression of his self as artist. If it is a mouth he may freely kiss, it is also a world in which he may find shelter; if it is a womb he may enter, it is also a space in which his troubled spirit may find both temporary rest and lasting expression.[48]

Of all his novels, it was for *The Sound and the Fury* that Faulkner felt "the most tenderness." [49] Writing it not only renewed his sense of purpose and hope;[50] it also gave him an "emotion definite and physical and yet nebulous to describe. . . .' "

---

[45] William Spratling, "Chronicle of a Friendship: William Faulkner in New Orleans," *The Texas Quarterly,* IX (Spring 1966), p. 38.

[46] See the works cited in note 42.

[47] See p. 415 of the second version of Faulkner's Introduction to *The Sound and the Fury* cited in note 7.

[48] See Irwin, *Doubling & Incest,* pp. 162–163.

[49] *Lion in the Garden,* p. 147.

[50] See *Faulkner in the University,* p. 67.

Caught up in it, he experienced a kind of ecstasy, particularly in the "eager and joyous faith and anticipation of surprise which the yet unmarred sheets beneath my hand held inviolate and unfailing. . . ." [51] Such language may at first glance seem surprising. For *The Sound and the Fury* is, as Faulkner once noted, a "dark story of madness and hatred," and it clearly cost him dearly.[52] Having finished it, he moved to New York, where he continued revising it. "I worked so hard at that book," he said later, "that I doubt if there's anything in it that didn't belong there." [53] As he neared the end for which he had labored hard, he drew back, dreading completion as though it meant "cutting off the supply, destroying the source. . . ." Perhaps like Rilke and Proust, he associated "the completed" with silence.[54] Having finished his revisions, he contrived for himself an interface of silence and pain. Happening by his flat one evening, Jim Devine and Leon Scales found him alone, unconscious, huddled on the floor, empty bottles scattered around him.[55]

What *The Sound and the Fury* represented to him, however, he had anticipated in *Mosquitoes*: a work "in which the hackneyed accidents which make up this world—love and life and death and sex and sorrow—brought together by chance in perfect proportions, take on a kind of splendid and timeless beauty." [56] In the years to come, he would think of his fourth novel as a grand failure. Imperfect success would always be his ideal. To continue his effort to match his "dream of perfection," he needed dissatisfaction as well as hope. If failure might drive him to despair, success might deprive him of purpose: "it takes only one book to do it. It's not the sum of a lot of scribbling, it's one perfect book, you see. It's one single urn or shape that you want. . . ." [57]

[51] See p. 414 of the second version of Faulkner's Introduction to *The Sound and the Fury* cited in note 7.

[52] Quoted by Coindreau, Introduction to *The Sound and the Fury*, *The Mississippi Quarterly*, XIX (Summer 1966), 109.

[53] Quoted in Blotner, *Faulkner*, pp. 589–590.

[54] See W. H. Auden, Sonnet XXIII, in "In Time of War," in W. H. Auden and Christopher Isherwood, *Journey to a War* (New York: Random House, 1938). Compare Auden, Sonnet XIX in "Sonnets from China," *Collected Shorter Poems, 1927–1957* (New York: Random House, 1966). See also *Absalom, Absalom!* (New York: Random House, 1936), pp. 373–374.

[55] See Blotner, *Faulkner*, pp. 590–591.

[56] *Mosquitoes*, p. 339.

[57] *Faulkner in the University*, p. 65. Compare *Soldiers' Pay*, p. 283.

Faulkner wanted, he once wrote Malcolm Cowley, "to be, as a private individual, abolished and voided from history." It was his aim to make his books the sole remaining sign of his life. Informing such statements is a definite need for privacy. But informing them, too, is a tacit conception of his relation to his art: that his authentic self was the self variously and nebulously yet definitely bodied forth by his fictions.[58] It is in this deeper rather than in the usual sense that his fiction is autobiographical. It is of his self expressive, which is to say, creative. "I have never known anyone," a brother wrote,

> who identified himself with his writings more than Bill did. . . .
> Sometimes it was hard to tell which was which, which one Bill was, himself or the one in the story. And yet you knew somehow that the two of them were the same, they were one and inseparable.[59]

Faulkner knew that characters, "those shady but ingenious shapes," were a way of exploring, projecting, reaffirming both the life he lived and the tacit, secret life underlying it. At least once he was moved to wonder if he "had invented the world" of his fiction "or if it had invented me. . . ."[60]

Like indirect knowing, however, imperfect success, which implies partial completion, carries several connotations. Both the decision to approach Caddy only by indirection and the need to describe the novel as a series of imperfect acts partially completed ally it with the complex. They are in part a tribute to epistemological problems and in part a sign that beauty is difficult—that those things most worth seeing, knowing, and saying can never be directly seen, known, and said. But indirection and incompletion are also useful strategies for approaching forbidden scenes, uttering forbidden words, committing dangerous acts. For Elmer Hodge, both his sister Jo-Addie and behind her "the dark woman. The dark mother," are associated with a "vague shape [s]omewhere back in his mind"—the core for him of everything

---

[58] To Malcolm Cowley, Friday [February 11, 1949], in *The Faulkner-Cowley File* (New York: Viking Press, 1966), p. 126. See Irwin, *Doubling & Incest*, pp. 171–172.

[59] John Faulkner, *My Brother Bill* (New York: Trident Press, 1963), p. 275.

[60] This quote is from a manuscript fragment in the Beinecke Library, Yale University. It is quoted in Blotner, *Faulkner*, p. 584.

he dreads and desires. Since attainment, the only satisfying act, is not only dangerous but forbidden, and therefore both can't and must be his aim, Elmer's life and art become crude strategies of approximation. The opposite of crude, the art of *The Sound and the Fury* is nonetheless an art of concealment as well as disclosure —of delay, avoidance, evasion—particularly where Caddy is concerned. Beyond Faulkner's sense that indirection was more passionate lay his awareness that it was also less dangerous. For him both desire and hesitancy touched almost everything, making his imagination as illusive as it is allusive, and his art preeminently an art of surmise and conjecture.

In *Flags in the Dust* he had taken ingenious possession of a heritage which he proceeded both to dismember and reconstruct. In *The Sound and the Fury* he took possession of the pain and muted love of his childhood—its dislocations and vacancies, its forbidden needs and desires. The loss we observe in *The Sound and the Fury* is associated with parental weakness and inadequacy —with parental frigidity, judgment, and rejection. In the figure of Dilsey Faulkner re-created the haven of love he had found in Mammy Callie; in the figure of Caddy, he created one he knew only through longing. If the first of these figures is all maternal, the second is curiously mixed. In the figure of the sister he never had, we see not only a sister but a mother (the role she most clearly plays for Benjy) and a lover (the possibility most clearly forbidden). Like the emotion Faulkner experienced in writing it, the novel's central figure comes to us as one "definite and physical yet nebulous. . . ." Needing to conceal even as he disclosed her, Faulkner created in Caddy Compson a heroine who perfectly corresponds to her world: like it, she was born of regression and evasion, and like it, she transcends them.

Pride and Nakedness
As I Lay Dying

by Calvin Bedient

I

The force of *As I Lay Dying* is in its opacity. Faulkner's novel has the particularity of real experience, and this is so rare a quality in modern art that we have forgotten how to appreciate it. So untranslatable, so irreducible to symbol and idea is the detail of the novel that one looks for analogies in painting and music; and even the sporadic explosions of reflective rhetoric in the book convey little more than a momentary and frustrated impulse to the "universal": they remain essentially opaque. For example, the construction "How do our lives ravel out into the no-wind, no-sound, the weary gestures wearily recapitulant: echoes of old compulsions with no-hand on no strings: in sunset we fall into furious attitudes, dead gestures of dolls" [1] has no value whatsoever as literal statement or meaning, particularly in the context, where it lies disconnected, florid, and obtrusive, like a bouquet found abandoned in the dust. These words function, instead, precisely as "furious attitude," as an expressive verbal gesture, a mood-painting; they are as immediate in interest as the sudden clenching of a hand or the swirls in a Van Gogh cypress.

In the sense intended by William Golding in *Free Fall*, *As I Lay Dying* is patternless, "translating incoherence into incoherence," [2] from life to art. The novel has a wonderful immunity to schematization; it is innocent of both a moral and a morality, and

---

Reprinted with permission from *Modern Language Quarterly*, 29 (1968), pp. 61–76.

[1] William Faulkner, *As I Lay Dying*, Vintage Book (New York, n.d.), pp. 196–97.

[2] Penguin Book (Harmondsworth, 1963), p. 7.

it seems to breathe out rather than posit a world view. Faulkner's novel does have, to be sure, a narrative movement and structure —a movement that, considering the fragmentation of narrative method, is remarkably steady, and a structure that is timeless, that answers to some unchanging psychological need: the journey undertaken and, despite great perils, completed. And yet, regardless of this, the book is open, both in the sense of making room for the incidental (indeed, the trivial [3]) and in the sense that it does not understand itself: it is essentially spectacle.

As I Lay Dying is to be "seen," not understood; experienced, not translated; felt, not analyzed. The malignity it portrays, both of the land and sky and of man, is aesthetic. Here suffering is above all a spectacle—to us, to the neighbors of the Bundrens (the chorus to the collective protagonist), and even to Anse Bundren, who looks upon each new misfortune as a show of the Opponent's ingenuity, the staging of Destiny. Is there, indeed, an organizer behind the spectacle? The novel does not help us to an answer. What it unfolds before us is simply the autonomy of misfortune; the brutal fact of its monotonous regularity and astonishing variety, of its farcical absurdity, of its tragedy; and questions of cause are not raised—they are extraneous. There is thus in the novel a fundamental silence that is truly terrible. For what is more mysterious, finally, than immediacy? Explanations tranquilize wonder, and *As I Lay Dying* contains no explanations.

The nakedness of form in this novel is the aesthetic equivalent of an act of courage; and despite its strong element of farce, the book is like tragedy in its refusal to mediate between destructive contradictions. The openness of *As I Lay Dying* is thus almost morally exhilarating; and yet it is appalling, too. For like its own Darl Bundren, the novel lacks defenses; it takes the world upon its flesh like a rain of arrows. Can one imagine a Faulknerian utopia? His books do not hold their heads so high as hope. *As I Lay Dying* is a prolonged cry of astonishment; everything within it is recorded as if with a soundless gasp. "Outrageous," say the neighbors when they are assailed by the odor of the rotting corpse; and the word echoes and expands until it has embraced everything in the book.

One could argue that *As I Lay Dying* is patternless to a fault—

[3] For example, the final words of Samson's monologue: "I have known him [MacCallum] from a boy up; know his name as well as I do my own. But be durn if I can say it" (p. 113).

that it is, in places, confused and self-destroying. The crucial monologue of Addie Bundren, for instance, is a marvel of dazzling unintelligibility. Why does she call herself "three" (herself, Cash, and Darl) when, as she says, Darl is her husband's child and not her own? By Cash's birth, she remarks, her "aloneness has been violated and then made whole again by the violation: time, Anse, love, what you will, outside the circle" (p. 164). But if Cash is still inside the circle with Addie, is her aloneness truly intact? Very often, the illogic of the characters is extreme, grotesque; it is not merely puzzling, but dizzying, and throws the mind down. And yet this grotesquerie possesses a kind of beauty—precisely the beauty of opacity. Like the pyrotechnic rhetorical reflections, the logical absurdities have a stubborn and assertive density that makes them analogous to the squiggles and clots of paint on modern canvasses; the book is entirely of a piece, opalesque all through.

It is for this reason that the thematics of *As I Lay Dying* are difficult to approach—or better, that it is questionable to speak of a thematics at all. At any rate, there is clearly no Ariadne's thread that will lead one through the labyrinth. But of course it is far from my intention to claim—what would after all be self-defeating —that the book cannot be discussed. The problem is that it can be discussed endlessly, since its patternlessness results, not in emptiness, but precisely in a continuous, turgid thickness of meaning, the significant indefiniteness of life itself. My purpose is simply to explore one of the dialectics of the novel as this is manifested in both the content and the form. I shall be bolder and assert that this dialectic is at the center of the book—not its theme, but its axis; not what the novel is "about," but a significant part of its substance and the determining principle of its form.

II

In *As I Lay Dying* life is conceived as the antagonist, living is "terrible," the protagonist self is alone: a naked and isolated consciousness in a broad land. This nakedness, this dreadful isolation, is already a kind of defeat, a form of abjectness, so that the utmost to be expected from the mind in its continual conflict with the world is simply a capitulation without dishonor: a surrender of everything, if need be, except pride. It is true that there are or appear to be, in the Faulknerian world, other "answers" [4] to aloneness—for example, Vardaman's mental revision of a reality his emotions cannot accept, and the physical "violation" of Addie's aloneness that comes with childbearing. Yet Vardaman's answer is transparently desperate, and Addie's seems to have the effect, not of breaking through her aloneness, but of expanding it; the circle of isolation remains inexorable. Thus the third term of this existential dialectic, the solution which remains after all others have failed, is pride, for pride is the only answer that stands upon, rather than attempts to evade, our inescapable nakedness.

The most remarkable quality of the very remarkable Bundrens —country people who feel their difference from "town folk"—is their fierce, their unexpected, their magnificently sustaining pride. Even Anse Bundren really seems to believe that he would be "beholden to none" (p. 218)—though in truth, of course, he often is. Like wounded animals that have instinctively found the herb that will cure them, the Bundrens have discovered pride; and each is typical, each is "universal," precisely in bearing, not as an idea but as a fact, the wound of nakedness, the solitary confinement and essential impotency of conscious being.

The fact and awareness of isolation is the very bedrock in Faulkner; it is given out direct as an odor. And it is the strength and beauty of *As I Lay Dying* that the form of the novel itself amplifies, that it is an aesthetic equivalent for, this truth. For each of the numerous monologues constitutes a new demonstration of the obvious: the fundamental isolation inherent in the very structure of consciousness.

Now let us take note of an apparent contradiction in the form and, at the same time, of its echo in the content. Obviously, each monologue is implicitly isolated, hermetically sealed from the others; yet the result of their grouping is, nonetheless, an appearance of mutual co-operation. *As I Lay Dying* is a composite narrative, a kind of unwitting group enterprise; and undeniably this apparent aspect of the form is as expressive as the actual technique of the accretion of fragmentary monologues. Considered as a whole, the novel expresses, through its form, Faulkner's pro-

---

[4] In using this term, I have in mind Addie Bundren's comment: "And when I knew that I had Cash, I knew that living was terrible and that this was the answer to it" (p. 163).

found feeling for the human group, above all for the family, which is presented as constituting its own fate: a kind of involuntary and inescapable group confinement, the inexorable circle in expanded form.

Human coherence in Faulkner, whether of the family or of the larger community, is presented chiefly as a response to the onslaughts of an opposing world. In the Bundrens, Faulkner lays bare the most primitive of the motives to community: society as a principle of survival. Shy and aloof as a herd, the Bundren family is held together, not by love, but by pride, which is its instinctive response to danger, including unfavorable public opinion. And if this herd is self-destructive, still it prefers its cannibalism to exposure to the world, to a nakedness synonymous with defeat.

The Faulknerian family is thus a kind of exacerbating protective covering, a hair shirt, to the "abject nakedness" of the individuals composing it. This accounts for the fact that family ties are so horrendously tense in Faulkner: they are the crackling bonds of a bitter necessity. At bottom, the Faulknerian family is a compulsive effort to end, to disguise, nakedness; but since nakedness is inescapable, this effort issues in hate. Thus if nakedness leads to community, it is also true that community leads to an aggravation of nakedness. The effort returns upon itself. Like the aesthetic form of the novel, the family only *appears* to transcend or resolve the fundamental isolation of the individual; in actuality, it is a terrible and frustrating unit of interlocking solitudes, atomic in structure like a molecule.

Yet the family is no more, if no less, terrible than nakedness. In the absence of other consolations, it may afford at least an illusion of "confidence and comfort"—words Darl uses when he defines the meaning that the coffin has for Addie (p. 5). Let us note that the coffin and the family are analogous forms, or better, that a dreadful yet desired confinement and covering is the form that accounts for both. Peabody helps us to this perception when, seeing Anse and Addie together, he observes of the latter:

> She watches me: I can feel her eyes. It's like she was shoving at me with them. I have seen it before in women. Seen them drive from the room them coming with sympathy and pity, with actual help, and clinging to some trifling animal to whom they never were more than pack-horses. That's what they mean by

the love that passeth understanding: that pride, that furious desire to hide that abject nakedness which we bring here with us . . . [and] carry stubbornly and furiously with us into the earth again. (pp. 44–45)

This little-noticed but important passage obviously extends into a paradigm of the behavior of the Bundrens on the journey to Jefferson, for they too, in their furious desire to hide their abject nakedness, drive from them those coming with sympathy and pity. More subtly, it explains the importance to Addie of the coffin, over the construction of which she attends, from her bedroom window, with an anxious and severe observation. To her, the coffin is a substitute for her family; it represents but a change of coverings.

Of course, for a while after death Addie clings to the family itself, and it is in this sense that she is not yet dead, that the entire journey takes place while she still lies "dying." Through her magnificent will, which is the instrument of her pride, she is thus doubly protected on her way to the grave, even in death covering her nakedness in the fierceness of her "modesty," which is but the pride, as it were, of her privacy. "For an instant," as the coffin is loaded on the wagon, "it resists, as though volitional, as though within it her pole-thin body clings furiously, even though dead, to a sort of modesty, as she would have tried to conceal a solid garment that she could not prevent her body soiling" (p. 91). It is as if even death could not conquer Addie's pride, though it constitutes the final and absolute nakedness. By means of the promise Addie exacts from her family to bury her in Jefferson, she prolongs even into death their customary relationship to her while she was living, which was to protect her, to encircle her with "her own flesh and blood." She is thus not so much carried as attended to Jefferson. Nor does she "die" until she is placed in the ground. Then at last she is abandoned and—as she might have foreseen—immediately forgotten, replaced at once by a new "Mrs. Bundren." By that time, however, she has punished her family just as she had intended [5]—punished it by

[5] "But then I realised that I had been tricked by words older than Anse or love, and that the same word had tricked Anse too, and that my revenge would be that he would never know I was taking revenge. And when Darl was born I asked Anse to promise to take me back to Jefferson when I died . . ." (pp. 164–65).

keeping it to herself a little longer, and in suffering, and for the reason that she had needed it, just as, in the instance of the deceit she practices for Jewel, she hated him "because she had to love him so that she had to act the deceit" (p. 123).

In Faulkner, then, pride binds but at the same time lacerates; there is a distance between people which, except in rare instances, cannot be closed, which, indeed, is maintained by pride itself. For pride is an expression of the aggressive instinct, a response and counterantagonism to the antagonism of destiny, to the painfully naked structure of being. The community that pride creates is at best an illusory one—the Bundrens on the road to Jefferson. And this deceptive community, overlaying a stark and irremediable personal nakedness, is mirrored in the form of the novel, which is real in its parts—its lonely monologues—but illusory as a "whole." In both the characters and the form that presents them, it is isolation that is basic and substantive.

III

Turning from the relationship of form to content, let us consider the two characters of the novel who embody the extreme ends of Faulknerian being: Darl Bundren, in whom nakedness has an absolute form, and his brother Cash, in whom pride attains to a constructive, humane, and stabilizing limit.

Alone among the Bundrens, Darl lacks the ingredient, the enzyme, of pride. Stricken in his very being, he is a demonstration of our natural emptiness, of a nakedness powerless to hide itself behind an "I." What is more, the vacuum of identity in Darl, unlike that of the mystic or the artist, cannot be seized upon and converted into a positivity; for although Darl is invaded by others as the mystic is inundated by God and the novelist possessed by his characters, those who occupy Darl do not replenish him, and naturally his consciousness deteriorates by a law of diminishing returns. Hopelessly open and undefended, at times even plural and familial, Darl's mind leaps barriers of space and flesh, flowing everywhere like the floodwaters of the river—but flowing because unformed, because it has no home in itself, no principle of containment.

This bitter gift and fatality, this plurality of being, Darl carries like a cross. If he is a freak, he is also a victim, and knows with characteristic lucidity what has made him the casualty he is. When Vardaman says, "But you *are,* Darl," the latter replies: "I know it. . . . That's why I am not *is. Are* is too many for one woman to foal" (p. 95). The point is that, unlike Jewel (whose "mother is a horse"), Darl has never been a foal, that is, sponsored; and as he here observes to Vardaman, it is his fate to be everyone except himself. He is *de trop,* a consciousness inhabiting the world as a kind of excess, baseless, and, as a result, pitilessly empowered to trespass upon the privacy of others.

Darl exists, but, because he is unloved, he cannot become *himself;* at least this is the explanation that he himself seems to favor. As Ortega has noted, love is choice in its very essence, a vital preference of this being over that one, a corroboration of the beloved; [6] and Darl knows that he has never been affirmed. "Jewel *is,*" Darl thinks at one point, "so Addie Bundren must be"; for the created postulates the creator. But Darl maintains that he has no mother, and the absence of the creator throws into doubt the reality of the created:

> In a strange room you must empty yourself for sleep. And before you are emptied for sleep, what are you. And when you are emptied for sleep, you are not. And when you are filled with sleep, you never were. I dont know what I am. I dont know if I am or not. (p. 76)

By thus equating being with consciousness, which sleep annihilates, Darl removes from existence its stability, giving it the flickering reality of a dream. "And so," he concludes, "if I am not emptied yet, I am *is.*" Only on that condition. For Darl has, he feels, no identity ("I dont know what I am") and thus no cord of continuity capable of withstanding the unraveling power of sleep. So the ending of the monologue falls with the force of a metaphor: "How often have I lain beneath rain on a strange roof, thinking of home."

Further, Darl's consciousness, in this passage, casts upon the world itself a desubstantiating shadow, so that for him objects too may appear suddenly orphaned:

> Beyond the unlamped wall I can hear the rain shaping the wagon that is ours, the load that is no longer theirs that felled

---

[6] José Ortega y Gasset, *On Love: Aspects of a Single Theme* (New York, 1957), p. 20.

and sawed it nor yet theirs that bought it and which is not ours
either, lie on our wagon though it does, since only the wind
and the rain shape it only to Jewel and me, that are not asleep
(p. 76)

More than this, their being is also subject, like his, to abrupt
cancellation: "And since sleep is is-not and rain and wind are *was*
[the load] is not" (p. 76). And although for the present the
wagon *"is,"* it too will surrender its reality when it has carried
Addie Bundren to Jefferson: "when the wagon is *was,* Addie
Bundren will not be" (p. 76). For Darl, then, being springs from
the mother ("Jewel *is,* so Addie Bundren must be"); disjoined
from Addie, the world and Darl appear equally unauthored,
existing without authentication, hovering on the verge of ex-
tinction.

Mercilessly unclouded by egoism, Darl's mind is the perfect
mirror of what surrounds him, which it reflects with a terrible
clarity. It is only his own identity that is obscure to Darl—the
failure of the mirror to reflect itself. In this novel, shapelessness
is the condition against which the characters must define themselves, and Darl cannot find his own shape. It is thus his destiny
to be, not himself, but the world. Since Darl neither acts (he is
called "lazy"), nor possesses anything that he can call his own,
nor is loved, he must fall back upon introspection to give him
identity. But, as Husserl observes, consciousness is itself empty;
we must be conscious *of* something to be conscious at all; [7] and
when Darl turns in upon himself, he finds nothing there. Tragically, Darl is not made present to himself as an *object* until he
is acted upon, literally apprehended by the world and conducted
to the insane asylum at Jackson (for, to be acted upon, one must
exist). But the Darl then given birth is a monster, a belated and
violent creation, who rightly laughs at the brutal comedy of his
birth, and who, with heart-breaking irony, is at last all affirmation: "Yes yes yes yes yes" (p. 243). At this parturition, the sus-
pected absurdity of the world finally declares itself unequivocally.
Appallingly, it answers to expectation. And yet to be so well
served is, after all, a kind of mercy. For Darl has at last discovered certainty: "Yes yes yes yes yes."

[7] See Edmund Husserl, *Ideas* (New York, 1967); Jean-Paul Sartre, *Being
and Nothingness* (New York, 1964), p. li.

If, on the one hand, Darl remains, even to the end, a transparent perceiver, he has become, on the other, a pure opacity. It is true, of course, that Darl was never perfectly transparent; earlier there is in him, for instance, the darkness of the body ("I could lie with my shirt-tail up . . . feeling myself without touching myself, feeling the cool silence blowing upon my parts" [p. 11]), and what appears to be an incestuous feeling for Dewey Dell asserts itself, through metaphor, on the train to Jackson. Ethereal as he is, moreover, Darl possesses, in addition, that subterranean, savage charge of energy which is necessary for life itself: "He and I look at one another," Darl says of Cash, "with . . . looks that plunge unimpeded . . . into the ultimate secret place where for an instant Cash and Darl crouch flagrant and unabashed in all the old terror and the old foreboding, alert and secret and without shame" (p. 135). Yet Darl *is* abashed at this naked core: that is his tragedy. Limitless, unclaimed, despairing of attaining shape, his very being longs to be undone: "If you could just ravel out into time. That would be nice. It would be nice if you could just ravel out into time" (p. 198). This decreation, however, is not permitted to Darl, whose fate it is to *see,* and who must endure even in madness a perception as pitiless as it is crystalline.

There is, of course, one point at which Darl *acts:* his setting fire to the barn that contains his mother's corpse. When this attempt fails, Darl is found, in tears, lying on the coffin, his passivity resumed, his mind more hopeless than ever. Darl's laughter at his seizure by the asylum authorities, Cash's insight, "This world is not his world; this life his life" (p. 250), and the tearful resurrender to nonentity over the putrescent body of his mother, taken together, suggest how unbearable the world must appear to a being absolutely naked to it, between whose capacity to suffer and the power of the world to inflict pain no selfhood and no love have intervened.

Though Darl's consciousness is so attentive and catholic that it seems at times to be a form of love, it is, for the most part, as neutral as photographic film. For Darl loves no one—except perhaps, in an unspeakably tormented way, Addie Bundren (as the barn-burning obscurely suggests)—and, until the end, he affirms nothing at all. On those few occasions when he displays strong feeling toward others, he is barbed and vindictive; for even he has a component of egotism, though only so much as is requisite for suffering. And just as he bitterly resents the woman who has caused his emptiness, so he resents those of her children who are enviably intense and narrow with their own being: Jewel and Dewey Dell. If Darl taunts them, he does so because they are so self-absorbed, because they *can* be self-absorbed, and from his aggressive insinuations one may understand that he would like to induce in them a portion of his own pain. Jewel and Dewey Dell, both truly flagrant and unabashed, are equally exposed to Darl, the first through the inexpressible intensity of his feeling for his mother, which renders him rigid, and the second, who is pregnant, through the unwelcome violation of her aloneness. Nor is it by chance that Darl gains and wields like a weapon secret knowledge of each: his clairvoyance is sharpened by his envy. At the end, when these two throw themselves upon Darl with ferocity, they are simply reasserting the privacy of their identities. The very fact that they have identities to defend proves their existential superiority to Darl; a battle between unequal opponents, the scene is cruel.

Perhaps Darl is finally a standing condemnation of the world. If "this world is not his world, this life his life," is it not because it is unloving where he wants its love, random where he wants its reason, savagely obtuse where he needs its understanding? Darl is not better than the world, only—by a kind of ontological error —more generous: though he receives nothing from his surroundings, he gives himself to them, just as he lends his eyes to the land that fills them. Doubtless, Cash is being sentimental when he says, "Sometimes I think it aint none of us pure crazy and aint none of us pure sane until the balance of us talks him that-a-way" (p. 223); and yet clearly this is true of Darl. Until he is seized, he is not truly insane; but then, sitting on the ground and laughing, bitter and manic, he does grant the world its victory and surrenders to the unreason at its heart. In his last monologue, which is tantamount to a ferocious, uncontrollable parody of all those earlier monologues in which his mind had seemed to belong to the family itself, he watches and attends "our brother Darl" (p. 244) on his departure to Jackson, and is puzzled by his laughter. Now that he sees "Darl," now that Darl exists for him, he cannot comprehend him. And perhaps he senses, as he speaks of our brother Darl in his cage in Jackson, that ultimately such laughter is beyond understanding.

It is against this dreadful nakedness that pride, in Faulkner, assumes its value. If Darl is our innate nakedness *in extremis,* impotent to defend itself, Cash exemplifies the pride that saves us and is itself the substance of identity; for the identity a man asserts is simply that part of himself he thinks well of.

As I Lay Dying brings to mind Conrad's *Heart of Darkness,* not only in the land that shapes "the life of man in its implacable and brooding image" (p. 44) and in the tensions it establishes between the shaped, moral surfaces of the mind and subterranean psychic energies (tensions aggravated, moreover, by a journey through a violent land), but also in its cautious celebration of the worker as hero. For Cash, like Marlow, is man defining himself, declaring his human dignity through the perfection of his work. Both heroes labor precisely in order to avoid being shaped by the violent land, or better, to avoid being shapeless; and in work each discovers the reality of himself. Whereas Marlow knows that work is man's defense against himself, a noble self-avoidance, Cash senses merely that the man is the work—an important but lesser insight. What Marlow tries to defend himself against is the darkness in himself; the darkness in Faulkner's novel, by contrast, is of the world. It is more than human, though it encompasses the human; and Cash is heroic (unassumingly and narrowly heroic) not so much in mastering himself as in contesting the amorphousness, the appalling anonymity, of existence itself.

For in the world depicted in Faulkner's novel, the hero's role must be to shape and to define. We see in Cash literally a rage for efficiency as he labors at the coffin, "his face sloped into the light with a rapt, dynamic immobility above his tireless elbow" (p. 72), working on into the night and the rain unfalteringly, as if "in a tranquil conviction that rain was an illusion of the mind" (p. 73). But neither at this time nor any other (a truth not generally grasped) does Cash's devotion to the perfection of his work dehumanize him: he is never the equivalent, say, of Conrad's Chief Accountant, whose books are kept in dazzling yet mean order only yards above a grove of death. On the contrary, Cash is always a figure nearer to Marlow, provincial and less profound, but humane and wise. Cash builds the coffin where his dying mother can see him because he loves her, as Jewel jealously perceives ("It's like when he was a little boy and she says if she had some fertilizer she would try to raise some flowers and he taken the bread pan and brought it back from the barn full of dung" [p. 14]); and such dogged, mechanically rationalized, and in the circumstances impractical efficiency indicates that his labor is basically an act of pride, the purpose of which is to assert the human in the teeth of its negation—the nothingness awaiting life, the shapelessness surrounding it. After Addie's death, when Cash (his ears deaf to the practical words of his father, his face composed) stands "looking down at her peaceful, rigid face fading into the dusk as though darkness were a precursor of the ultimate earth, until at last the face seems to float detached upon it, lightly as the reflection of a dead leaf" (p. 49), he takes in at once what he and his mother are up against and returns immediately to work. Against such dematerialization of the human, the construction of the coffin, which looks so merely mechanical, is actually a passionate protest, a fierce assertion of human value. Built under the inimical pressure of time, but nonetheless perfected beyond practical reason, the coffin is to death what *As I Lay Dying* itself is to the artless world: a product of love, a preserving form, and in its craftsmanship a predication of human dignity.

From first to last Cash is the most human of the Bundrens— and also the most humane. The notion that Cash develops during the course of the narrative "from unimaginative self-containment to humane concern" [8] has taken hold despite obvious objections: the gross improbability of such a development in a man in his late twenties within a nine-day period and, more important, the textual evidence to the contrary.[9] "The increasing range of Cash's awareness," writes Olga Vickery, "is suggested by his growing sympathy with Darl." [10] But, on the contrary, the point to note is that Cash's sympathy with Darl, which was strong from the first, actually meets with a check as the novel progresses: it comes up against a moral judgment.

For though Cash's pride is not in itself dehumanizing, it neces-

[8] Irving Howe, *William Faulkner,* 2nd ed., rev. (New York, 1962), p. 188.

[9] See pages 124–25, where Cash is shown to be extraordinarily sensitive and sympathetic, and surprisingly worldly-wise, at a period that antedates the present time of the novel.

[10] "The Dimensions of Consciousness: *As I Lay Dying,*" in *William Faulkner: Three Decades of Criticism,* ed. Frederick J. Hoffman and Olga W. Vickery (East Lansing, 1960), pp. 239–40.

sitates, as a safeguard, a morality that is inevitably rigid. Of the kinds of strength represented in the novel—the violence of feeling in Addie and Jewel, the imperturbable, maudlin self-centeredness of Anse, the wild-seed egoism of Dewey Dell, the rational stability of Cash—it is only the latter which is moral in tendency, leading to the correction of life by mind. The strength of Cash is ultimately the strength of conviction. When he declares that men who cannot "see eye to eye with other folks" must be considered crazy (p. 223), clearly he is assuming a kind of tacit social contract, according to which men work and construct their buildings and shape their lives with the understanding that others will not hinder them or destroy the fruits of their labor. Those who fail to honor this contract are morally blind, that is, "crazy." "I dont reckon nothing excuses setting fire to a man's barn and endangering his stock and destroying his property," Cash says. "That's how I reckon a man is crazy" (p. 223). What Cash opposes is not simply the destruction of material property, for property is never simple. There is always the man *in* the property to take into account, the value it possesses from having absorbed part of the human life that shaped it: "there just aint nothing justifies the deliberate destruction of what a man has built with his own sweat and stored the fruit of his sweat into" (p. 228).

Like Marlow, then, Cash values a good job because it creates human value, or rather, it is valuable because it is a human creation. The meaning of work is that it is an essentially human expression; and its value is that it allows a man to be proud of himself as a creator. But where Marlow also values work for its binding effect—workers become brothers—Cash, an American very much on his own, prizes work solely as a source of human identity and pride. Life as it gets lived, certainly as the Bundrens live it, is a "shoddy job" (p. 227), a judgment that includes not only Darl's burning of the barn, but also the attack made upon Darl by Jewel and Dewey Dell. To Cash, a neat job does more than testify to man's capacity for shaping; it is also a symbol of discipline and decency, of a renunciation of aggression. Thus for Cash, life, like the building of a barn, is what you make of it, and the shamefulness of the present, its shoddiness, really stems from a failure of pride, of man's imagination of his value. Only recently, Cash implies, have people moved away "from the olden right teaching that says to drive the nails down and trim the edges well always like it was for your own use and comfort you were making it" (p. 224). Why is this teaching "right"? Because a man defines himself, not by what he builds, but by the way he builds it: "it's better to build a tight chicken coop than a shoddy courthouse, and when they both build shoddy or build well, neither because it's one or tother is going to make a man feel the better nor the worse" (p. 224). And if ultimately the self-definition of man matters, it is because, naked as man is, he has nothing else to claim as his own.

Both Marlow and Cash are forced to judge as evil the actions of men of whom they almost feel themselves to be accomplices, for just as Marlow acknowledges the "fascination of the abomination," [11] so Cash had thought more than once that "one of us would have to do something" (p. 223) to get rid of the corpse. In noble contrast to the vicious men around them, each judges with a sense of necessity, in the name of civilization, and at real cost to himself. But it is precisely here that we come up against the negative limits of pride; for the final relationship of Cash to Darl is one of unbending (though not insensitive) pride to abject nakedness. The response the book itself makes to Darl's nakedness, the response it elicits from the reader, is that of a disarmed compassion unadulterated with judgment. "It was bad so," Cash says of Darl's laughter. "I be durn if I could see anything to laugh at. Because there just aint nothing justifies . . . deliberate destruction . . ." (p. 228). The point is not that Cash is incapable of perceiving abject nakedness, for it is this that he describes when he says, "It's like there was a fellow in every man that's done a-past the sanity or the insanity, that watches the sane and the insane doings of that man with the same horror and the same astonishment" (p. 228). What is significant is that Cash cannot *afford* his own insight into abjectness. For compassion dissolves pride, it is utterly passive—at its fullest, it is a recognition of man's ultimate, existential defeat. On the other hand, though the novel carries us beyond Cash into the impotent heart of understanding, into a compassion beyond social principle and responsibility, it will not allow us to judge pride, either. What it says, rather—even though the fact that Cash, the technician, has broken his leg for the second time and lies helpless as Darl is

[11] Joseph Conrad, *Heart of Darkness*, in *Three Short Novels*, Bantam Book (New York, 1960), p. 5.

apprehended—is that finally the world is too much even for the proud and that there is no limit to the demand life makes upon our compassion.

IV

Let us return to our examination of the relationship between form and content in Faulkner's novel. We have noted in the subject matter a polarity of nakedness and pride, and in the aesthetic form an answering nakedness. Let us now see whether there is also, in the technics of the novel, a complementary pride. *As I Lay Dying* is primarily naturalistic in technique. The device of the narrative soliloquy is a means of presenting the mind in its immediacy, and in this sense it directly serves the ends of realism. Let us acknowledge, further, that the basic impulse underlying the book is unmistakably a yearning for reality. And yet it would be untrue to claim that Faulkner's novel lacks all traces of the dehumanization often observed in modern art. In his seminal essay on this trend, Ortega pungently remarked that all style involves dehumanization, for style necessarily deforms reality; and it was the aim of modern poetry, as Ortega saw it, to substitute style for reality.[12] I have remarked already upon the turgidity and opacity of Faulkner's rhetorical style. Now let us take this observation to its limit: Faulkner's metaphorical prose is, at its densest, not so much a mimetic instrument as the preening expression of the pride of the imagination in itself. This is to say that Faulkner's very language is proud, and proud precisely as a defiantly "free" response to the threat always present in the perilous nakedness of the self and the world.

When, for example, Darl says of the vultures that they hang in the sky "in narrowing circles, like the smoke, with an outward semblance of form and purpose, but with no inference of motion, progress or retrograde" (p. 216), or when Peabody defines death as "no more than a single tenant or family moving out of a tenement or a town" (p. 43), the language gets in the way of the reality it describes, or better, the language here secretly flouts and overcomes reality, achieving a proud independency. Or consider the description of Vardaman's face at his mother's death:

[12] *The Dehumanization of Art and Other Writings on Art and Culture,* Doubleday Anchor Book (Garden City, N.Y., 1956), pp. 23, 32.

"From behind pa's leg Vardaman peers, his mouth full open and all color draining from his face into his mouth, as though he has by some means fleshed his own teeth in himself, sucking" (p. 48). It is the simile that is primary, and the reality referred to exists principally as a pretext for the image: an image which is, in truth, not a description but an invention, a subjective idea. In all these instances, Faulkner's prose is distended to make room for the imagination. And the result is a style at once grotesque, as though somehow maimed, and proud, as if totally free to make of itself what it will.

The very grotesqueness of the style is a demonstration that language is not free, that it is governed by certain laws. And as a rule Faulkner's language bends, if not bows, to necessity, admitting the authority of reality. But plainly Faulkner's style is impatient of law, and harbors a resentment toward the duty of mimesis. In its attempts to liberate itself, it moves toward its own self-defeat, at times failing to convey any meaning at all. Proud as it is, it represents, like Cash's pride, an ambiguous triumph over nakedness: its strength is at the same time an impotence, a refusal to admit, and perhaps an inability to tolerate, the naked power of the world. As in the polarity, then, between proud and naked being in the novel, there is between the openness of the form and the opacity of the style an unremitting tension, a contradiction that testifies, on the one hand, both to man's hunger for reality and to his nerve for the truth, however invidious it may be, and, on the other, to his proud and imaginative spirit—to his ambition to create an object, whether a building or a prose, that is his own.

Toward a Supreme Fiction: *Absalom, Absalom!*

by Donald M. Kartiganer

In *Light in August* Faulkner made the first of his most significant attempts to free himself from the idea of the necessary failure of fictions, of the unbridgeable distance between any human construct and reality. He did this not by asserting a referential relation between formulation and fact but by suggesting new ways of fictional meaning. Joe Christmas is a character in whom illusion and flux are wedded together. His enactment of the roles of black and white is a process of making into flesh the ungrounded fable of his origins. The figure of his life remains a mystery, a metaphor, for it revolves around a center—the blackness—which may be imaginary. Indeed the power of the figure resides in that very possibility, and in the fact that Joe is aware of it and does not conceal it. This possible invention of the blackness that gives Joe his special distinction and his special agony is not an evasion of complexity, as in the case of Quentin Compson's fantasy of incest, "symmetrical above the flesh." It is rather the means by which Joe confronts and illuminates that complexity, his own and his society's. Joe comes to exemplify the activity of the supreme fiction that Faulkner is trying to create: the fiction that claims both the precariousness and the relevance of forms, not as opposition but as a dynamic whose terms feed on and fuel each other.

Absalom, Absalom! is another and even more successful attempt to construct a significance of fictions without giving up the sense of a fundamental discontinuity between art and life that is basic to the modern. . . . At the center of *Absalom, Absalom!* there is a known fact, like a real stone enduring centuries of words: in 1865 a man named Henry Sutpen, the son of Thomas Sutpen and Ellen Coldfield, killed a man named Charles Bon. The fact is inhuman not only because it has to do with violent death but because it is without meaning; it covers everything with chaos. This fact is what makes imagination necessary; and imagination is limitless, with the single exception that it cannot drive the fact from existence, from having occurred.

The lives of Miss Rosa Coldfield, Mr. Compson, Quentin Compson, and Shreve McCannon, retelling the story of the Sutpen family in 1909–1910, take root and grow into unique shapes through the different ways they approach this fact. Each must invent the structure that will satisfy the conditions of fact and the conditions of the self as well. The novel is one of four "educations"; the narrators must each learn the processes by which they can master imaginatively the enigma of murder in 1865.[1] The test of that mastery is the degree to which imagination and

---

[1] According to Blotner's account of the writing of *Absalom, Absalom!*, it is clear that from its origins as a short story called "Evangeline," begun in 1926, through his resumption of the tale in January 1934 as *A Dark House* (also, for a time, the working title of *Light in August*), to the novel's final form, Faulkner was concerned with the problem of telling. First "I" and "Don," then "Chisholm" and "Burke," finally Quentin and Shreve take the roles of two men trying to understand the past: "[Faulkner] was continuing to work at the problem that had perplexed him from the start: not the events in the lives of Sutpen and his children, but how to relate and interpret them." Joseph Blotner, *Faulkner: A Biography* (New York: Random House, 1974), 1:890.

Between January 1934 and January 1936, when he completed the manuscript, Faulkner was besieged by his usual financial problems. He had to put the novel aside to write most of the stories of *The Unvanquished,* which he called "a pulp series," and *Pylon,* written largely in the last three months of 1934; he also worked on movie scripts for Howard Hawks. Yet, when the manuscript was done, Faulkner said to a Hollywood associate, " 'I think it's the best novel yet written by an American' " Blotner, *Faulkner,* 2:927.

I am indebted to Hyatt Waggoner's essay on *Absalom, Absalom!* in *William Faulkner: From Jefferson to the World* (Lexington: University of Kentucky Press, 1959), pp. 148–69, one of the first to explore the novel in terms of the creation of history. Another study, by James Guetti in *The Limits of Metaphor* (Ithaca: Cornell University Press, 1967), suggests that the novel is a failure because its subject, the failure of the imagination, is beyond literary art. I do not agree with Guetti's conclusions, but his account of the novel and the rigor of his argument make it one of the major essays on the subject.

fact can coincide in a supreme fiction: it is fact metamorphosed into a figure for subjective desire, yet it is still fact. . . .

[Each narrator, in other words, must tell that version of the Sutpen story which he or she needs to tell—the version that will both explain the facts and satisfy some personal desire: symbolically purge an anxiety or justify a life that is not without its frustrations and bitterness. Their insights into history are self-serving ones, which they "validate" first by acknowledging an apparent contradiction, then by subtly reconciling that contradiction with the original pattern.

Miss Rosa, for example, interprets the story as a gothic drama revolving around a Satanic being, Sutpen, whose violence and viciousness not only explain *"why God let us lose the War,"* but also provide Rosa with an apologia for her own paralyzed, aborted life. Her subsequent consideration of Sutpen's possible humanity, undermining this view, fades before his brutal conditions for their impending marriage: Rosa retreats both to her spinsterhood and the demonic interpretation of history.

Mr. Compson, disillusioned, world-weary, appropriately sees the story as the product of an unmeaning fatality: " 'a horrible and bloody mischancing of human affairs.' " Finding in Charles Bon a cynicism that surpasses even his own, Compson is yet able to reconcile Bon's final gesture of altruism—the refusal, according to Compson, to renounce the octoroon mistress—with the sense of fatalism that has guided all the rest of Bon's acts, and which also serves to justify Compson's life of impotence. The violent outcome of the story must remain a mystery: " 'we are not supposed to know' "—an interpretation of history that complements and confirms the fundamental cynicism of its creator.

In presenting the story through these personal and necessarily distorting perspectives, Faulkner dramatizes the creativity of the interpretive act, the process by which meaning emerges from the meeting of history with the most private and vested interests. But the novel does not rest merely as a series of subjective exploitations of fact. If the narratives of Rosa and Compson are finally no more than strategies for self-exoneration, then the tales told by Quentin and Shreve are something else: fictions that, while never wholly escaping their origins in personal need, come to embody a convincing, if fragile truth.*]

* The paragraphs in brackets summarize an argument made at greater length in a section of *The Fragile Thread* omitted from this selection.—Ed.

If there is truth in the narration of Quentin and Shreve, it does not depend on a closeness to historical fact, but on the vitality of the telling and the passionate involvement of the narrators with their subject and with each other. In terms of form, this part of *Absalom, Absalom!* is the climactic moment in Faulkner's career, for it is here that his essential style of fragmentation, of isolated narrators and actors placed at odd intervals on the rim of a single event, moves toward its most profound meaning.

Unlike the other narrators, Quentin and Shreve present what is largely a cooperative version of the Sutpen story. For Miss Rosa and Mr. Compson the listener of a tale is no more than a receptacle for the interpretation the teller is trying to press; for Quentin and Shreve listening and telling are identical actions: "It was Shreve speaking, though . . . it might have been either of them and was in a sense both: both thinking as one, the voice which happened to be speaking the thought only the thinking become audible, vocal; the two of them creating between them, out of the rag-tag and bob-ends of old tales and talking, people who perhaps had never existed at all anywhere." [2] This engagement of the boys with each other is both metaphor and means of their engagement with the past, enabling them to pass beyond defense and self-justification to something we are prepared to call truth.

Imagining begins, however, in private need, and Quentin and Shreve, like Miss Rosa and Mr. Compson, must begin their narration of the Sutpen history in the shadow of their own personalities, coloring the tale with their youth, their distance from the past, their situation as freshmen at Harvard. The time is now January 1910. Shreve approaches the story with a heavy wit: " 'You mean she was no kin to you, no kin to you at all, that there was actually one Southern Bayard or Guinevere who was no kin to you? then what did she die for' " (p. 174). He quickly retells the story he has just heard in a few pages of parodic exaggeration: of " 'this old dame' " (p. 176) and " 'this Faustus, this demon, this Beelzebub . . . who appeared suddenly one Sunday with two pistols and twenty subsidiary demons' " (p. 178), who fiercely erected his minor kingdom and, just as fiercely, destroyed it. Shreve sees Sutpen as a " 'mad impotent old man' " (p. 180)

---

[2] William Faulkner, *Absalom, Absalom!* (New York: Random House, 1951), p. 303. Subsequent page references will be to this edition.

who deliberately frustrates his own ambitions. And Quentin responds with his own device for keeping himself detached both from these matters and his Canadian roommate: *"He sounds just like father. . . . Just exactly like father"* (p. 181).

Following, however, the story of Charles Etienne (mostly from Mr. Compson in chapter 6) and Sutpen's own version of his life (mostly from Grandfather in chapter 7), the two boys move into their own invention. They decide that Charles Bon must have been the older half-brother of Henry and Judith, determined either to marry his half-sister or to win recognition from his father, Thomas Sutpen, who, for some unknown reason, withholds it. The basis for their assumption that the threat of incest, not bigamy or the blind vengeances aroused by a demon, is the true cause of Henry's murder of Bon is never unequivocally explained, but it seems to be the result of Quentin's visit with Miss Rosa to Sutpen's Hundred in September 1909. Explaining to Shreve how Mr. Compson comes to know the incest motive, when in his own narrative he attributes all to bigamy and the " 'bloody mischancing of human affairs,' " Quentin says that he himself was the one who gave Compson the new information, " 'The day after we—after that night when we—' " (p. 266).

Regardless of this evidence, however, the important fact here is that Quentin and Shreve can expand and elaborate on the incest theme because it so richly suits the condition of their own youth: sons still seeking their maturity, potential lovers still dreaming of passions they cannot admit are usually confined to books. Whatever facts may exist here, the romantic tale of siblings and lovers which Quentin and Shreve evolve goes well beyond such facts. Their story is similar to the stories of Rosa and Compson in that this is the tale they can most afford to tell, a magnificent yet self-indulgent exploration of love and courage, of defiance and honor. The enigma of murder in 1865, which Rosa explains in terms of demonic powers and which Compson attributes to fatality, becomes with Quentin and Shreve a tale of star-crossed love and the quest for identity. It is the tale we would expect from two boys "who breathed not individuals now yet something both more and less than twins, the heart and blood of youth" (p. 294).[3]

[3] I disagree with Joseph Reed's contention that Quentin and Shreve's metaphors, unlike Miss Rosa's and Mr. Compson's, "are open-handed, with

Their story has all the trappings of a Byronic romance. First
there is Charles Bon: the gallant, troubled young man isolated
by his mother for some unknown reason; the lover torn with
incestuous desires he is still prepared to restrain for the sake of
honor; the son who demands from his mysterious father the nod
of recognition that will send him on his way, a fugitive from his
desire yet the owner at last of his identity. And there is Henry
Sutpen: the younger brother, the acolyte trying desperately to
catch up with his model. He is born into one world and follows
his hero into another, attending him, even as he must guard
their sister from him.

In the heat of this romantic re-creation in little matters, the
objective narrator tells us, that the boys imagine Bon and Judith
walking that Christmas in 1860 in a garden surrounded with
"jasmine, spiraea, honeysuckle, perhaps myriad scentless unpick-
able Cherokee roses," despite the fact that it is winter and the
garden devoid of bloom. "But that did not matter because it had
been so long ago"; it does not matter "so long as the blood
coursed—the blood, the immortal brief recent intransient blood
which could hold honor above slothy unregret and love above
fat and easy shame" (p. 295).

" 'And now,' Shreve said, 'we're going to talk about love' "
(p. 316). This is the brunt of the first and longest phase of Quentin and Shreve's narration: a story of love and youthful heroism,
intensified because it is also a story of potential incest. By inter-
preting the facts in this way, they free Charles Bon of the callousness and fatalism with which Compson has described him. But in
doing so, the boys encounter the necessary crisis of their narration, the possibility that this is a story not so much of love as of
exploitation. For if Bon is the half-brother of Judith and eventually realizes this fact, as the boys allow he does, then his actions
toward Sutpen take on the quality of extortion. It could be
charged that he is willing to use Judith as a human instrument in
order to gain his recognition from the father.

Insofar as the boys are using this historical material for imaginative self-service, it is necessary for them to deal with this possi-

---

nothing self-indulgent or self-serving about them" *(Faulkner's Narrative*
[New Haven: Yale University Press], p. 165). For much of their story the
two boys, like the earlier narrators, are telling the tale most comforting to
them.

bility of exploitation on Bon's part. If he is to be their Byronic hero, representing in the middle of the nineteenth-century values and possibilities attractive to the youths of 1910, then he can hardly be the callous rogue who uses the love of his sister to attack his father. Their problem here is again the requirement of symbolic resolution: if they are to enjoy the solace of symbolic form, then they must overcome some self-erected barrier, in this case the possible dishonor of Charles Bon. Shreve takes most of the initiative here. Charles Bon *did* not want recognition from Sutpen, Shreve admits, but he *also* loved Judith.

Quentin resists Shreve's argument for much of their narrative, as if eager for a purer love than this. Yet Shreve gradually hammers home his point, emphasizing both the fervor of Bon's quest for recognition—" 'there would be that flash, that instant of indisputable recognition between them and he would know for sure and forever' " (p. 319)—*and* the growing intensity of his attraction to Judith: " 'It would be no question of choosing, having to choose between the champagne or whiskey and the sherbet, but all of a sudden . . . you find that you dont want anything but that sherbet and that you haven't been wanting anything else but that' " (p. 323). Shreve even uses the incest as evidence of the love of Bon for Judith—the impossibility of his being able to restrain it—and thus further excuses him from any possible charge of calculation. Finally, the love and the quest for recognition are involved with each other, for the measure of Bon's earnestness for the one is taken by his willingness to sacrifice the other: " '*Yes. Yes. I will renounce her; I will renounce love and all; that will be cheap, cheap, even though he say to me "never look upon my face again; take my love and my acknowledgment in secret, and go" I will do that*' " (p. 327).

The motive behind this retelling is the symbolic guarantee that adolescent notions of love and honor still operate in the world. By conceiving the story as they do, Quentin and Shreve conjure up a fiction in which these notions are not names but living factors. It is the *father,* not the young men caught up in this irresolvable dilemma, who is made to bear the deepest moral censure of the story. For it is he, according to the two boys, who withholds recognition from his eldest son, thus ensuring the final disaster.

But the motives of Quentin and Shreve are more personal and specific than this need to give fictional life to certain abstract values. For Quentin there is the additional problem of his complex relationship to the South. Proud of his heritage yet ashamed of its transgressions, Quentin participates in this retelling of the Sutpen story in the hope of ridding himself of his ambivalence. For despite the urgent cry with which he concludes the novel, it is clear that in certain ways Quentin *does* hate the South, finding in the Sutpen story a legacy of violence and hatred, of courage exacted in an unworthy cause, of grace and courtesy undermined by inhumanity.

Quentin's strategy here, aided by Shreve, is to shift the emphasis of the story to the sons, Henry and Bon, seeing them (as he must try to see himself) as the unwitting and faultless victims of the brutality of the father. By explaining the murder of Bon as a tragedy of incestuous love, Quentin can resolve his own and Henry's guilt in the necessary defense of honor and purity. Sutpen's refusal to recognize Bon, and thus prevent incest, gives Bon no choice: he *must* (for love and honor) insist on going through with the marriage. Henry Sutpen, Quentin's special alter ego, must then murder his friend and brother out of devotion to a code that transcends brotherhood. The actions of *both* sons are justified by Quentin and Shreve, and the concluding episode of violence is also justified by a difficult yet finally admirable allegiance to purity. Bon's love for Judith may be sincere enough, and Sutpens' rejection of him cruel and irrational, but Quentin's Henry Sutpen still has the larger responsibility of protecting his sister, even at the cost of his brother's life, against the violation of a universal, rather than a merely Southern, sanction against incest.

Both sons then, Henry especially, become the victims of circumstance, in whose wake they appear not only guiltless but brave. Through this strategy Quentin can see himself in a similar way, absolving himself of guilt for his own role and responsibilities as a Southerner.[4]

---

[4] Quentin and Shreve's interest in the possible incest between Bon and Judith often reminds readers of Quentin's preoccupation with incest in *The Sound and the Fury,* as if the two novels were parts of a single whole. The link between the two novels is a basic assumption of John T. Irwin's *Doubling and Incest/ Repetition and Revenge: A Speculative Reading of Faulkner* (Baltimore: The Johns Hopkins University Press, 1975). Although Irwin's book is one of the most provocative studies of Faulkner in existence, a penetrating discussion of Faulkner's work as a whole and of the idea of repetition in narration and life, I believe his close linking of the two Quen-

Shreve also has his special purpose in becoming actively involved with the Sutpen story. His personal investment will seem less to us than Quentin's, and yet the investment is real enough to allow him to participate fully in this retelling of the tale. For all his superficial cynicism, Shreve's growing interest in the story

---

tins forces him into some essential misreadings of *Absalom, Absalom!* The most crucial of these is his placing of Quentin at the center of the novel and the subsequent minimization of the importance or drama of the act of narration by Miss Rosa, Mr. Compson, and Shreve: "the other three only function as narrators in relation to Quentin" (p. 26). The brunt of my own discussion is that all three are involved in acts of narration that take their form from personal needs, that there are four acts of narrative repetition in this novel, not one. Irwin ignores the fact that Henry's incestuous desires for Judith are emphasized more by Mr. Compson than by Quentin (see pp. 79, 91–92, 96–97, and 99); and his suggestion that Bon is motivated more by a desire to gain recognition from Sutpen than by his love for Judith is contradicted by Shreve, the whole point of whose narration is to exonerate Bon from just such a charge. Irwin also assumes that there is a "true reason" (p. 119) for the murder of Bon, which Quentin knows and Compson does not, thus drastically reducing the importance of the novel as being about the imaginative act and its ability to invent (or repeat) the truth of the past. There is also the fact that the characterization of Charles Bon and his dual pursuit of recognition from Sutpen and the love of Judith is, to a large extent, dependent on Shreve. Is he also repeating the events of *The Sound and the Fury?* Most important of all is the great difference in character between the two Quentins, one of whom is trapped in the fable of incest he has created as a substitute for his impotence, while the other completes, with Shreve, an imaginative breakthrough into the past which neither Mr. Compson nor Miss Rosa has been able to make. The two novels are different, with completely different conceptions of the powers of imagination, and this is a difference that Irwin neglects. In *Absalom, Absalom!,* of course, Quentin never mentions Caddy. Faulkner had reasons for using his character again. In a letter to Hal Smith he wrote, "I use him because it is just before he is to commit suicide because of his sister, and I use his bitterness which he has projected on the South in the form of hatred of it and its people to get more out of the story itself than a historical novel would be. To keep the hoop skirts and plug hats out, you might say" (Joseph Blotner, ed. *Selected Letters of William Faulkner* [New York: Random House, 1977], p. 79.) What is important to Faulkner here is that the novel should be told from a critical although not unsympathetic point of view, so as to avoid the frequent sentimentality of historical fiction. Perhaps the soundest strategy on this point comes from Jean-Jacques Mayoux in "The Creation of the Real in William Faulkner," in Frederick J. Hoffman and Olga W. Vickery, eds., *William Faulkner: Three Decades of Criticism* (East Lansing: Michigan State University Press, 1960): "One needs, it seems to me, to forget the other Quentin while searching for the meaning of *Absalom, Absalom!*" (p. 167).

betrays his suspicion of the emptiness of his own life, a suspicion he makes explicit at the beginning of the last chapter of the novel: " 'Wait. Listen. I'm not trying to be funny, smart. I just want to understand it if I can and I dont know how to say it better. Because it's something my people haven't got. Or if we have got it, it all happened long ago across the water and so now there aint anything to look at every day to remind us of it.' " Shreve ponders a loss he can scarcely define—" 'What is it? something you live and breathe in like air?' "—and yet which he knows has something to do with " 'indomitable anger and pride and glory' " (p. 361). Almost as deeply as Quentin confronts his ambivalence toward the South, Shreve confronts an absence, something about love of land and heritage and community which, as a Canadian, he feels is no longer a living part of his character.

It is no wonder then that Shreve identifies so closely with Charles Bon, the one who, according to Shreve, is himself ruthlessly cut off from the heritage that is his, and is helpless to wrest from his father the sign that will return it to him. The complication of incest is able to provide Shreve, as it does Quentin, comfort for his inner grief, because it so romanticizes Bon's alien situation, transforming him into a giant Byronic figure. What better balm for the man without heritage than to see himself as *possessing* it, even as he is so hopelessly cut off from it? Shreve's Charles Bon is the man stripped of his past, yet *in actuality* the eldest son, the adored, the skillful, the brilliant hero of his own alienation, who rides to his death because he can neither have nor give up the woman he loves.

For Quentin and Shreve, then, as for Miss Rosa and Compson, this re-creation of the past becomes a source of symbolic consolation, a strategy with which to relieve the pressures of private anguish. Despite the intensity of all these tales and the investment being made, and despite the willingness to deal with some imagined crisis on which to test their aesthetic strength, the fact remains that they are all examples of imaginative manipulation for their creators' ends.

Nor can these interpretations be separated from the theme of exploitation that is so prominent everywhere in *Absalom, Absalom!* Depending, of course, on whose version of the story is operative, we see Thomas Sutpen exploiting a whole community, especially the Coldfield family, in order to gain his land and respectability; or we see Sutpen himself, along with other poor whites, exploited by a privileged class of landowners. Sutpen puts aside his first wife, not to mention his last mistress, and Charles Bon "uses" Judith to attack his father. Such exploitation, disregarding the integrity of another being, is also true of much of the narration in the book, involving an imaginative exploitation of people and facts long dead. And surely it is no accident that this exploitation fails to convince the reader of its validity.

But the scale of sensibility depicted in this novel does not end with art as manipulation. For the crucial fact of the Quentin-Shreve narration is that the boys eventually assert the *failure* of what they have created.

The italicized passages from pages 346 to 350 describe Henry Sutpen's agonized *acceptance* of the incestuous marriage of Bon and Judith. He accepts the fact that Bon has done all that honor demands in giving Sutpen the chance to recognize him and thus prevent the marriage. And this acceptance on Henry's part is also Quentin's, for this italicized section is the single voice of Quentin and Shreve, Henry and Bon: "two, four, now two again, according to Quentin and Shreve, the two the four the two still talking . . ." (p. 346). What we discover is that Henry does *not* murder Bon because of the threat of incest.

This reversal is the most extraordinary development in the novel. It is art breaking loose from the confines of calculation into a kind of freedom. The whole purpose of Quentin and Shreve's narration, up to this point, has been to establish incest as the basis for the act of murder in 1865. Just when they have succeeded in giving that motive a large measure of imaginative support—the lawyer, Charles's mother, the quest for recognition from Sutpen—and have also kept Bon and Henry morally unblemished, Quentin and Shreve cooperatively dismiss incest as the cause of the murder. They decide that Henry was willing to accept it. " *'Dont try to explain it,'* " Henry says, " *'Just do it.'* . . . *'Do I have your permission, Henry?'* and Henry: *'Write Write,'* " (p. 349).

Henry's willingness to accept an incestuous marriage is a moment of temporary reconciliation, not only between Henry and Bon but between Quentin and Shreve, for it constitutes Quentin's acceptance of Shreve's argument that this *is* a story of love, not extortion. It is as if, for one moment, all the conflicts which Quentin and Shreve have imagined in the past and are actually living in 1910, have been eliminated. Henry will endure this social violation: " ' "But kings have done it! Even dukes!" ' " (p. 342); and Charles Bon will either marry Judith or force the father to kill him. He will have either his heritage or his recognition.

But this reconciliation is, of course, complete illusion. Whether Henry accepted incest or not, Charles Bon is in fact dead, at Henry's hands. For Quentin and Shreve to create this acceptance then, and still remain in the same world as the fact of murder in 1865, they must find another explanation. This moment of reconciliation, therefore, is not that at all; it is merely the boys' cooperative recognition that their tale must move on.

And with this sudden twist in the story the Byronic play and the manipulation come to an end. For the time has come now to move from an art that re-creates the past through the screens of present, personal need to an art of "becoming" the past, of transforming one's own life and the past into metaphors for each other.

Quentin and Shreve are striving for resolutions that so far are unknown in the various tales of *Absalom, Absalom!* These creations out of the past, these shadows called "Henry" and "Bon," are now being forced into a new arena, into an identification with Quentin and Shreve that is beyond the ordinary uses of metaphor, an identification of creator and created that must be the largest understanding of both: the candor of knowing the self through its perfect image in the imagined past. Henry and Bon are revealed to us as the incarnations of their creators. Invention becomes a repetition, a reenactment of imagined acts that confers upon them reality. The art product, strategy no longer, binds its creators to itself with the cords of their own creation.

The invention of Bon's Negro blood is the great imaginative leap of the novel, and it comes about primarily because of what has been happening to Quentin and Shreve during the bulk of their narration: the growing sense of communion, of the created tale as a cooperation of minds, the speakers giving themselves gradually up to each other as the only means of giving themselves to that past they are trying to comprehend. This is narrative as a marriage of minds: "it did not matter to either of them which one did the talking, since it was not the talking alone which did it . . . but some happy marriage of speaking and hearing wherein each before the demand, the requirement, forgave condoned and forgot the faulting of the other" (p. 316).

The coming together of the boys (there is nothing comparable to this in the other narratives) is the mirror of their imaginative engagement with the past, an engagement so profound as to give their meanings the status of facts in our minds. By this crossing into each other's lives, Quentin and Shreve emotionally propel themselves into communion with the lives of Bon and Henry as well: "the cold room where there was now not two of them but four, the two who breathed not individuals now yet something both more and less than twins, the heart and blood of youth" (p. 294). Out of their imaginative capacity for the one emerges the other; the one is the flesh of the other. The past is finally *known* in the dynamics of love, which becomes for Faulkner the power of the imagination to break down temporarily the fact of separation, of distance between knower and known .

Shreve's initial flippancy diminishes: " 'No . . . you wait. Let me play a while now'. . . . This was not flippancy either. It too was just that protective coloring of levity behind which the youthful shame of being moved hid itself" (p. 280). The boys begin alternating in the narration, "He did not even falter, taking Shreve up in stride without comma or colon or paragraph" (p. 280), until it is not a matter of alternation any more, but a single voice that speaks for both: "since for all the two of them knew he had never begun, since it did not matter (and possibly neither of them conscious of the distinction) which one had been doing the talking. So that now it was not two but four of them riding the two horses through the dark over the frozen December ruts of that Christmas Eve" (p. 334).

There has been much interest in how this climactic version of the Sutpen story comes about; how do Quentin and Shreve discover the blackness in Charles Bon? Cleanth Brooks has suggested that the boys by no means invent this story, but that Quentin discovered it the night he and Miss Rosa went out to Sutpen's Hundred.[5] There is some textual evidence, if ambiguous, to this

[5] Brooks, *William Faulkner: The Yoknapatawpha Country* (New Haven: Yale University Press, 1963), pp. 436–38. See also Millgate, *The Achievement of William Faulkner* (New York: Random House, 1966), pp. 323–24. In his examination of the manuscript of *Absalom, Absalom!*, Gerald Langford has discovered that Faulkner originally did not intend to withhold the knowl-

effect, yet the implications of such a reading are rather disastrous
for the novel, for it means that Quentin knows the full truth
about Charles Bon *all the time* he and Shreve are having their
passionate and absorbing conversation. This would not only make
Quentin a hypocrite of psychotic proportions, but maneuvers
Faulkner into the position of deceiving his reader for no good
purpose. It is the objective narrator who says during the boys'
retelling of the story that one speaks for the other and that finally
they are *thinking* as one. Yet until its climax this cooperative
re-creation is ignorant of Bon's part Negro blood, and conse-
quently presents Bon as being also ignorant of it. On page 308
Bon, referring to his mistress, speaks lightly of a " ' "little matter
like a spot of negro blood" ' "; on page 321 he refers to " '*whatever it was in mother's [blood] that he could not brook*' "; and
on page 346, the chief obstacle to the marriage with Judith is
still the problem of incest. Bon, of course, can be ignorant of his
own blood only because Quentin and Shreve, who are telling his
story, are themselves ignorant of it.

And yet there is some reason to think that Quentin *does* find
out the secret in September 1909, before he ever meets Shreve.
Brooks cites the passage in which Quentin tells Shreve that it
was he who supplied Compson with information about Bon's
paternity (see p. 266). That Quentin learns about Bon's Negro
blood on the same night at Sutpen's Hundred seems at least possible. There is also an earlier passage, not mentioned by Brooks,
when Quentin is relating Sutpen's conversation about his first
wife with Grandfather: " 'He also told Grandfather, dropped
this into the telling as you might flick the joker out of a pack of
fresh cards without being able to remember later whether you
had removed the joker or not, that the old man's wife had been
a Spaniard' " (p. 252). Only someone who knows that Bon is part
black could grasp the significance here—and Quentin is doing the
talking.

If Quentin has known of Bon's black blood since September
then why doesn't he simply give Shreve this information instead

---

edge of Bon's origins until the end of the novel. That he finally chose to do
so is not an argument for or against the "truth" of Quentin and Shreve's
interpretation, but it does emphasize the importance of that interpretation,
making it the climax of the book (*Faulkner's Revisions of "Absalom, Absalom!"* [Austin: University of Texas Press, 1971]).

of going through the process of inventing what he already knows? The answer here is, I think, central to Faulkner's notions of the imagination and of the way truth is known. Between that italicized passage in which Henry accepts the incestuous marriage (p. 349)—thus sweeping away the basis of their whole explanation of the murder—and the italicized passage in which the fact of blackness first emerges clearly (p. 355), Shreve returns to that significant September night, 1909. For now he too knows the deepest truth of the Sutpen story and he knows how *Quentin* has come to know it: " 'And she didn't tell you in so many words how she had been in the room that day when they brought Bon's body in and Judith took from his pocket the metal case she had given him with her picture in it; she didn't tell you, it just came out of the terror and the fear . . . and she didn't tell you in the actual words because even in the terror she kept the secret; nevertheless she told you, or at least all of a sudden you knew' " (pp. 350–51).

Presumably, what Clytie is *not* telling Quentin at this point is that Henry Sutpen is upstairs, but it is this kind of wordless communication, and the intuitive grasping of truth it necessitates, that must be the means by which Quentin has learned the secret of Bon's mixed blood. Yet this last truth is something that Quentin can really *know,* can possess as a truth of the Sutpen family, only with the aid of Shreve and the communion that is created between them. Only then can he know what perhaps he has always known but could not admit to knowing, could not grasp except in the images of imaginatively realized truth.

The whole narrative of Quentin and Shreve, then, has been the process by which Quentin draws Shreve, the remote Northerner who exists a whole country apart from these Southern facts and legends, into the cooperative telling of truths Quentin cannot bear to face alone. Shreve, as his name denotes, is involved in an elaborate confession; he is the instrument through which Quentin comes into the full *imaginative* possession of what previously he has known only in fact. Quentin may be said to "use" Shreve, even as most of the characters in the Sutpen story have made use of other human beings. Shreve himself, it should be added, has been guilty of a similar act, since he is clearly using Quentin and the South not only to satisfy his curiosity—"*Tell about the South. What's it like there. What do they do there*" (p. 174)—but in order to indulge his own romantic notions of love and honor.

But "use" between the two boys is different from what it is
elsewhere in the novel, even as one of the chief moral conclusions
of their narration has to do with the special use Bon makes of
Judith. Manipulation, according to Quentin and Shreve, has in
that case been redeemed by love. Shreve insists, for example,
that Bon's substitution of the octoroon's picture for Judith's is an
act not of callousness or vengeance but of devotion: " ' "it will be
the only way I will have to say to her, *I was no good; do not
grieve for me*" ' " (p. 359). This is an interpretation Quentin and
Shreve can believe in because it is true of themselves: their own
exploitation of each other is redeemed by the depth of their
communion. And the visible sign of *that* redemption is the tale
that they have finally succeeded in telling.

The capacities of the imagination, in other words, are irrevocably rooted in our moral life. Quentin and Shreve can conceive
of an enduring love because they have created it between themselves, and the reverse is also true. Still further, and what is most
shocking and most moving of all, they have come to imagine the
motives for the murder of a brother by thrusting themselves into
brotherhood and then *experiencing* the resentment and regret
that only this union can produce. The last chapter of the novel
plays out, in the bitterness and mockery the boys express, the
extraordinary love-hate implicit to the earlier, and completely
imaginary, scene when Henry discovers that Charles Bon is part
black (pp. 351–58). This is the scene which concludes with its
invitation to murder: "—*You will have to stop me, Henry.*" The
past yields up its truth only when the imagination propels the
two boys into a repetition of the moral crises of Henry and Bon.
Imagination imprisons Quentin and Shreve within the shapes of
their imagining. They create those shapes in order to make
grandly visible what they have become; they reenact an invented
past in order to release it into meaning.

In making their momentous leap from the theme of incest to
that of miscegenation, Quentin and Shreve separate themselves
from Mr. Compson and Miss Rosa, for theirs is the only version
of the story that has expanded itself just at the moment of its
apparent completion. The tale as a rendering of the past into a
stable unchanging artifact becomes the tale as organic flesh and
blood, alive with the presence of change.

For Quentin the truth he has dared to imagine is the fullest
truth of his ambivalent relationship to the South, the truth of

human violation. Loving the South, conscious of its heritage, of a tradition in which one would die for one's land, Quentin yet forces himself to endure the dishonor and shame, the murderous denial of human responsibility. His despair is not over his hatred for the South, but over his love, for he cannot reconcile himself to its moral failures or to that moral superiority of Charles Bon with which Shreve has ended the tale. Quentin's agony becomes completely that of the Henry Sutpen he has imagined.

This last Henry is not the defender of a sister's chastity or a family's honor, but the murderer of the black man who is his brother. It is not incest now, the violation of an ancient taboo, but miscegenation that is the key to this history; and Quentin is much too candid to confuse Henry's resistance to it with a justifiable defense of honor and virtue. Henry's dismay at Bon's blackness is Quentin's own. For Quentin, trying to imagine truth in 1910, blackness rather than incest is the only adequate motive for murder. And this blackness becomes the fiction we believe in, for Quentin has not merely imagined its horror for Henry Sutpen; he has lived it.

The intense brotherhood of the tale of 1865 is the brotherhood in this freezing room in 1910. Shreve is the foreign intruder, the counterpart to Charles Bon, and Quentin is Henry Sutpen, the despair-ridden defender of his own shame. Together they create and live once more the brotherhood that attempts to defy the divisions of man. The symbolic form is not strategy but the visible contours of a young man's anguished soul; the only consolation is the tragic recognition of oneself.

Shreve, the co-creator of all this, endures the final separation of Charles Bon and *himself* from a heritage to which he has become imaginatively joined. No longer, however, can Bon face this separation as the Byronic hero glorious in his alienation; now he is only the lost being who horrifies the family whose acknowledgment he seeks: *"—He must not marry her, Henry"* (p. 354).

As victim, Shreve's Bon can own the last bravery: " 'And he never slipped away,' Shreve said. 'He could have, but he never even tried' " (p. 358). His is the last gesture as well, the altruism of carrying the octoroon's picture in order to save Judith from grief. Shreve heatedly insists on this, and Quentin accepts. But for Charles Bon the gesture is death; and for Shreve it is the eternal distance between himself and these matters, these bloody affairs of " 'anger and pride and glory.' " It is the distance, too, from the Southern stranger with whom he has reconstructed the tale, but who will at the end drive him, like any trespasser, from its boundaries.

The last pages of chapter 8 are the novel's climax, firing the unformable, unknowable heart of being human and the cold, enduring images of art into the violent oneness of a tragic form. Nineteen ten and 1865 are one, the two narrators and their completely realized shadows are one, the image is everything and everything is implicit to it: the creators and their creating and their creation all one in the realization of truth.

> Because now neither of them were there. They were both in Carolina and the time was forty-six years ago, and it was not even four now but compounded still further, since now both of them were Henry Sutpen and both of them were Bon, compounded each of both yet either neither, smelling the very smoke which had blown and faded away forty-six years ago from the *bivouac fires burning in a pine grove, the gaunt and ragged men sitting or lying about them, talking not about the war yet all curiously enough (or perhaps not curiously at all) facing the South.* . . .
>
> —*You are my brother.*
>
> —*No I'm not. I'm the nigger that's going to sleep with your sister. Unless you stop me, Henry* (pp. 351–58).

This is the novel's triumph of created image, measured by its ability to thrust its creators into a reality they have not anticipated. The tragedy of this triumph is that it can breed only the destruction of what gives it life: illusion becomes the voice of disorder and violence, love issues forth as fratricide, passionate communion devours itself in murder.

The fullness of form: communion shatters itself on the truth it utters. Its supreme victories are always its defeats.

In the last chapter of the novel occurs the painful disintegration of the communion between Quentin and Shreve that has resulted in the most compelling version of the Sutpen history. The fiction realized, there is an inevitable wrenching apart by both Quentin and Shreve, as if in retreat from those truths of the self that their imaginative venture has revealed to them. Just after

Shreve has offered to cover the shivering Quentin with over-
coats, repeating Bon's act of covering Henry with his cloak (p.
346), they retreat into callousness and defensiveness. Shreve's confession that there is in the South " 'something my people haven't
got,' " something that he would like to learn about, is answered
by Quentin, " 'You cant understand it. You would have to be
born there' " (p. 361), a statement that dismisses the meaning of
everything they have done together. Shreve replies by summing
up the whole story with a vicious insensitivity, calculated to de-
tach himself completely from these matters in which he has obviously invested so much, *revealed* so much, of himself—as well as
to punish Quentin for appearing to reject that investment: " 'So
it took Charles Bon and his mother to get rid of old Tom, and
Charles Bon and the octoroon to get rid of Judith, and Charles
Bon and Clytie to get rid of Henry; and Charles Bon's mother
and Charles Bon's grandmother got rid of Charles Bon. So it
takes two niggers to get rid of one Sutpen, dont it?' " (pp. 377–
78).

And he concludes with his comments on the mixed-blood Jim
Bond: " 'I think that in time the Jim Bonds are going to conquer
the western hemisphere. . . . and so in a few thousand years, I
who regard you will also have sprung from the loins of African
kings' " (p. 378). The lines may be read as a reflection of Faulkner's own racism, yet coming after the whole Sutpen story, and
coming with such rednecked callousness, this would be an unfair
indictment not only of Faulkner's morality but his artistry as
well. The lines characterize Shreve, not Faulkner; their largest
significance is hardly their sociology but the terrible impasse that
has suddenly emerged between Shreve and Quentin. With a per-
versity that may reflect the awesome letdown from relationship
to isolation, from communion to alienation, Shreve is taunting
Quentin, building upon a fear of blackness the Northerner always
assumes exists in the Southerner. He concludes with a question
that surely pertains to a "fact," an authentic aspect of Quentin,
but is wholly absent of imagination, not to mention generosity:
" 'Why do you hate the South?' " (p. 378).

This is the working out of the divisions implicit to the images
of chapter 8, the return of the two boys, despite all that love and
imagination can humanly perform, to those privacies of being
where image and meaning are lost in the soul's confusion and
sorrow. The center of chapter 9 is the literal confrontation be-

tween Quentin Compson and Henry Sutpen. This is all truth; it
contains no conjecture and, therefore, no metaphor:

> *And you are—?*
> *Henry Sutpen.*
> *And you have been here—?*
> *Four years.*
> *And you came home—?*
> *To die. Yes.*
> *To die?*
> *Yes. To die.*
> *And you have been here—?*
> *Four years.*
> *And you are—?*
> *Henry Sutpen.* (p. 373)

The scene is so grim and naked, so free of the imagination's
insight, that it seems the most factual but the least true of any
scene in the novel. This is fact stripped of art, the fusions of a
supreme fiction now dissolved, as is necessary, back into the
reality that fails to mean. And yet it *is* reality, what the eye has
seen; and it colors everything that has come before with the tint
of irrelevance. Art, this wealth of words, is disturbed, wrenched
askew, by the shocking, disappointing revelation of what is merely
real. Present encounters past; but the voice, once so rich and
full, is now just this side of silence.

In chapter 9 reality, emptied of metaphor, of its Reality, is
what is left. Form and meaning have been achieved, and yet the
creators themselves remain; except for Miss Rosa, they are still
talking. The collective illusion does not fully encompass the continuing history; we remember now its origins in subjectivism,
the conjectures piled one on the other. But more than this we see
that the meanings which have been won, the total sympathy of
creators and created, are now disintegrating into callousness, sim-
plistic summary, the hysterical denial.

There is an anguish communicable only in the fullest achievement of form, the tragic form that draws its power from the fact
of its impending destruction. The tragic art ultimately turns on
itself, allowing once again to rise the dark knowledge—the original meaninglessness of murder—it has tried to illuminate. The
words summon the very silence whose truth they would deny.

The fictional image survives, nevertheless, in memory. It is what we have: Henry and Bon brought to life by their identity with their creators, riding south in tattered gray to Sutpen's Hundred. Wearied with the years of war, still fumbling their way through the fragments of old dreams and old moralities—the sister's flesh Bon will give up for the word from the father, the incest Henry will condone—they find themselves at last at the gates of Bon's blackness, which can be neither given up nor condoned. The image, created in order to assuage, to resolve the inarticulate sorrow, again opens wide with murder in 1865 and its symbolic repetition in 1910.

At the bottom of this modern tragedy is the inability of one man to speak to another, some inviolable privacy at the center that imagination and love, feeding on absence, bring forth in the splendid contours of language and pattern, but which finally returns Bon and Henry, Quentin and Shreve, *Absalom, Absalom!*, to the wordless fact of a dumb and secret despair.

Aesthetics of the Rural Slum:
Contradictions and Dependency in "The Bear"

by Susan Willis

Faulkner's period cannot be adequately understood in terms of a general history of the American 30s or in terms of the narrower concerns of rural populism. His work, like that of modernism in general, has its genesis in a society whose traditional organization is being transformed by global changes in capitalism. Only by situating Faulkner's writing in relation to the historical conflicts that erupted into a rural agricultural society defined by slave labor as well as sharecropping as it was affected by financial investment and industrialization can we grasp the social meaning of his formal "innovations."

The recent and exciting work being done in what is now generally termed dependency theory, specifically that of Andre Gunder Frank and Immanuel Wallerstein, has a great potential for literary analysis in general, and Faulkner in particular. What distinguishes dependency theory from other economic theories of underdevelopment is the way it sees the underdevelopment of the Third World as a direct result of contact with capitalism. In so doing, it understands dependency in terms of a global system where different modes of production define degrees of dependency and constitute a synchronic dialectic.

As yet, little has been done in the application of dependency theory to literary analysis. However, it raises the possibility of understanding the texts of the Third World in a way not possible for other criticism generated in the First World. Faulkner's position as a Southerner suggests the necessity of seeing his work in terms of dependency, and what makes dependency theory so useful for literary analysis is that it defines the historical contradic-

A longer version of this essay appeared in *Social Text 2* (Summer 1979), pp. 82–103. Reprinted with permission from the editors of *Social Text*.

tions of domination in terms which can then be related to the form and language of the literary text.

While dependency theory might be applied to any of Faulkner's works, and some offer obvious examples of dependency rewritten as literary practice (particularly *Absalom, Absalom!*, where Caribbean colonialism functions as pretext for the fiction), I have chosen to work with "The Bear." Because the history of dependency is in some ways less obvious in this text, its revelation will be all the more significant and meaningful in relation to Faulkner's other works. Moreover, "The Bear" poses a special problem which traditional modes of literary criticism have never dealt with successfully; namely, the discordant and disruptive nature of the story's fourth section. If the story consisted only of the first three sections and the last, it would tell the moving tale of Ike McCaslin's coming of age, played out against the yearly bear hunt and the gradual disappearance of the wilderness. However, the interruption of Section IV, which focuses on the McCaslin family genealogy and Ike's desire to give up the family domain, complicates the text and throws into question the seeming simplicity of the story's other sections.

Wilderness/Commissary

Initially, the difference between the story's sections is defined by the spatial juxtaposition of two wholly distinct worlds: the wilderness and the commissary. Each of these separated worlds is described as an interior space in which the individual is shut off from the outside world. Ike's first impression of the wilderness is of "the tall and endless wall of dense November woods under the dissolving afternoon and the year's death, somber, impenetrable (he could not even discern yet how, at what point they could possibly hope to enter it . . .)." [1] A similar sense of closure informs the description of the commissary, its densely packed space evoked by the careful enumeration of its contents; the building itself, heavy with the same impenetrability which defined the forest wall, "the solar-plexus . . . the square, galleried, wooden building squatting like a portent above the fields" (p. 255).

[1] William Faulkner, *Go Down Moses* (New York: Random House, 1942), pp. 194–195. All page references will be to this edition.

The juxtaposition is enhanced by the very different social relationships pertaining to each of the worlds: on the one hand, the
community of the hunt, and, on the other, family relations. In
this context, it is important to bear in mind that the kinship
group which traditionally informs Faulkner's work is the extended, rather than the nuclear family. Even the smallest family
unit, such as Charles Mallison's (*Intruder in the Dust*), includes
the very important maternal uncle, Gavin Stevens. Clearly, the
notion of the extended family has its roots in the rural culture
of the South; for Faulkner, it represents a positive social factor.
This is true even in relation to the Snopes clan, where, notwith-
standing the humor and derision it occasions, family cohesion
between the successive waves of invading Snopes is held in admiration. Indeed, what appears to be a serious transgression of the
bond of kinship (Mink's murder of Flem) testifies, instead, to its
strength. Here, murder is a just retribution for Flem's earlier
abandonment of several of his kinsmen and his final refusal to
come to Mink's aid.

In the wilderness world of "The Bear," the extended family
has been altered to produce the community of the hunt. This is
possible because the importance of wealth and power in determining social relations partially yields to the criterion of the
experience and ability required for the hunt. To be sure, Major
de Spain and General Compson are still the most powerful members of the group. However, as their relationship to Ike demonstrates, they, along with McCaslin Edmonds, function like uncles
or fathers of the material order. Ike's wilderness extended family
also includes a spiritual father in Sam Fathers and something of
a brother in Boon, who, like a child, needs to be chaperoned on a
trip to town.

As often occurs in Faulkner, the notion of social perfection
epitomized by the community of the hunt, is an all male society.
The portrayal is obviously steeped in a sexism which implies that
the only way to eliminate conflict is to eliminate women; nevertheless, the image of masculine society also taps a reservoir of
positive imagination, and serves as a Utopian element in Faulkner's text. This is expressed in the refuge it offers the tormented
individual wishing to escape pain and conflict in the real world
and finding solace in the male group. This is true in *Sartoris*
where young Bayard, after recklessly causing the death of his
father in an auto accident, seeks out the Campbell family retreat.

And it is true in "The Bear" where the community of the hunt, enclosed within the wall of wilderness, is, for a time, sheltered from the drastic changes wrought by progress.

"The Bear"'s' other world—that of the commissary—lacks Utopian content, and instead operates like a reality principle. Painfully guilt-ridden, the extended family is overburdened with fathers—all of them defined by blood relationship. First, there is Ike's real father, Theophilus (Buck) McCaslin, who died when Ike was only five years old, but whose relationship to his son is undeniably recorded, not, as one might expect, in the Family Bible, but in the ledgers of the family commissary. Then there is Ike's grandfather, Carothers McCaslin, the perfect stereotype of the plantation owner, whose way of life was for his sons and grandson an abomination which they would strive to negate (the sons, by freeing their slaves and giving them the manor house while they slept in a log cabin, and Ike, by "relinquishing" his ancestral claim to the land and choosing, instead, the life of a tradesman). Finally, there is McCaslin Edmonds, Ike's cousin and titular father, who not only raised Ike from childhood but, as their dramatic confrontation in the commissary demonstrates, clearly occupies the position of the father—McCaslin speaking with the voice of reason, attempting, like a father, to understand Ike's motives and at the same time dissuade him from what he sees as family and class suicide.

While both worlds are defined by paternalistic systems, clearly none of Ike's blood relatives stand to him in the way that Sam Fathers does. Why this is true is apparent in a comparison of the legacies pertaining to each social system. On the one hand, Sam Fathers, who has taught Ike from the depths of his wilderness experience, bequeaths his son the deep and personal understanding of the spirit of the wilderness.[2] Something of this spirit moves Ike to recognize the importance of giving Sam Fathers a tribal funeral and it conditions his spontaneous greeting to the snake, " 'Chief,' he said, 'Grandfather' " (p. 330). Furthermore, because Sam Fathers' legacy is of the spirit, it generates a sense of whole-

---

[2] The text makes an important distinction between Sam Fathers, who, owning no land, has no material legacy to give, and old "Ikkemotubbe, the Chickasaw chief, from whom Thomas Sutpen had had the fragment [of land] for money or rum or whatever it was" (p. 255). Later we shall see how a system of exchange based on money defines the historical world and would, in terms of the wilderness ideal, represent a form of contamination.

ness, which the subsequent incursions of business interests into the wilderness cannot totally eradicate.

In contrast, the legacies left by Ike's blood fathers are all in coin and paper. Moreover, these material bequests, defined by the market system itself, are subject to fluctuations in the economy. For instance, the cup of gold coins left by Ike's maternal uncle, Hubert Beauchamp, is reduced, through years of economic hardship, to a coffee pot filled with I.O.U.'s. The fact that Ike keeps the coffee pot, uses it, and assigns it the same symbolic importance as a gift from one of his wilderness fathers (General Compson's powder horn) attests to the strength of the wilderness community in Ike's system of desire.

The true nature of the legacy in the world of the commissary goes much deeper than its inscription on ledger papers, scraps of I.O.U.'s, and golden coins. These only mediate the real burden of family history which Ike is heir to. The system of blood relationships transcribed in the family ledgers reveals as Ike's true inheritance: the guilt of his family's incest and miscegenation and the responsibility for its expiation. In the context of his genealogical inheritance, Ike's attempt to "relinquish" his birthright is futile. While he might choose to give up paper and coin—title to the land and the wealth it produces—he cannot erase the history of exploitation which these material objects symbolize. In the same way, he cannot negate the children of his black half-brother.

Myth and History

The distinction between the text's two worlds is made tangible by the use of two very different narrative modes. The narrative mode of the wilderness is myth, whose principal elements are the yearly confrontation with nature and Ike's initiation into the mysteries of the hunt and the tribal brotherhood. In contrast, the most basic element of the commissary narrative is the document, particularly the transcriptions from the ledgers.

Significantly, these two narrative modes—the mythic and the documentary—correspond to two different ways of experiencing history. However, within the story there seems to be a strong ambivalence toward knowing history at all. First of all, the moving tale of the wilderness functions to contain and compensate for the discordant historical content of Section IV. Then, even in this section where the mode of narration is historical, the text attempts to keep history out. This is evident in Ike's defensive withdrawal from history's intrusive staccato on the ledger pages into a cloud of poetic rhetoric. The reason why the experience of history has become problematical and painful can be understood by defining the historical specificity of each mode and the relationship to history which each implies.

The undeniable historicity of Faulkner's mythic mode is first evident when his story is read in relation to the tradition of the southern folktale. The nineteenth century tale, "The Big Bear of Arkansas"[3] is but one example in a rich tradition of legends (anglo, red, and Black) based on bear hunts, many of which include the three key elements of Faulkner's story: bear, dog, and child. The fact that "The Bear" has a number of folkloric predecessors does not diminish the importance of Faulkner's version. Conditioned by the tendency to valorize the "originality" of a work, traditional criticism fails to recognize that the importance of a story like "The Bear" lies in its continuation of the rich cultural tradition. The author reworks the tale and its historical context in relation to his own historical and social situation. No matter how much the story may attempt to negate history with myth, it remains grounded in the flow of history.

The mixed iconography of the natural order imprints the effects of history on the mythic mode itself. Nature has long since been contaminated by contact with culture, which is why Ben is not, as many critics believe, an embodiment of the pure state of nature. Ben's "trap-ruined foot," his most frequently mentioned physical trait, testifies to the long history of conflict between the natural and cultural orders. The blurred edge where these two worlds meet is defined by trespass; Ben oversteps the laws of the natural order by devouring domestic stock, and the men infringe upon the natural system by bringing guns and other machinery into the wilderness.[4]

Just how deep the history of trespass goes is evident in the narration itself:

[3] This story by Thomas Bangs Thorpe is included in the "Cultural Roots" chapter of the *Bear, Man, and God* anthology. The story tells of an exceptionally large and wily bear, and the equally exceptional hunter and his dog, who, over a period of years, finally succeed in killing the bear.

[4] Significantly, Ike's integration with nature is possible only after he has given up the trappings of culture—his compass, watch, and rifle.

the long legend of corn-cribs broken down and *rifled,* of shoats
and grown pigs and even calves carried bodily into the woods
and devoured and traps and deadfalls overthrown and dogs
mangled and slain / and shotgun and even *rifle* shots delivered
at point-blank range yet with no more effect than so many peas
blown through a tube by a child. (p. 193—italics and slash, mine)

Here the mixing of nature and culture conditions the basic
structure of the narrative so that, in what is essentially a string of
grammatically equal signifiers, the shift from Ben's incursions
into the realm of culture to man's trespass on the natural order
occurs between narrative segments of equal value, so as to be
nearly imperceptible. Furthermore, the double meaning of the
word "rifle," which makes it possible to apply the same word to
both Ben and his hunters, suggests the extent to which Faulkner's
so-called "nature myth" is, in fact, a hybrid.

At the center of the conflict between nature and culture is
Ben himself, who

[leaves] a corridor of wreckage and destruction beginning back
before the boy was born, through which sped, not fast but
rather with the ruthless and irresistible deliberation of a locomotive, the shaggy tremendous shape. (p. 193)

The fact that Ben is compared more than once to the locomotive,
which itself comes to represent the invasion of business interests
into the primal world of the wilderness, demonstrates that the
adulteration and transformation of nature by history has already
been accomplished before the story begins.

The penetration of history into what Faulkner would like to
see preserved as the privileged state of nature also predates Ike's
initiation in the community of the hunt and conditions his earliest thoughts about the wilderness:

It ran in his knowledge before he ever saw *it. It* loomed and
towered in his dreams before he even saw the unaxed woods
where *it* left *its* crooked print, shaggy, tremendous, red-eyed,
not malevolent but just big, too big for the dogs which tried to
bay *it,* for the horses which tried to ride *it* down, for the men
and the bullets they fired into *it;* too big for the very country
which was *its* constricting scope. *It* was as if the boy had
already divined what his senses and intellect had not encom-

passed yet; that doomed wilderness whose edges were being constantly and punily gnawed at by men with plows and axes who feared *it* because *it* was wilderness, men myriad and nameless even to one another in the land where the old bear had earned a name, and through which ran not even a mortal beast but an anachronism indomitable and invincible out of an old dead time, a phantom, epitome and apotheosis of the old wide life which the little puny humans swarmed and hacked at in a fury of abhorrence and fear like pygmies about the ankles of a drowsing elephant—the old bear, solitary, indomitable, and alone; widowered childless and absolved of mortality—old Priam reft his old wife and outlived all his sons (pp. 193–194—italics mine).

This passage shows how the categories of nature and culture overlap. There are two movements, first towards the confusion of nature and culture, then towards their separation and reconstitution—all of which turns on the use of the indefinite pronoun "it." The first nine uses of "it" refer to the hybrid image Ben/locomotive which connotes the adulteration of nature. The integrity of the natural order is further eroded because "it," being indefinite, depersonalizes its referent, Ben, who would otherwise be known by name. In the fluctuation between the personalization and depersonalization of nature, the ability to conceive of it in any coherent way has become problematical.

However, an abrupt and again imperceptible shift occurs with the line, "It was as if. . . ." Here the indirect use of the pronoun brings about a change in the narration which dehybridizes the image and reconstitutes the oppositional elements of the image as separate entities (the wilderness and man, nature and culture, pre-history and history). In this context, Ben is no longer the beast/machine, but an old bear living out his solitary immortality.

Both the hybridization of images and the abrupt shift in referent suggest a great deal of ambivalence on the part of the author towards the material of his narration. However, the reader tends to accept the conflicted language as natural, rather than as an index of the jarring incongruities in the narration itself. All of this testifies to an extremely dexterous management of conflict in Faulkner, which can be understood by more closely examining the relationship between Faulkner's story and the folk tale. What differentiates "The Bear" from its oral predecessors is that for traditional society history is present. Both the storyteller and the tale serve a social and historical function—the tale, to inscribe the community in the flow of history, and the storyteller, to preserve and teach the lessons of history to an essentially non-literate population.[5] In this experience of history, the historical event has not yet become reified, but is held in a sort of continuum of daily experience by the relationship between the storyteller and the community of listeners.

However, for Faulkner, the situation is radically different. What the narrative mode of Section IV suggests is that history, now manifested by fact and document, has become divorced from daily experience. In this context, the storyteller becomes a storywriter, whose function is to collect historical data and decode the historical document.

In Section IV of "The Bear," Ike's interpretation of the ledgers parallels the work of the modern writer and duplicates an earlier attempt by his father and uncle to assemble the same fragments into historical knowledge. The fact that so many of Faulkner's works are defined by the need to reconstruct history, apparent in so much of Faulkner's writings, betrays the inability to any longer experience history directly and the haunting remembrance of what this relationship to history was in traditional society. Indeed, we might compare the Faulknerian narrative to a model kit, where information about the past is given in bits and pieces and the characters, along with the reader, work to assemble the separate fragments in a meaningful way. For instance, the archaeological work of the characters in "The Bear" duplicates on a small-scale the tremendous effort waged in *Absalom, Absalom!* by Quentin and his roommate, Shreve, to make sense out of "the rag-tag and bob-ends of old tales and talking." [6] The text is thus an historical construct, a version of the past which is as close as anyone can get to "real history."

"The Bear" involves two very different ways of relating to and knowing history: the direct, unmediated manner characteristic of the mythic mode, and the reconstructed version of the historical mode. The juxtaposition of the two reveals that the tradi-

---

[5] For an account of how the oral tradition is related to its social context, see Albert Lord, *The Singer of Tales* (Cambridge, Mass.: Harvard University, 1960).

[6] William Faulkner, *Absalom, Absalom!* (New York: Random House, 1964), p. 303.

tional relationship to the past, typical of the Southern small town, is passing out of existence. In its place has evolved a more problematical relationship to the past, which in turn derives from a very different form of social organization. The integrity of the small town is being broken down by its relationship to the South's recently developed industrial centers and to consumer society in general as they centralize social life and flatten out cultural difference.

All of Faulkner's work is conditioned by the social effects of historical transition. At one level, transition is expressed as an ambivalence toward history, while at another level, it directly informs the text's imagery. The disappearance of traditional society is expressed by the destructive drive of the bear/locomotive through village and farmland. To emphasize the point, Faulkner invents yet another locomotive, the log train whose incursion into the virgin timber land makes it the representation of exploitative progress. Seen both as the bearer of progress (desired social betterment) and of destruction (the unmastered transformation of the known world), the image of the log train may be equated with capitalism itself, which represents the most revolutionary and at the same time most destructive mode of production. The fact that Major de Spain, formerly the most powerful representative of the plantation system, has been bought out by the logging company suggests that the text be read in relation to historical transition produced by the intervention of capital. Such a reading demands a more meaningful interpretation of the story's basic opposition.

The Plantation vs. Industrial Capitalism

The juxtaposition between two worlds, the wilderness and the commissary, is in fact the coded form of the historical opposition between the plantation system and industrial capitalism. The text sets out to maintain a binary opposition between neutral terms, presenting the wilderness and the commissary as spatial opposites. As each becomes contaminated with history, their neutrality dissolves, nature and culture overlap, and the tremendous impact of historical transition transforms the text into an allegory of dependency. The truth of the text's two worlds is a dialectic between unequal modes of production.

Within the system of dependency, the locomotive at once sym-bolizes the invasion of capital from the outside and constitutes a mediation between unequal worlds. The path of the log train, winding its way out of the wilderness to Hoke's saw mill where it connects with the Memphis train, traces geographic relationships which are historically determined. The significance of geography provides a key for understanding what would otherwise be a gratuitous episode in the story: the whiskey buying trip which Ike and Boon take to Memphis. While one aspect of the trip to the city is that it develops the theme of Boon's childlike inno-cence, this alone cannot explain what is essential about the epi-sode. Ike and Boon go to Memphis to buy supplies. The trip demonstrates that the wilderness community is neither self-contained nor self-sufficient, but dependent on the outside world. The recognition of a direct link between the wilderness and the centers of commerce explodes once again the myth of nature and its illusory isolation.

The reference to Memphis, positioned on the outside periphery of the story's geographic space, is hardly an arbitrary allusion. Even a cursory reading of Faulkner's work reveals the frequent mention of this city, just far enough away to be distant, yet close enough to be included in the familiar world—noticeably different but not strange. In social terms, Memphis is seen as the locus of all that is unwholesome: gamblers, criminals, loose women, and prostitutes. Memphis seldom occupies the center; the Faulknerian text decentralizes its focus by displacing the city to the periphery, in order to emphasize, instead, the rural community. Yet the city's dominance is always discernible; life in the small towns of Faulkner's fiction hinges on its relationship to the distant city. This dominance lies precisely in the economic disparity between the city and its outlying towns, and is registered in the logic of the associations in Ike's first impressions of Memphis itself:

> The street was busy. He watched the big Norman draft horses, the Percherons; the trim carriages from which the men in the fine overcoats and the ladies rosy in furs descended and entered the station. (p. 233)

The progression from the street, busy with commerce (which the text, clinging to its natural imagery, describes in terms of draft horses), to the finery of the men and women who benefit from the city's economic superiority, provides for a striking contrast with the hunters' boots and khaki, mud and unshaven faces. Then too, the fact that the city dwellers are disembarking at the station, dressed in their best and bound for what one imagines are even finer cities, suggests that while Memphis enjoys a position of dominance in relation to its small sphere, it in turn occupies an inferior position in a larger geographic and economic context.

The story's geographic points thus map out a system of relationships between unequal worlds: the wilderness, the plantation and its hinterland, the village, and the city. Holding the map together is the ascending chain of domination which determines the logic of the system. The wilderness, its wealth of raw materials expropriated by the logging industry, is economically inferior to the village, which in turn (and as inevitably as the railroad lines which connect them) is inferior to the city. The economically determined geography of "The Bear" suggests in microcosm Andre Gunder Frank's notion of dependency as a chain whose alternating links respond to the contradiction of expropriation from the *satellite* and appropriation by the *metropolis*.[7]

Because Faulkner is dealing with a period of historical change the map is based on a complicated dialectic between two economic systems. The industrial capitalist system which manifests itself in the city, village, and wilderness system, is paralleled by the older plantation system whose chain of domination includes the wilderness, the rural hinterland, and the plantation. The two systems come together at their most basic point: the wilderness. For in either system production initially involves the extraction of raw materials. That everyone has a stake in the wilderness is clearly demonstrated in "The Bear" as representatives from all levels of both systems converge to participate in the hunt: Indians, "swampers," plantation owners and their retainers, townspeople and businessmen.

That Faulkner's work reveals such remarkable insight into the nature of dependency is closely related to the influence of economic transition during the peak years of his creativity. Essen-

---

[7] For an overview of Frank's thesis, including an explanation of the terms satellite and metropolis in relation to the contradictions of dependency capital, see his *Capitalism and Underdevelopment in Latin America* (New York: Monthly Review Press, 1969).

tially, the 30s represented for the south the culmination of a process of upgrading from *periphery* to *semiperiphery*.[8] Generally speaking, the change in the economic status of the South was produced by its transition from the production of raw materials (principally cotton) to the production of a labor force [9] (black and poor white) for export to northern industrial cities. What facilitated this change was the increasing development of more peripheral areas in the Third World for the production of raw materials and the steady effort on the part of the North, from the post-Civil War period to the end of the Depression, to incorporate the South in its production machine. The culmination of this process occurred during the 30s, precipitated by the collapse of the rural economy and the flight of the work force to the industrial cities. What we sense then in Faulkner as a confrontation between unequal worlds is closely related to the lived experience of historical change, as an older form of agrarian dependency is rapidly being replaced by a newer form of industrial dependency.

An understanding of the social dialectic of dependency regrounds the interpretation of key textual features and operations. The function of Section IV of "The Bear" becomes manifest once we recognize that the confrontation between Ike and his cousin could only have taken place in the commissary. The form of labor control in the semiperiphery is, as Wallerstein shows, wage labor and money rents.[10] The mode of production is sharecropping not slavery. Indeed, sharecropping has been the one most durable form of production in the South. Existing during slave times, it superseded the abolition of that institution to become the dominant agrarian mode. Only very recently has industrialization re-

---

[8] For the most part, I base my understanding of dependency on Immanuel Wallerstein's analysis of global capitalism, *The Modern World System* (New York: Academic Press, 1974). Wallerstein's more refined conceptualization of dependency based on the periphery, semiperiphery, and core provides a way of accounting for the differences and changes in the Third World, which is lacking in Frank's formula.

[9] From the standpoint of the southern microcosm, the flight of blacks and poor whites to the North can be interpreted as a form of migration, necessitated by the collapse of the rural economy. However, from the point of view of global economics, the need for workers in the industrial cities parallels the need for raw materials. Both are expropriated and incorporated into the production process. In this sense the supplying of a labor force represents a form of production.

[10] Immanuel Wallerstein, *The Modern World System*, pp. 102–103.

placed sharecropping as the means by which poor whites are incorporated in the production process. "The Bear" is truly a tale of the semiperiphery, and the commissary is indeed the text's "solar-plexus." In a sharecropping economy, the commissary represents the seat of labor control and the place of the laborer's yearly reckoning. This contrasts directly with the slave labor system where control emanates from the manor house. Faulkner's most graphic representation of this form of labor control occurs in *Absalom, Absalom!* when the ragged, white-trash boy, Thomas Sutpen, is turned away from the front door of the plantation mansion, and told to go around to the back by a splendidly dressed black servant. Given the economics of sharecropping, the ledger notations reproduce the heartbeat of the system and suggest that what is really at stake is the whole definition of social class.

The ledgers document the transition from a peripheral to a semiperipheral economy brought about by the adoption of a money economy. This has tremendous ramifications for the system of land ownership. Whereas the mode of production in the periphery strictly differentiates the class of owners from the class of producers, land-ownership in the semiperiphery will always be a locus of uncertainty. As long as money is the determining factor, a number of producers will accede to the class of owners. The disposition of land-ownership at the end of "The Bear," in which Ike is no longer a landowner while Sophonsiba's Negro husband is, describes a world vastly different from that of the plantation where racial exclusion and the absence of a money economy make such a situation impossible.*

---

* Faulkner's response to dependency is complex and often expressed figurally. For instance, the theme of legitimation takes on a deeper meaning when read as a social metaphor generated by the economics of dependency. Ike's reconstitution of the relationship between Carothers McCaslin and his mulatto child, Tommy's Terrel, is cast in terms specific to the semiperipheral situation, where money mediates social relationships:

> "So I reckon that was cheaper [the legacy] than saying My Son to a nigger," he thought. "Even if My Son wasn't but just two words" (pp. 269–270).

The legacy in coin that Carothers McCaslin leaves his black heirs represents a form of recognition permissible in the social economy of the semiperiphery. The fact that Carothers McCaslin does not endow them with his name and that Ike himself is childless signals the end of the recognized McCaslin line. For the semiperiphery, real authority can never be achieved; it necessarily resides elsewhere. In its absence, money fills the gap.

If we plot the four main character positions according to Greimas's formula for the generation of meaning in narrative,[11] we define the deep social contradictions produced out of the transition from a peripheral to a semiperipheral economy.

Ike	WHITE⟷BLACK	Lucas
	(inheritance prescribed) *(inheritance denied)*	
McCaslin	NOT BLACK⟷NOT WHITE	Sam Fathers,
	(inheritance not denied) *(inheritance not prescribed)*	Boon

What one critic has described as a strong sense of "irresolution" [12] in the text is in fact produced by the narrative's frantic attempt to imagine and fill every possible structural category— a strategy which suggests an implicit awareness of historical contradiction, given the social categories which the characters represent. The diagram presents the characters as they ideally ought to be. According to the social laws of the dominant plantation system, Ike, the white descendant in the male line, is ideally the inheritor, while Lucas, the black, is ideally not an inheritor. The same class system which excludes on the basis of caste defines McCaslin (a non-black) as a possible inheritor and assigns the marginals (Sam Fathers and Boon) (not white, but also not black) the ambiguous status, "inheritance not denied." Thus, Sam Fathers, the aristocrat of his category, is allowed to inherit the spiritual world of nature. On the other hand, Boon, the plebian, represents a problem for the text. The rules of class and caste do not quite apply to a plebian who, because he is not black, cannot be immediately excluded. Boon is thus portrayed in ambiguous terms: a giant of a man, but childlike. He is allowed to fulfill a

[11] A. J. Greimas, *Du sens* (Paris: Seuil, 1970). See the chapter: "Les Jeux des Contraintes Semiotiques."

[12] Walter J. Slatoff, "The Edge of Order: The Pattern of Faulkner's Rhetoric," in *Faulkner: Three Decades of Criticism,* ed. Frederick Hoffman and Olga W. Vickery (East Lansing: Michigan State University Press, 1960), pp. 173–198. Slatoff takes the point of view that "Faulkner seems very anxious to keep pieces from fitting together." This is contrary to general critical opinion and much in line with our own findings. However, while Slatoff demonstrates the lack of resolution in the texts themselves, he cannot explain satisfactorily why this is the case, and in the end, attributes irresolution to Faulkner's "temperament."

function in both the worlds of nature (as the killer of Ben) and the world of commerce (as sheriff at Hoke's).

While the generation of the characters has its fundamental logic in the ideal of the plantation system, none of the characters as they are developed in the text wholly corresponds to the ideal. This is because history enters into the system—as it must—and transforms the narrative logic in relation to Faulkner's own historical context. The opposition between the author's historical period and that of the plantation system subverts the ideal categories, and strains the narrative logic to the breaking point.

In textual practice, then, Ike, Lucas, and McCaslin represent a reversal of the narrative ideal. Ike, who ought to fulfill the laws of patrilinear descent, denies his inheritance by "relinquishing" his title, and then, because he is childless, negates the system as a whole. The reversals which inform the other two character positions (McCaslin and Lucas) are mirror images of each other. McCaslin is an acceptable inheritor on the basis of caste, even though his matrilinear descent should have excluded him. In contrast, while Lucas qualifies on the grounds of patrilinear descent, he is denied on the basis of caste. Lucas' cash legacy demonstrates how semiperipheral economics subverts what would otherwise be strict social prohibitions.

The Attempt to Resolve Contradiction: Myth and Mediation

The Greimasian formula, recast in terms of its historically determined reversals and modifications, demonstrates how the narrative, in a frantic attempt to avoid confrontation with its inherent contradictions, gives full vent to the generative process. Categories are combined in every possible way, producing the great range of character types which occur in "The Bear." However, the generative process itself, does not resolve contradiction, which is what the text desperately wants but cannot possibly achieve. At every level, the underlying contradictions which shape the history of the semiperiphery find their way into the text.

The semiperiphery, midway between economic opposites, is that peculiar area of dependency which wants not to appear dependent. The textual attempts to eliminate contradiction evoke the desire for integration with the core. The semiperipheral text thus differs from the more discordant texts from the periphery, where the irresolution of contradiction produces obvious and disruptive discontinuities best expressed by Fanon's emblematic title "black faces and white masks."

Given the contradictions of dependency in the rural slum, real resolution could only be attained in radical historical transformation. In its absence, the Faulknerian text is a many layered expression of the desire for resolution. At rock bottom, two very different strategies frame this desire and encompass all previously defined textual juxtapositions, oppositions, and contradictions—namely, *myth* and *mediation*.

Myth in Faulkner is a direct expression of dependency. As such, it is defined by various textual features which move toward but never achieve the resolution of contradiction. This understanding of myth suggests a basis for defining the similarity between Faulkner and a great many contemporary writers from other dependent areas. Indeed, Faulkner has often been compared with Claude Simon, in France, and Gabriel García Marquez, of Colombia. While common critical opinion attributes the basis for their similarity to literary influence, this explanation cannot account for the fact that, while Faulkner has so many foreign disciples, he has very few in his own country. The real reason for the similarities is a shared response to dependency. Given the now almost total assimilation of the South by the North, dependency analysis helps to explain the lack of Faulknerian heritage in this country.

The significance of dependency is suggested in an interview with two of Faulkner's most frequently cited disciples: García Marquez and Vargas Llosa. Here Marquez explains:

> I think it is the method. The Faulknerian method is very effective for telling about the Latin American reality. Unconsciously, this is what we discovered in Faulkner. That is to say, we were living this reality and we wanted to tell about it and we knew that the European method wouldn't work and neither would the traditional Spanish one; and all of a sudden, we found that the Faulknerian method is extremely well suited for telling about this reality.[13]

---

[13] Marquez made this statement in a joint interview with Mario Vargas Llosa, published as "La Novela en América Latina," in *Imagen y Literatura*, ed. Carlos Milla Batres (Lima: Ediciones Universidad Nacional de Ingeniería, 1968).

Faulkner's "method" is so appropriate for expressing the reality of the Third World precisely because of its recourse to myth. Myth creates a Utopian space within which contradictions that have their basis in the real world are transformed into more manageable textual problems. Once inside the mythic space, the text generates a number of features which evoke the resolution of contradiction. Often the very use of language plays with the notion of synthesis. This is evident in "The Bear" where Ike's "pride" and "humility" are made compatible. Faulkner's invention of the page-long sentence—his most recognizable stylistic trait—evokes, with its unbroken, lyrical rhythm, the very nature of Utopian wholeness. No matter what the language, be it the original English, or the Spanish and French of his followers, the lengthy, convoluted Faulknerian sentence has become the sign and structure of myth itself.

The long Faulknerian sentence is built on an accumulation of separate but equal parts. Faulknerian sentences are in fact simple sentences, expanded to incredible lengths by appended words (generally epithets) and phrases (invariably adjectival and participial). Significantly, the appendage sentence is an extreme manifestation of the avoidance of hypotaxis. It represents a rejection of rigid grammatical structure, resulting in a loosening of sentence structure and an overall opening up of the text. These sentences contrast with the social claustrophobia which so preoccupies the narrative. The stifling small town, inbred and incestuous families, the spontaneous eruption of violence and the long festering jealousies which typify the Faulknerian text and readily suggest an overwhelming sense of closure are paradoxically described in lengthy and loose paratactical sentences, free of the contingencies of hypotaxis which might otherwise seem a more appropriate vehicle for the narration.

To solve the apparent discontinuity between closed and open in Faulkner, let us again consider the nature of myth as it seeks to resolve contradictions through the creation of a textual totality. The notion of totality can take two very different forms, and the fact that both occur in Faulkner suggests the intensity of the desire to achieve wholeness even though it results in the tension between closed and open. Totality in its closed form is defined by incest. The negative and ungratifying form, it shuts out the world and retreats to the totality of one. Conversely, totality in its open form is all inclusive, like Shreve and Quentin's historical and geographic construct, limitless and unstructured like the sentences themselves. While this is the gratifying or polymorphous form of totality, both forms, because they deny contradiction —either by excluding it in the closed form, or by making everything equal to itself as in the open form—are appropriate to myth.

Another feature of the mythic text is its substitution of the family genealogy for history ordered by linear time and event. The function of the McCaslin family tree or Marquez's Buendía family genealogy (which is so complex as to suggest a pastiche of the device) is to provide an alternative means of conceptualizing history. While family-oriented history corresponds to the sense of community in the literature of dependency, its denial of historical process provides an unsuccessful means of opposing historical explanations for dependency generated from the dominant point of view.

Finally, because the mythic space only provides for the acting out of resolution, none of its features can be truly gratifying. In the final analysis, the recourse to myth is a compensatory reaction whose eloquent expression voices the lack of resolution in the real world.

The failure of myth in no way lessens the text's desire for resolution, which, in a feverish burst of frustration and creativity, manifests itself in a second strategy for resolution: mediation. In "The Bear" mediation occurs at moments of extreme polarization and is generally embodied in the character Ike. Nowhere is this more clear than in the confrontation between McCaslin and Boon over the question of Sam Fathers' death. Significantly, the incident occurs at the end of Section III and marks the moment of transition from the wilderness world to the commissary. Moreover, the confrontation has very little to do with Boon's credibility when asked if he helped end Sam Fathers' life; rather, it signifies the end of the natural order and the origins of history. Not only does the episode take place over the very graves of Sam Fathers and Lion, but Boon himself is made to represent the last vestige of the natural order. Twice the author remarks the "black scoriations" on his face, tattoos of his hand-to-claw struggle with Ben. Finally Boon's identification with nature is made complete, and he becomes the embodiment of Ben:

> Then Boon moved. He turned, he moved like he was still drunk and then for a moment blind too, one hand out as he blundered

toward the big tree and seemed to stop walking before he reached the tree so that he plunged, fell toward it, flinging up both hands and catching himself against the tree and turning until his back was against it, backing with the tree's trunk his wild spent scoriated face and the tremendous heave and collapse of his chest, McCaslin following, facing him again, never once having moved his eyes from Boon's eyes. "Did you kill him Boon?" (pp. 253–254).

His heaving, blundering movements, the great heave of his chest, poised erect, his back against a tree, Boon mirrors Ben's final moments.

In direct opposition to him is McCaslin, clearly the representative of the world of law and order, and thrust between the juxtaposed pair is Ike:

Then the boy moved. He was between them, facing McCaslin; the water fell as if it had burst and sprung not from his eyes alone but from his whole face, like sweat. "Leave him alone!" he cried. "Goddamn it! Leave him alone!" (p. 254).

The tremendous emotional impact of the confrontation overwhelms Ike, whose flood of tears suggests the longed for release which only the true resolution of contradiction can provide. But resolution is not forthcoming. And Ike's tears represent the desperate futility of his position as mediator. The fact that he is portrayed as a child, a "boy," enhances the poignancy of his effort and underscores his emotionally laden appeal, "Leave him alone. . . . Goddamn it! Leave him alone."

With these words left to reverberate through the text, the narrative abruptly (though imperceptibly) shifts to a wholly new world and narrative mode. The first indication that a transformation has taken place is Ike's transition from boyhood to adulthood: "then he was twenty-one." The content of this new world is defined by the terms of yet another juxtaposition—this time between Ike and his cousin, who confront each other, not over the "wilderness," for nature has passed out of existence, but over the "tamed land."

To understand what has happened in the shift from Section III to IV, it is necessary to note the mechanics of the transformation. Ike's intervention between Boon and McCaslin, rather than bringing about the desired resolution, has the opposite effect of heightening contradiction. Ike's intervention effectively eliminates one of the terms of the opposition, nature, and renews the polarization at another level, history. Ike, the erstwhile mediator, is thus redefined as one of the terms of an historical contradiction. The heartbreaking futility of the recourse to mediation results in an even more profound contradiction.[14]

The function of myth and mediation define a text very different from that commonly attributed to Faulkner. The Faulknerian world is not an organic unity, but a tormented disunity inscribed within the oppression of dependency. Torn apart by contradiction and frustrated by the attempts at resolution, the text produces the creative richness of myth and the gripping futility of mediation.

[14] An article by David H. Stewart, "Ike McCaslin, Cop-Out," included in the *Bear, Man, and God* anthology, also raises the question of mediation: "It is his frenzied mediations that many critics have mistaken for actual commitment, negative or positive . . ." (p. 220).

Faulkner's Last Phase

by Gary Lee Stonum

Almost all the novels of Faulkner's last decades address a single, complex problem: the fate of design. Just as the earlier writings had developed according to progressive reinterpretations of the arrested-motion principle, so the work of Faulkner's last phase looks to the stranger who is to receive what has been arrested.[1] After about 1940 Faulkner persistently asks what the consequences are to be of the personal, cultural, and literary structures that men produce. The same question is implicit in Faulkner's earlier writings, of course, for he often depicts the plight of those who inherit the forms of the past (Quentin Compson and Bayard Sartoris) and of those who survive the collapse of fictions they have lived by (Harry Wilbourne and the tall convict in *The Wild Palms*). Beginning with *The Hamlet*, however, Faulkner much more explicitly asks how one is to endure, how to go on when the structures one has made for experience prove inadequate. The question is made more urgent by the knowledge that burdens Quentin and his creator in *Absalom,*

Reprinted from Gary Lee Stonum, *Faulkner's Career: An Internal Literary History*, with minor emendations made by the author for this edition. Copyright © 1979 by Cornell University. Used by permission of the publisher, Cornell University Press.

Faulkner's works are cited parenthetically in the text of this essay and identified by the following abbreviations: *H, The Hamlet* (New York: Random House, 1940); *M, The Mansion* (New York: Random House, 1959); and *T, The Town* (New York: Random House, 1957).

[1] The idea of arrested motion, which has long been recognized as a key motif in Faulkner's earliest writings, receives its fullest and most general expression in a 1955 interview. "The aim of every artist is to arrest motion, which is life, by artificial means and hold it fixed so that 100 years later when a stranger looks at it, it moves again since it is life." James B. Meriwether and Michael Millgate, eds., *Lion in the Garden: Interviews with William Faulkner, 1926–1962* (New York: Random House, 1968), p. 253.

Absalom!, the knowledge that all such structures are flawed and that even so they may continue to exert a crippling pressure on subsequent generations. Immediately and expressly at stake in the last phase is the possibility of surmounting the despair that has claimed Quentin.

In the openly didactic spirit of Faulkner's late fiction, the questions of enduring and of the fate of design can fairly be described as posing the problem of values. What are values, and how are they found or made? What is their relation to the cultural designs and discursive structures that literary fictions subsume, investigate, and transmit? Almost every major character in the works after 1940 is directly seeking either to challenge or to maintain existing value systems and the institutions in which they are embodied. In addition to the characters of the Snopes trilogy and those such as Charles Mallison and Gavin Stevens who also appear prominently in other works, one can point to Ike McCaslin, Lucas Beauchamp, Nancy Mannigoe, and all the principal characters in *A Fable.*

Value is a central concept for both linguists and economists. In the Snopes trilogy Faulkner's continuing attention to the structures of language and of social discourse is joined by and then fused with an increased attention to the structures of economic interchange. He understands that in all these areas the question of value concerns the bonds established between persons when they exchange words, commodities, and sexual favors. He understands also that these bonds find their most important manifestations in cultural patterns, social and economic institutions, and literary fictions. Value, then, is the term that denotes the character of such bonds and the quality of the relationship they establish.

The concern for the consequences of design and for the values that are institutionalized in social structures directly implicates the work of the writer. It calls into question his responsibility for the literary fictions he produces. Though Faulkner continues announcing that he writes without regard for the possibility that his books will be read, in practice his fiction is at this time directly concerned with its relationship to readers and to the culture in general. (During these same years Faulkner allows himself to become a public figure and a spokesman for both his region and his nation: he begins writing essays and public letters, he tours several parts of the world for the State Department, and he speaks at length about his writing and his personal views in classroom talks and interviews.) The writer has discovered himself to be a purveyor of values, and he now requires himself to attend to the consequences of the ones he transmits, transforms, or criticizes in his writing.

The Town and *The Mansion* complete what *The Hamlet* began, a discrediting of all established social institutions and cultural forms. The available forms of human interaction are exposed as both empty and all-powerful. On the one hand, Flem succeeds in taking control of Jefferson's civic institutions and perverting the values they were meant to secure. His chief opponent, Gavin Stevens, a defender of the established forms of honor and propriety for their own sake, finds that a stand in favor of such forms usually works to Flem's advantage. The genteel customs Gavin desperately clings to and the law he upholds as an officer of the court serve not as bulwarks against Flem's advance but as structures that Flem can easily manipulate for his own ends. On the other hand, once Flem reaches his pinnacle and has fully consolidated his control over these structures, he finds that he possesses nothing of real value to him. Instead he is entombed by the very structures he has struggled so long to appropriate.

Gavin Stevens is patently a quixotic figure, especially in *The Town*. He makes continual recourse to "poets' dreams" as the source of his values and of his faith in established forms, but he is frequently willing to help compromise his own ideals rather than to see their formal embodiments fall entirely (*T* 226). Thus he fights a gallantly absurd duel with De Spain over the "principle that chastity and virtue in women shall be defended whether they exist or not" (*T* 76). More important, his defense of established forms makes him Flem's accomplice in several of the latter's most crucial stratagems: obtaining entry into Jefferson society, railroading Montgomery Ward Snopes to the penitentiary, and arranging a church burial for the suicide Eula.

The continual failure of Gavin's attempts to oppose Flem exposes the secret complicity between the two. Both men depend on established codes, and both are willing to impose them on others. Much of the battle between the two is waged over Eula and Linda, and both men try in different ways to coerce the

women into acting in public according to codes the men determine.

Both the emptiness of official structures of human interchange
and their imprisoning power are represented by Flem's situation
in *The Mansion*. President of the bank, owner of an antebellum
mansion, and nominally the most powerful man in Yoknapatawpha
County, Flem is "completely complete" (*M* 154). But he has sacrificed to those public forms whatever capacity he may ever have
had to enjoy them. "When he had nothing, he could afford to
chew tobacco; when he had a little, he could afford to chew gum;
when he found out he could be rich provided he just didn't die
beforehand, he couldn't afford to chew anything" (*M* 66). We see
him always "chewing steady on nothing"; along with his sexual
impotence, the "little chunk of Frenchman's Bend air" on which
his jaws continually work becomes the image for the emptiness at
the center of his official control over the community's institutions
(*M* 157).

In part we can assimilate Flem to the many other fictional
characters who have given over the direction of their own desire
to others. *"He had sacrificed everything . . . to gain the only prize
he knew since it was the only one he could understand since the
world itself as he understood it assured him that was what he
wanted because that was the only thing worth having"* (*M* 240).
Official forms and established institutions play the role of the
mediator for Flem in the operation of what René Girard has
called triangular desire; like the characters Girard analyzes, Flem
discovers the desired object, the mansion, to be his "mausoleum"
(*M* 359).[2] Once he has attained the goals defined by others, he
becomes incapable of answering the question Montgomery Ward
poses: "Jesus, you do want to stay alive, don't you. Only, why?"
(*M* 70).

Ratliff in *The Hamlet* and Gavin in *The Town* despair at the
powerlessness of forms to preserve human values or to secure
positive human relations. The dark vision now becomes the discovery that such forms by themselves carry no values and establish no relations at all. Flem's isolation and emptiness are
duplicated in *The Mansion* by the experience of his putative

---

[2] René Girard, *Deceit, Desire, and the Novel,* Yvonne Freccero, trans.
(Baltimore: John Hopkins University Press, 1965).

daughter Linda, whose dependence on organized structures links Faulkner's theme to wider currents of twentieth-century history. Faulkner presents her membership in the Communist party, her patriotic work in the war against Hitler, and her well-meaning but abstractly motivated civil rights work as memorials to her dead husband and ineffective replacements for their marriage. She becomes in her deafness someone who lives "outside human time," a Keatsian "bride of quietude and silence striding inviolate in the isolation of unhearing" (*M* 236, 230). Thirty years before, such a figure would have represented a desired aesthetic transcendence for Faulkner, but now it denotes a terrifying alienation from all human interchange, even, at the end, with her protector Gavin. "She just stood, our eyes almost level, looking at me out of, across, something—abyss, darkness; not abject, not questioning, not even hoping" (*M* 238).

Established forms, rather than serving as instruments of social intercourse and embodiments of humane values, prove to be the graveyard of once vital relations and values. Forms refer only to bygone value; the institutions that Flem commands are only petrified remnants. His antebellum mansion is the now vacant symbol of a once meaningful society. Gavin recognizes the reason for this, at least conceptually, during his one climactic moment of insight in *The Town*. "Because the tragedy of life is, it must be premature, inconclusive and inconcludable, in order to be life; it must be before itself, in advance of itself, to have been at all" (*T* 317–318). The Motion—Faulkner now begins to capitalize the word—and creative energy that genuinely establish human relationships always precede the forms in which we retrospectively see the relationships.

Like the designs of Sutpen and his interpreters in *Absalom, Absalom!*, social forms in the trilogy seem both inescapable and incapacitating. Flem and Gavin's battle and their secret complicity is, in fact, another version of the relation between Sutpen and Quentin. Like Gavin and Quentin, we grow up in the midst of structures that appear to provide our only worthy relations to others and thus we become their confused and stymied defenders. Or, like Flem and Sutpen, we appropriate them from the outside and are made over in their image. Unless we are as strong and lucky as Sutpen and can die before understanding how completely devoid of values the established forms are, we find ourselves in despair, like Gavin at the end of *The Town,* overtaken by paralysis, like Flem near the end of *The Mansion,* or suffering from both, like Quentin in *Absalom, Absalom!*

The literary counterpart to this situation is not so emphasized in *The Town* and the earlier part of *The Mansion* as in *The Hamlet;* it is nonetheless easy enough to see. Faulkner finds himself with a strong conviction about the values that ought to be manifest in human relationships. All of them are traditional humanistic values: courage, kindness, honor, and the like. But every traditional or invented literary fiction in which he attempts to represent these values turns out to be at best inadequate or incomplete and at worst an accomplice in the betrayal of those values. Frontier humor in *The Hamlet* not only proves insufficient for representing life in Frenchman's Bend, but its use by Ratliff and the others as an operative cultural myth makes them that much more defenseless against Flem Snopes. The same may be said about the dreams of Gavin Stevens's poets.

The story of Mink Snopes in *The Mansion* offers the counter to this desperate situation and the first step in the strategy by which Faulkner seeks to go beyond the constraints of determinate literary forms without abandoning the specificity of the fluid materiality they organize. By the time Mink leaves prison he has been systematically deprived of any place in the society or any role within the culturally sanctioned forms of exchange. Because he is so much an anachronism in the modern world that has grown up during his imprisonment, Mink is rightly terrified of falling prey to laws and customs that have arisen in his absence. Now a man reduced to what is uniquely his own, Mink serves as an inverse mirror to his relative Flem. Flem, who begins by exerting a sheer will to power, ends up imprisoned by having given over his will to established forms of power; Mink, who begins firmly if unhappily placed in a network of kinship relations, economic obligations, and traditional customs, loses all such structured relations in the actual prison at Parchman and is left only with a fierce will to assert his bond with Flem.

In one respect Mink is a paragon of self-reliance, but his is not an Emersonian reliance on the self to be complete unto itself. His independence is a capacity to be able, without depending on established forms of relationship, to insist upon his relatedness to others. Mink asserts his selfhood not as a principle of autonomy but as part of a relationship to Flem. Flem's original outrage to

Mink had been a violation of the "ancient immutable laws of simple blood kinship," but by the time Mink gets out of prison the recognition he intends to elicit from Flem is something different (*M* 5). It is both more primitive, since it is the fundamental recognition of mutual selfhood between persons, and also more a product of Mink's own creative effort, since it is brought fully into being only at the moment when the two men confront each other.

Mink's self-reliance is also qualified by an ambiguous and perhaps somewhat suspect religious vision, which turns on the distinction Faulkner means to establish between trust and dependence.[3] When Mink commits the murder that first sends him to prison, the cold-blooded ambush of Jack Houston, he is already very much the proud, self-reliant loner. But he firmly believes he can depend on *"them—they—it,* whichever and whatever you wanted to call it, who represented a simple fundamental justice and equity in human affairs, or else a man might just as well quit" (*M* 6). Suffering Houston's insolence has gained him the "right to depend on *them* which he had earned by never before in his life demanding anything of them" (*M* 6–7).

By the time Mink leaves prison and sets off to kill Flem, however, his dependence on *"them"* to secure justice for him has been supplanted by a less clearly defined trust. Like Ratliff and the others who have come from Frenchman's Bend, he refers now to Old Moster, a figure who is for Mink less a genuinely external force than an emanation of Mink's own "confidence" (*M* 100). Mink's faith in Old Moster is, in effect, a trope for his ability to go on hoping that he will have the opportunity to depend on himself. Mink is thus able to do successfully what Ratliff recommends: "So what you need is to learn how to trust in God without depending on Him. In fact, we need to fix things so He can depend on us for a while" (*M* 321).

The elusive semantic margin between trusting and depending marks the difference between assuming the responsibility to create new value and relying upon forms in which such value has been previously established. The distinction is crucial to the last phase of Faulkner's career, for it turns the question of the fate of designs that always prove inadequate back upon the designer's

[3] The same distinction appears in *Light in August*. Joe Christmas prefers McEachern's abstract and impersonal dependability to the kindness of Mrs. McEachern, who insists on trusting Joe.

responsibility to keep on working the design and transforming it. The same personal fashioning of value can be seen in Aunt Molly's arrangement of a funeral for her grandson in *Go Down, Moses* and Nancy Mannigoe's actions in *Requiem for a Nun*. In *Snopes* also, although the bond that Mink creates is accomplished by a murder and the revitalized human relationship lasts only for the brief moment of recognition between Mink and Flem (while Flem waits silently for the other to fire his pistol a second time), Mink's action is clearly a triumph. Against all odds and almost entirely from his own resources, Mink has created an authentically mutual relationship where before there had been only the empty form of distant kinship and Flem's lifelong refusal of mutuality.

The burden of Mink's actions falls on Gavin Stevens, and so more heavily does the burden of Linda's furtive complicity in the murder. Gavin is required at last to take a responsibility upon himself that violates the forms he has before so carefully and ineffectually tended. At the point where established forms seem most to have crumbled, he proves capable of envisioning a new and very different kind of human relatedness. Having seen his image of Linda's perfect fidelity and grief shattered, having seen her betray his trust in her, and having then taken responsibility for her action to the point of condoning murder and even delivering at her behest a packet of getaway money to Mink, Gavin finds that he no longer needs to defend the official institutions of Jefferson or to think in terms of abstract moral categories.

> "There aren't any morals," Stevens said. "People just do the best they can."
>
> "The pore sons of bitches," Ratliff said.
>
> "The poor sons of bitches," Stevens said. "Drive on. Pick it up." [*M* 429]

Gavin's phrase, "the poor sons of bitches that have to cause all the grief and anguish they have to cause" (*M* 430), climaxes a refrain that runs throughout *The Mansion*. Like Brother Goodyhay and Miss Reba, Gavin and Ratliff mean by it "all of us, everyone of us" (*M* 82). Envisioned for the first time here is a fundamental human relatedness that includes all mankind, victim and victimizer alike, in a single community. It is a community of suffering and striving: a striving that Mink and even Flem exemplify and a suffering that both of them cause and endure. Human bonds within such a community arise not from the performance of prescribed functions in an established structure but from the ongoing effort of individuals continually involved in the work of transforming relationships and values. Value thus comes from the energy, the motion, that the individual puts into its creation. But as a part of Motion, the individual is already part of a universal community, from the well-nigh cosmic perspective that Gavin has begun to glimpse and that the trilogy now advances.

Faulkner moves here toward the elision of the middle term in the series that runs from the person to the society to mankind. The forms and institutions of a specific society, Frenchman's Bend or Jefferson, establish that society as a discrete unit by defining boundaries, excluding what is outside, and classifying what is inside.[4] Over against such societies and encompassing them without either contravening or supporting their specific codes, Faulkner sets a vision of community which is deliberately indefinite, inclusive, and undifferentiated. Frenchman's Bend and Jefferson, past and present, and Mink and Flem all become fundamentally indistinguishable from this perspective. All belong to the persistence of human motion and effort within a world of flux and change. The motion of life within a flux of specific cultural forms becomes, in fact, the object of Faulkner's simultaneously celebratory and melancholy vision. Both the successes and the failures of human effort to establish relations and to maintain cultural forms are ultimately transitory, but the effort persists. In motion, in a refusal of stasis and despair, are discovered the sources of a vitality that both causes all the grief and anguish and affords a continuing hope of overcoming them.

Faulkner's vision of mankind's endurance appears within a definable literary context. The conclusion of *The Mansion* rewrites the entire trilogy as an elegy, here specifically a pastoral elegy. As for Milton and Shelley, elegy is for Faulkner ultimately a celebratory genre. But the speakers in "Lycidas" and "Adonais" must first grieve for what has passed before they can achieve a vision of the enduring or the eternal. Their eventually joyful vision transforms and, in effect, repudiates the initial grief. In

---

[4] Cf. Charles Mallison's comment on Jefferson: "Ours was a town founded by Aryan Baptists and Methodists, for Aryan Baptists and Methodists . . . not to escape from tyranny as they claimed and believed, but to establish one" (*T* 306–307).

Faulkner's version, however, the lamentation for what has been lost and the celebration of what is discovered to endure occur simultaneously. Neither response offers a higher order of truth. By contrast to the durable conventions of elegiac verse, in which the victory of the eternal over the temporal and mutable is trumpeted, Faulkner insists joy and grief are both to be found in time. Mink, Faulkner's humble counterpart to Shelley's Adonais, is not exalted as a new god or translated into the divine spirit but interred among all those who have been part of motion and change.

Ultimately the community to which Mink belongs is the community of those who have been. It is into a pantheon of the dead who have suffered and striven that Mink enters at the close of the novel in a virtuoso passage of celebratory prose.

> He could feel that Mink Snopes that had had to spend so much of his life just having unnecessary bother and trouble, beginning to creep, seep, flow easy as sleeping; he could almost watch it, following all the little grass blades and tiny roots, the little holes the worms made, down and down into the ground already full of the folks that had the trouble but were free now, so that it was just the ground and the dirt that had to bother and worry and anguish with the passions and hopes and skeers, the justice and the injustice and the griefs. [*M* 435]

Faulknerian man becomes himself for having walked upright, for having taken the bother to struggle against the seductive pull of the earth in order to create value in his life. The pull of the earth then becomes an earned caress and the dissolution of death a reward for his striving. It is Mink's refusal to give up, his capacity to go on struggling for value, that earns his place among all the others of legend and song.

> All mixed and jumbled up comfortable and easy so wouldn't nobody even know or even care who was which any more, himself among them, equal to any, good as any, brave as any, being inextricable from, anonymous with all of them; the beautiful, the splendid, the proud and the brave, right on up to the very top itself among the shining phantoms and dreams which are the milestones of the long human recording—Helen and the bishops, the kings and the unhomed angels, the scornful and graceless seraphim. [*M* 435–436]

These final phrases repeat the words used in *The Hamlet* to describe the earth that Ike Snopes walks upon with his beloved (*H* 213). Like Mink, Ike is an outcast and to the others in Frenchman's Bend only marginally human. But on the edge of society, away from its forms, Ike has created a life worthy of the lushly idyllic prose Faulkner bestows upon him. Ike's bizarre love story is the genuine pastoral within the nominally pastoral community of Frenchman's Bend. He has truly gone outside the culture when he steals Houston's cow. But as the ornate and highly literary language of his story is meant to suggest, what lies outside an established culture may be not nature but the more humane culture Ike himself founds. It is thus the least of Faulkner's characters in the trilogy, Mink and Ike, who are the exemplary figures for the genuinely human capability that goes beyond the established structures of society and is ultimately the base on which those more transitory and partial forms are established.

The same understanding can be observed in most of the other novels of Faulkner's last phase: in *Requiem for a Nun* certainly, and quite baldly in the declamatory passages of *A Fable,* but also in the elegiac structure of the otherwise more somber *Go Down, Moses.* Faulkner's elegiac vision receives its fullest, most impressive expression in the final chapter of *The Mansion,* however, a chapter that looks back over the entire trilogy and transforms its meaning. The chapter looks back on Faulkner's entire career, in fact, for he has been careful to include in *The Mansion* a last retelling of stories from the whole span of his fiction and to make brief allusions to an even larger number of novels and tales. Events from Faulkner's earliest Yoknapatawpha novels—*Sartoris/ Flags in the Dust, The Sound and the Fury,* and *Sanctuary*—are rehearsed once more. Even relatively obscure short stories such as "Uncle Willy" and "Shingles for the Lord" are recalled.

Mink's death in the last chapter is a secular version of elegiac apotheosis. The chapter's affinity with pastoral elegy is further sustained by an insistently autumnal tone. Mink, Gavin, and Ratliff are all old men now. The Frenchman's Bend in which they meet is not the "rich river-bottom country" of *The Hamlet* (*H* 3) but a land of eroded farms awaiting the winter.

> The sun had crossed the equator, in Libra now; and in the cessation of motion and the quiet of the idling engine, there was a sense of autumn after the slow drizzle of Sunday and the

> bright spurious cool which had lasted through Monday almost;
> the jagged rampart of pines and scrub oak was a thin dike
> against the winter and rain and cold, under which the worn-out
> fields overgrown with sumac and sassafras and persimmon had
> already turned scarlet [*M* 417].

From this local autumn emerges an autumn of the cosmos and
also the autumn of Faulkner's career.

> Stevens found the fading earthen steps again, once more up and
> out into the air, the night, the moonless dark, the worn-out
> eroded fields supine beneath the first faint breath of fall, wait-
> ing for the winter. Overhead, celestial and hierarchate, the
> constellations wheeled through the zodiacal pastures: Scorpion
> and Bear and Scales; beyond cold Orion and the Sisters the
> fallen and homeless angels choired, lamenting [*M* 433].

The elegiac form with which the trilogy concludes differs from
the numerous other literary forms, fictions, and genres employed
elsewhere in the three volumes. It both is and is not the final
form of *Snopes* and a last fiction to which all the others in Faulkner's work are assimilated. It is final in the sense that it explicitly
concludes the trilogy and implicitly concludes the career, thus
taking upon itself all that has gone before. It is final also in that
it has a kind of privileged status in relation to forms which have
gone before.

Yet is is not strictly comparable to these others. It is not a way
of arresting motion or (to paraphrase another of Faulkner's descriptions of fiction-making) a means of stopping life's motion
and holding a light up to it. Unlike designs that intervene upon
motion and that thereby shape life actively, elegy responds to the
many shapings of life. Elegy thus serves as a meta-fictional frame
for all fictions and fiction-making, just as the community of mankind serves to frame all particular social structures. Elegy celebrates arrest and motion as constant forces that can never be
exhausted or united in a single, final, and total design; likewise,
it mourns the expense of these forces in the endless search for
resplendent permanence, the search that had inaugurated Faulkner's career forty years before.

Faulkner's writing career thus concludes by demonstrating that
its task, the making of fictions and the structuring of experience,
can never be concluded. In fact, Faulkner wrote one more novel

before he died. *The Reivers* is like a detail from the panels in *Go Down, Moses* or the mural in *Snopes*. It represents a boy's coming of age as the comic conflict between the designs inherited from his parents and those of his own that he is trying to establish for the first time. The comedy ends by showing these designs as fundamentally compatible, this being the structural counterpart to the comic tone, and by presenting itself as the boy's narration many years later to his own grandson. The process goes on; designs are established and then passed on as narratives to be adopted, transformed, or rejected by those who come after.

To say this in another way, Faulkner's career does not come to a point of closure or fasten upon some conclusive program that would designate finite boundaries for his work. He creates no supreme fiction. The writing does end at a moment when Faulkner has recently surveyed his entire past output and defined the place at which the career has arrived. That definition, however, is not a breaking of the pencil that completes the task or abandons it, but a passing of the baton to the future, to the stranger a hundred years hence.

Chronology of Important Dates

1897   Born September 25, New Albany, Mississippi.

1902   Family moves to Oxford, Mississippi.

1915   Quits school in eleventh grade after several years of increasing resistance.

1916–17   Works at odd jobs and mixes in student activities at the University of Mississippi. Begins drawing and writing poems in the aesthetic manner.

1918   After Estelle Oldham's engagement, leaves Oxford and stays in New Haven, Conn., then enlists in the Royal Air Force (Canada). War ends with Faulkner still in training as cadet pilot. Returns to Oxford.

1919–20   First published poem appears in *The New Republic*. Enrolls as special student at University. Publishes poems and drawings in student publications, and writes verse play, *The Marionettes*, for student drama group.

1921   Moves to New York City, where he clerks in bookstore. Returns to Oxford to become postmaster of the university post office.

1924   Publication of first volume of poems, *The Marble Faun*, subsidized by Phil Stone.

1925   Moves to New Orleans and associates with *Double Dealer* group, including Sherwood Anderson. Writes *Soldiers' Pay* with Anderson's encouragement. Sails for Europe in July and stays in Paris, working on "Elmer." Returns to Oxford, December.

1926   Publication of first novel, *Soldiers' Pay*.

1927   Publication of second novel, *Mosquitoes*. Early work with Snopes materials. Writes *Flags in the Dust*, first Yoknapatawpha novel, which is rejected by publishers.

1928   Writes and revises *The Sound and the Fury.*

1929   Publication of *Sartoris,* a cut version of *Flags in the Dust.* Writes first version of *Sanctuary.* Marries Estelle Oldham after her divorce from Cornell Franklin. Begins *As I Lay Dying* while working night-shift in power plant of University. *The Sound and the Fury* published, October.

1930   Begins sale of stories to prominent magazines. Buys antebellum mansion in Oxford, Rowan Oak. Publication of *As I Lay Dying.* At work revising *Sanctuary.*

1931   Birth and death (after nine days) of daughter Alabama. Publication of the revised *Sanctuary. These 13* published (stories).

1932   *Light in August* completed and published. Takes first job in Hollywood, as MGM contract writer.

1933   Publication of *A Green Bough* (poems). Birth of daughter Jill. Begins flying lessons and purchases first airplane.

1934   Begins work on projects that will become *Absalom, Absalom!* and *The Unvanquished.* Publication of *Doctor Martino and Other Stories.*

1935   At work on *Absalom, Absalom!. Pylon* published. Brother Dean dies in crash of plane Faulkner had given him. Returns to Hollywood.

1936   *Absalom, Absalom!* completed and published. Begins year-long stay in Hollywood.

1938   Publication of *The Unvanquished.* Purchase of Greenfield Farm. Writes *The Wild Palms* and starts work on Snopes trilogy.

1939   *The Wild Palms* published. Elected to National Institute of Arts and Letters.

1940   Publication of *The Hamlet.*

1942   Publication of *Go Down, Moses.* Returns to Hollywood on long-term contract with Warner Brothers. Screen credits for *To Have and to Have Not* and *The Big Sleep.*

1946   Publication of *The Portable Faulkner,* edited by Malcolm Cowley, begins revival of Faulkner's American reputation.

1948   Writing and publication of *Intruder in the Dust,* Faulkner's first book in six years. Elected to American Academy of Arts and Letters.

1949   Publication of *Knight's Gambit* (stories).

1950   *Collected Stories* published. Receives American Academy's Howell's Medal for Fiction. Travels to Stockholm to receive Nobel Prize.

1951   Beginning of frequent international travel. Publication of *Requiem for a Nun*. Receives Legion of Honor.

1954   Publication of *A Fable,* completed after ten years of work.

1955   Official recognition continues with National Book Award and Pulitzer Prize for *A Fable.* Begins State Department tours that will take him to Japan, Greece, and Venezuela.

1955–56 Series of letters and articles on integration.

1957   Begins term as writer in residence at University of Virginia. Publication of *The Town.*

1958   Returns to University of Virginia as writer in residence.

1959   Publication of *The Mansion.*

1962   Visit to West Point. Receives Gold Medal for Fiction of National Institute of Arts and Letters. *The Reivers* published, June. Dies July 6, at Oxford, after injury in fall from horse.

Notes on Contributors

RICHARD H. BRODHEAD, the editor of this volume, teaches English and American Studies at Yale. He is the author of *Hawthorne, Melville, and the Novel* and of essays on various aspects of American fiction.

CALVIN BEDIENT teaches at the University of California at Los Angeles. He is the author of *Architects of the Self: George Eliot, D. H. Lawrence, and E. M. Forster* and *Eight Contemporary Poets*.

CLEANTH BROOKS's many works include *Modern Poetry and the Tradition, The Well Wrought Urn, William Faulkner: The Yoknapatawpha Country* and *William Faulkner: Toward Yoknapatawpha and Beyond*. He is Professor of English Emeritus at Yale.

IRVING HOWE, who teaches at the City University of New York, has written on many literary and cultural subjects. His works include *William Faulkner: A Critical Study, Politics and the Novel*, and *World of Our Fathers*.

JOHN IRWIN is the author of *Doubling and Incest/Repetition and Revenge, American Hieroglyphic*, and a volume of poetry, *The Heisenberg Variations*. Formerly editor of the *Georgia Review*, he now teaches at Johns Hopkins University, where he directs the Writing Seminars.

DONALD M. KARTIGANER teaches at the University of Washington. He is the author of *The Fragile Thread: The Meaning of Form in Faulkner's Novels*.

HUGH KENNER, Chairman of the Department of English at Johns Hopkins, is the author of many books, including *The Invisible Poet: T. S. Eliot, The Pound Era, A Homemade World*, and *Joyce's Voices*.

DAVID MINTER has written *The Interpreted Design as a Structural Principle in American Prose* and, more recently, *William Faulkner:*

His Life and Work. Having taught for many years at Rice, he is now Professor of English at Emory University and Dean of Emory College.

GARY LEE STONUM teaches at Case Western Reserve University. He is the author of *Faulkner's Career: An Internal Literary History.*

SUSAN WILLIS is at work on a study of Caribbean and Latin American literature, *The Poetics of Dependency.* She is currently teaching English and Afro-American Studies at Yale.

DAVID M. WYATT is the author of *Prodigal Sons: A Study in Authorship and Authority.* He teaches at the University of Virginia.

Selected Bibliography

Bibliographies and Guides to Research

Meriwether, James B., *The Literary Career of William Faulkner: A Biographical Study.* Princeton: Princeton University Press, 1961.

Bassett, John, *William Faulkner: An Annotated Checklist of Criticism.* New York: David Lewis, 1972.

McHaney, Thomas L., *William Faulkner: A Reference Guide.* Boston: G. K. Hall, 1976.

Meriwether, James B., "William Faulkner," in *Sixteen Modern American Authors: A Survey of Research and Criticism,* ed. Jackson B. Bryer. Durham, N.C.: Duke University Press, 1974.

Reviews of new Faulkner scholarship are available annually in *American Literary Scholarship: An Annual,* ed. James Woodress (Durham, N.C.: Duke University Press) and the (Summer) Special Faulkner Issue of *The Mississippi Quarterly.*

Materials Especially Useful for the Study of Faulkner's Fiction

Blotner, Joseph, ed., *Selected Letters of William Faulkner.* New York: Random House, 1977.

Cowley, Malcolm, ed., *The Faulkner-Cowley File; Letters and Memories, 1944–62.* New York: Viking Press, 1966.

Faulkner, William, *Essays, Speeches, and Public Letters,* ed. James B. Meriwether. New York: Random House, 1965.

Gwynn, Frederick L. and Joseph L. Blotner, eds., *Faulkner in the University.* Charlottesville: The University Press of Virginia, 1959, reprinted 1977.

Meriwether, James B., and Michael Millgate, eds., *Lion in the Garden: Interviews with William Faulkner, 1926–62* New York: Random House, 1968.

Biographies and Critical Biographies

Blotner, Joseph Leo, *Faulkner: A Biography,* 2 vols. New York: Random House, 1974.

Minter, David, *William Faulkner: His Life and Work.* Baltimore: Johns Hopkins University Press, 1980.

Selected Critical Works on Faulkner

Bleikasten, André, *Faulkner's As I Lay Dying,* trans. Roger Little. Bloomington: Indiana University Press, 1973.

—— *The Most Splendid Failure: Faulkner's The Sound and The Fury.* Bloomington: Indiana University Press, 1976.

Brooks, Cleanth, *William Faulkner: The Yoknapatawpha Country.* New Haven: Yale University Press, 1963.

—— *William Faulkner: Toward Yoknapatawpha and Beyond.* New Haven: Yale University Press, 1978.

Brown, Calvin, *A Glossary of Faulkner's South.* New Haven: Yale University Press, 1976.

Gray, Richard J., *The Literature of Memory: Modern Writers of the American South.* Baltimore: Johns Hopkins University Press, 1976.

Guerard, Albert J., *The Triumph of the Novel: Dickens, Dostoyevsky, Faulkner.* New York: Oxford University Press, 1976.

Guetti, James L., *The Limits of Metaphor: A Study of Melville, Conrad, and Faulkner.* Ithaca: Cornell University Press, 1967.

Harrington, Evan, and Ann J. Abadie, eds., *Faulkner, Modernism, and Film.* Jackson: University Press of Mississippi, 1979.

Hoffman, Frederick J., and Olga W. Vickery, eds., *William Faulkner: Three Decades of Criticism.* East Lansing: Michigan State University Press, 1960.

Howe, Irving, *William Faulkner: A Critical Study* (3rd ed.). Chicago: University of Chicago Press, 1975.

Irwin, John T., *Doubling and Incest/Repetition and Revenge: A Speculative Reading of Faulkner*. Baltimore: Johns Hopkins University Press, 1975.

Jenkins, Lee, *Faulkner and Black-White Relations: A Psychoanalytic Approach*. New York: Columbia University Press, 1981.

Jehlen, Myra, *Class and Character in Faulkner's South*. New York: Columbia University Press, 1976.

Kartiganer, Donald M., *The Fragile Thread: The Meaning of Form in Faulkner's Novels*. Amherst: University of Massachusetts Press, 1979.

Kawin, Bruce F., *Faulkner and Film*. New York: Frederick Ungar, 1977.

Kenner, Hugh, *A Homemade World: The American Modernist Writers*. New York: Knopf, 1975.

King, Richard H., *A Southern Renaissance: The Cultural Awakening of the American South, 1930–1955*. New York: Oxford University Press, 1980.

Kinney, Arthur F., *Faulkner's Narrative Poetics: Style as Vision*. Amherst: University of Massachusetts Press, 1978.

Matthews, John T., *The Play of Faulkner's Language*. Ithaca: Cornell University Press, 1982.

McHaney, Thomas L., *William Faulkner's The Wild Palms: A Study*. Jackson: University Press of Mississippi, 1975.

Millgate, Michael, *The Achievement of William Faulkner*. New York: Random House, 1966.

Pitavy, François, *Faulkner's Light in August,* trans. Gillian E. Cook. Bloomington: Indiana University Press, 1973.

Polk, Noel, *Faulkner's Requiem for a Nun: A Critical Study*. Bloomington: Indiana University Press, 1981.

Schoenberg, Estella, *Old Tales and Talking*. Jackson: University Press of Mississippi, 1977.

Slatoff, Walter J., *Quest for Failure: A Study of William Faulkner*. Ithaca: Cornell University Press, 1960.

Stonum, Gary Lee, *Faulkner's Career: An Internal Literary History*. Ithaca: Cornell University Press, 1979.

Wagner, Linda W., ed., *William Faulkner: Four Decades of Criticism*. East Lansing: Michigan State University Press, 1973.

Warren, Robert Penn, ed., *Faulkner: A Collection of Critical Essays*. Englewood Cliffs, N.J.: Prentice-Hall, 1966.

Wittenberg, Judith Bryant, *Faulkner: The Transfiguration of Biography*. Lincoln: University of Nebraska Press, 1979.

Wolfe, George H., ed., *Faulkner: Fifty Years After the Marble Faun*. University, Ala.: University of Alabama Press, 1976.

Wyatt, David M., *Prodigal Sons: A Study in Authorship and Authority*. Baltimore: Johns Hopkins University Press, 1979.

Index